Civil Peace and
Sacred Order

Civil Peace and Sacred Order

LIMITS AND RENEWALS I

Stephen R. L. Clark

CLARENDON PRESS · OXFORD
1989

Oxford University Press, Walton Street, Oxford OX2 6DP
Oxford New York Toronto
Delhi Bombay Calcutta Madras Karachi
Petaling Jaya Singapore Hong Kong Tokyo
Nairobi Dar es Salaam Cape Town
Melbourne Auckland
and associated companies in
Berlin Ibadan

Oxford is a trade mark of Oxford University Press

Published in the United States
by Oxford University Press, New York

British Library Cataloguing in Publication Data
Clark, Stephen R.L. (Stephen Richard Lyster)
Civil peace and sacred order: limits and renewals
1. Society. Philosophical perspectives
I. Title
301'.01
ISBN 0-19-824446-0

Library of Congress Cataloging in Publication Data
Clark, Stephen R. L.
Civil peace and sacred order / Stephen R.L. Clark.
Contents: v. 1. Limits and renewals.
Bibliography: v. 1., p.
Includes index.
1. Political science—Philosophy. 2. Political obligation.
3. Philosophy. I. Title.
JA74.C57 1989   320.5'2—dc 19   88–36620
ISBN 0-19-824446-0

Computerset by Promenade Graphics Ltd., Cheltenham
Printed and bound in
Great Britain by Biddles Ltd,
Guildford and King's Lynn

Acknowledgements

Edwin Muir's poem, 'The Debtor', is quoted from *Collected Poems of Edwin Muir*, by permission of Faber and Faber Ltd., and Oxford University Press, New York.

Kathleen Raine's poem, 'Isis Wanderer', is quoted by permission of Kathleen Raine.

'Glyn Cynon Wood' is quoted from Gwyn Williams's *Welsh Poems: Sixth Century to 1600* by permission of Faber and Faber Ltd.

W. B. Yeats's poems, 'The Seven Sages', 'The Two Trees', 'The Irish Airman foresees his death', and 'Supernatural Songs IX' are quoted by permission of A. P. Watt Ltd. on behalf of Michael B. Yeats and Macmillan London Ltd., and of Macmillan New York.

Preface

I gave the lectures on which this first volume of *Limits and Renewals* is based in the spring of 1987, in Cambridge. I am grateful to the Stanton Lectureship electors for giving me the opportunity and incentive to put my particular brand of anarcho-conservatism on paper. I also lectured on these topics in Manchester University in 1987, and read a paper on the religious dimensions of liberalism to a workshop on liberalism held in St Andrews in 1987. Other papers, on the care of church buildings or the wider environment, on nuclear deterrence, slavery, ancient ideals of wisdom, or the rights of children, have all been tried out on audiences in Glasgow, Liverpool, London, and other British universities. I am grateful to all my auditors and critics, and expecially to Graham Bird (in Manchester), Nicholas Lash, Stephen Sykes, Dorothy Emmet, Brian Hebblethwaite, Malcolm Schofield, Renford Bambrough, and the Principal and Fellows of St John's College (in Cambridge) for their hospitality and good sense. Others of my friends and sometime colleagues, notably John Skorupski, Dudley Knowles, Gordon Graham, Raymond Frey and Gillian Clark will recognize long-standing preoccupations. Flint Schier, who died young and bravely a few weeks ago, would have found much to criticize, and perhaps a little to commend. He is much missed.

This volume is conceived as the first of a trilogy. The second volume will deal, as did my 1987 Stanton Lectures, with the structure of the soul; the third, with the structure of reality—both in a traditional and theocentric context. Since it is one of my central contentions that political philosophy, philosophy of mind, and metaphysics are interdependent disciplines, I must hope that readers will have the patience to wait for the resolution of some riddles, and take the trouble to reflect upon the matters discussed in this volume in the light shed (so I hope) in later volumes. I make no apology for not setting out my thoughts *more geometrico*: it is sometimes a necessary discipline to require students of philosophy to spell their arguments out from scratch, but it would be historically false and philosophically naive to think that such 'geometrical' methods are the source of the great philosophers' power to challenge or convert. What passes for rigorous argument is often only the exposition of current prejudice, 'making a dictionary of words'; what challenges prejudice must sometimes seem discursive or tangential precisely because the words 'we' use make one, socially approved reality seem all there is or could be. My thesis is that current preoccupations and vocabulary can best be challenged from below, from the long tradition of 'pre-modern' thought. Fashionable challenges to Enlightenment Thought regularly neglect that perennial philosophy that enlightenment sages sought to overthrow. Succinctly: Marxist or sub-Marxist 'radicals' are right to identify political ideology in modern or post-modern philosophies of mind, state, and universe; where they are wrong is in failing to locate the real challenge to that ideology, namely 'the last, lost giant, even God, risen against the world'.

That reference may serve as reminder or due notice that I see no reason to restrict my reading or quotation to those few thinkers admitted to polite philosophical society. Chesterton's *Orthodoxy* deserves as much attention as the texts preferred, without any clear attempt to justify the choices, in our customary syllabuses. Yeats offers as interesting a commentary on Berkeley and the world. Kipling should be taken seriously as a thinker, not patronized as a poet. These were journalistic hacks? But so were Mill, or Hume, or Hobbes. Their real crime, for a profession that practises methodological atheism and prefers to be 'progressive', lies in their enthusiastic traditionalism. But progressive secularists have no monopoly on truth or right reason, and should be glad to be reminded even of the faith they flee. Professional philosophers, 'progressive' or otherwise, ought always to remember that most of the great texts we study were actually written by people who would not now be regarded as 'professional philosophers', and that we betray our calling if we behave as if only 'professionals' can now reason to any good effect. In drawing on a wider literary field than many of my professional colleagues, I may seem to be writing only 'popular philosophy'. Obviously—in a sense—I hope I am: but I deny that this is less exacting, or less interesting, than the kind of philosophistry that reduces the great questions to a parlour game played only by 'State-kept schoolmen'!

Lourdes McGunigle deserves my gratitude for typing most of this volume; Samuel and Dorothea for arguing back, and Verity for re-acquainting me with children's literature (anarcho-conservative in essence); Gillian Clark, for academic and personal assistance (and forbearance) over sixteen years.

S. R. L. C.

Liverpool,
8 July 1988

Contents

FIFTH. Whence came our thought?

SIXTH. From four great minds that hated Whiggery.

FIFTH. Burke was a Whig.

SIXTH. Whether they knew or not.
　　Goldsmith and Burke, Swift and the Bishop of Cloyne
　　All hated Whiggery; but what is Whiggery?
　　A levelling, rancorous, rational sort of mind
　　That never looked out of the eye of a saint
　　Or out of a drunkard's eye.

SEVENTH. All's Whiggery now,
　　But we old men are massed against the world.

SIXTH. What schooling had these four?

SEVENTH. They walked the roads
　　Mimicking what they heard, as children mimic;
　　They understood that wisdom comes of beggary

(From The Seven Sages: Yeats 1950: 272 f.)

I

Reason, Value, and Tradition

The Calling of an Anglican Philosopher

University lecturers, especially in small departments, sometimes have to restrain their creative imagination, and content themselves with putting some small collection of received theories and techniques on show. Sometimes our job seems to be to perform a series of conjuring tricks, pulling grotesque conclusions from the hat of cunningly sophistical argument and then revealing the nature of the sophistry. We can rarely afford the luxury of developing any one particular theme as our very own, and may often give the impression that the sole office of philosophy is to disillusion, to immunize against enthusiasm (see Clark 1984: 3 ff.). It was therefore especially delightful, though also profoundly alarming, to be set free, by my election to the honourable post of Stanton Lecturer in the Philosophy of Religion, to try to live out my God-given vocation as a philosopher, if only on a verbal level! Instead of a conjuror I would wish to be, or at least to imitate, the Mage: 'The Mage in us turns over his kaleidoscope and all is unexpected, more true, more beautiful. It depends only upon us to see, the joy of the world is at our doors if only we would want it' (Sat prem 1968: 326). That kind of *Gestalt* shift of view cannot be produced by argument alone, but argument can at least prepare the way, and make some record of the journey.

Inevitably, I must remain a showman: what I have to say may be regarded—even by myself in other moods—as only one of the 'nine and sixty ways of constructing tribal lays'. It is, as Plato said (*Laws* 719 C), the task of the poet to give voices to those who disagree with each other, and with the 'common sense' of their society. Any literary artist—a class which includes philosophers—can echo Yeats's plea for a world 'where a man is heard by the right ears, but never overheard by the wrong, and where he speaks his whole mind gaily, and is not the cautious husband of a part; where fantasy can play before matured into conviction' (Yeats 1955: 231). It is my earnest, and underlying, belief that we ought not to second-guess ourselves too frequently. What I have to say may be in error, but we shall never know whether or not it is until the thesis is developed as clearly and imaginatively as may be. Even those of you, who may well be the majority, who find yourselves adamantly opposed to the claims I shall be making, may profit from a full-blooded and shameless exposition of the creed you reject: how shall you understand even your own doctrines until you see what the opposing doctrine is?

That doctrine is, simply, traditional theism of a kind that has in the past been identified as of the essence of Anglicanism (though there have been others to suspect or boast that Anglicans always prefer not to think too clearly about their doctrine), though I approach it by a route that some may find surprising.

The characteristics of this type of Christianity are—a spiritual religion, based on a firm belief in absolute and eternal values as the most real things in the universe—a confidence that these values are knowable by man—a belief that they can nevertheless be known only by whole-hearted consecration of the intellect, will and affections to the great quest—an entirely open mind towards the discoveries of science—a reverent and receptive attitude to the beauty, sublimity and wisdom of the creation, as a revelation of the mind and character of the Creator—a complete indifference to the current valuations of the world-ling. (Inge 1926: 33.)

Or in Morgan's words:

In [the Anglican Church's] generally platonist and sacramental outlook the dogma of the incarnation holds together God and the world, faith and history, doctrine and spiritual practice. . . . Continental antitheses are rejected: only a catholic can be a good protestant (i.e. one must respect the ancient tradition), and only a protestant can be a good catholic (i.e. one must also dare to be criti-cal of the tradition, to be a theologian). (Morgan 1980: 11.)

Clearly, I am in good company in supposing that such a metaphysically serious, traditional religion is worth expounding. But—although there are encouraging signs to the contrary—it has sometimes seemed that dutifully 'modern minds' take it for granted that no such 'platonist and sacramental' doctrine can be true. Even Christian theologians some-times seem to have abandoned all serious philosophical interest in the doctrines they profess to examine, or even to teach. The questions they seem to ask are not 'What does this doctrine mean, why should we believe it, is it true?', but 'What does it mean to us, how do we feel about these words, is it relevant to modern man?'. Even those who do attend to intellectual history do not regard it as normative. Studying the 'making of Christian doctrine' is 'like reading a debate about the movement of the planets before the invention of the telescope' (Wiles 1967: 1 f.; see also p. 166). 'We live in an age for which the later Platonism of the 4th century A.D. is almost—almost, but not quite—as alien an outlook as the eschatological expectations of late Judaism' (Wiles 1976: 157)—from which somewhat ethnocentric observation Wiles apparently concludes that, whatever insights may be culled from the Fathers and however often we must remind ourselves of past debates, 'the great doctrinal definitions of the early Church . . . the outcome of a closely contested process of reasoning' (Wiles 1967: 159) should be abandoned merely because they are (allegedly) 'foreign to our [*sic*] way of thought' (Wiles 1967: 113).

Most of us are victims of this century's extraordinary attack of amnesia. Some of us, lay theologians, philosophers, and journalists alike, treat doctrines that stem from the profound and difficult exploration of mundane and extra-mundane realities as if they were new apophthegms, without background or history. What some carefully phrased dogma 'means' to a relatively ignorant 'modern' (by which is meant an educated Westerner who has shown no dangerous signs of religious enthusiasm) is held to be all that matters. Cupitt's charge that 'Anglo-Saxon philosophy' is unhistorically minded (Cupitt 1980: 75) is a considerable exaggeration, true only of a few, sometime fashionable thinkers (almost as exaggerated, some may think, as the converse notion that present-day theologians are forgetful of the faith!), but he does thereby point to an error into which any of us may slip. Others of us realize, with Wiles (1967: 159), that the doctrines had definite and historically important meanings, but take it for granted that such 'statements whose truth and falsity can be determined only in terms of a world-view that is dead and gone can hardly be . . . statement[s] of direct relevance to subsequent ages' (Wiles 1967: 9). Why the world-view should be thought 'dead and gone' remains unexplained. To ask anyone, whether fashionable agnostic or would-be believer, to try and understand Philo of Alexandria,[1] or Plotinus, as a necessary propaedeutic to the understanding of the Chalcedonian or Nicene definitions or their favourite hymns, is obscurantist. Either they had nothing true to say, or else the truth in what they did say was distorted by doctrinal and metaphysical assumptions which 'we' know quite well to be false.

---

[1] Wiles, from whose writings no student of these matters could fail to profit, himself ignores Philo, and seems to treat both 'the Greek World' and intertestamental Judaism as monoliths. If 'the main trend of contemporary philosophical thought was eclectic in

Platonism, according to many theologians, was a great mistake, and we who come after are able and entitled to rephrase orthodoxy in non-Platonic mode, extracting the 'real meaning' of the Gospel from its alien shell. 'If only the Lord had arranged for Jesus Christ to be born in twentieth-century Europe or America: how much more accurately would we have understood his message, how much more righteously have treated him!'. Not that anyone actually says this: who could keep a straight face?

By contrast, the three volumes united under the general title of *Limits and Renewals* constitute my attempt to restate theocentric traditionalism as the one true rival of 'modernist error'. Other writers than I have found fault with modernism, and sought to restate a mainstream, trinitarian orthodoxy, whether in Thomist or Modern Continental style. My own enterprise owes less to Thomas Aquinas, Heidegger, or Whitehead than to the Platonic and Aristotelian thought from which those worthies themselves sought sustenance. I am, by temperament and training, a classical philosopher—which is why, like the ancients, I see nothing odd about appealing to the writings of poets as well as of philosophers. 'Poets were once considered learned men—not simply intuitive or prophetic, but learned. It was possible, and it still is possible, to see them either as philosophers or purveyors of philosophy' (White 1970: 2). Great poets, at least, like Homer, Shakespeare, Hopkins, Kipling, Chesterton, or Yeats (the list is not exhaustive), are worth attending to—not for the 'poetic feeling' they induce, but for the truths they teach. The same applies to the Gospel-writers: I had rather see them listened to as thinkers, than praised as 'poets'. What I have come to believe is that much of what even sympathetic commentators have treated as mythological or metaphorical can actually be given a serious and literal sense; that it is possible to be even more 'conservative' than normal conservative theologians precisely by being more 'radical' than normal 'radical philosophers'. It is worth adding that although I often use the terms 'liberal' and 'modernist' pejoratively, it should not be assumed that I therefore disapprove of all 'liberal' actions. On the contrary, my complaint is often that fashionably 'liberal' theories are inadequate to defend 'really liberal' intuitions and policies. What I am seeking to do is expound traditional theism in its relation to Society, the Soul, and the Universe—an enterprise that

character' (Wiles 1967: 117), perhaps that was because the greatest saints and thinkers thought, like Inge, that the divine *Logos* incorporates all truth, while at the same time recognizing that each of us now only knows in part, and prophesies in part.

would be merely pretentious were it not for the fact that my betters
have already done most of the work.

During much of our history, insight has often come through the recitation and
rearrangement of materials from tradition . . . A florilegium was an explicit
refusal to be 'original', and its originality and creativity must therefore be
sought in its repetition of the standard formulas, not apart from that repetition . . . A florilegium is a mosaic, all of whose tiles have come from somewhere else; a myopic examination of the tiles, or of the spaces between the
tiles, misses the whole point, which is in the relation of the tiles to one another
and of the mosaic to other mosaics. (Pelikan 1984: 74.)

This first volume is to do with 'Preventing the Ruin', not only of Great
Britain—which was George Berkeley's aim—but of any human polity.
To give you some idea of what to expect, 'he who makes it his business
to lessen or root out from the minds of men [a religious fear and awe of
God] doth in effect endeavour to fill his country with highwaymen,
housebreakers, murderers, fraudulent dealers, perjured witnesses and
every other pest of society' (Berkeley 1948: vi. 219 f.).

Dogmas of Liberal Modernism

Traditional theism is the doctrine I intend to expound. But there is
little chance that this will be understood, or acknowledged as a viable
option in the 'modern world', as long as my readers take certain methodological assumptions so much for granted that they hardly notice
them. It is those easy assumptions that lead even believing Christians
to conclude that the Fathers spoke from within an alien world-view
that 'we' cannot or should not now recover. Either that world is long
since gone, or else it lingers only 'in the more backward countries of
the Third World or the socialistic block' (Cupitt 1980: 17). 'We' know
better. Self-styled moderns, proclaiming their allegiance to a consciousness that 'is, or seeks to be, free, self-aware and entirely undog-
matic' (Cupitt 1982: 10), are often astoundingly parochial! So, to put
my cards firmly on the table, let me declare at the outset that the following doctrines, which I take to be definitive of 'liberal modernism',
seem to me to be not merely doubtful but entirely and even obviously
erroneous:

　1. No one ought to believe or ask others to believe anything more
than she can herself demonstrate on the basis of her own personal
knowledge.

2. No one ought to believe or ask others to believe (and no 'truly modern person' will believe or ask others to believe) anything that will be believed to be incompatible with 'modern knowledge' or fashionable opinion.

3. No one ought to believe any positive doctrine that cannot be verified by 'the scientific method', although it is obligatory to believe all opposing negative doctrines.

4. Long-established beliefs and practices have no greater claim on our practical and theoretical allegiance than newly minted ones, and may properly be dismissed as obsolete even if there is no definite evidence against them.

5. No one can be obliged either to do or to believe anything that she herself can at the moment see no reason to do or to believe.

6. No one ought to believe that there are any obligations 'laid down from above', except perhaps an obligation to be 'sincere', and no one ought ever to advance her own moral opinions to another.

7. All modern persons must acknowledge that the body of genuinely true propositions is entirely value-free, and that the world is only seen aright when it is seen without any emotional affect.

8. No modern person should think anything more important than 'personal relationships'.

9. No modern person should think anything more important than 'this-worldly' ties or give credence to 'dualistic' or 'other-worldly' philosophies.

These doctrines do not form a coherent set, but something like them seems to be part of received wisdom amongst the pontificating classes. Bambrough's Dictionary of Received Ideas (*Philosophy* 62 (1987), 129 f.) offers a similarly incoherent collection. Perhaps some of them can be reworded so as to convey some partial truth—we have, after all, Blake's word for the thesis that 'every thing possible to be believ'd is an image of truth' (Blake 1966: 151); perhaps all of them together can, with sufficient ingenuity, be reformulated into a single coherent doctrine—'corrected liberal modernism'. In the absence of any such well-formulated creed, I am as entitled as would-be modernists to guess what it would have to be like: the corrections needed would, in my view, so radically alter 'modernism' as to lead it back to the perennial philosophy I wish to present! Of the dogmas I have identified not one is rationally compelling, most are ridiculous, and several would actually be destructive even of the scientific enterprise if they were consistently applied. I have been told that some of them, at least, are not as fashionable as once they were: I would gladly believe this true were it not that the schools still send us students coached to profess them. In this first chapter of the first volume, I shall try to outline what is wrong with the dogmas of liberal modernism as I have stated them and what rational framework of thought and action I shall put in their place.

The Politics of Rationality

The first modernist dogma that I mentioned, that no one ought to believe anything more than she can herself demonstrate on the basis of her own personal knowledge, is a version of the Cartesian principle. Everything that can, logically, be denied, ought to be doubted, even if no one in her right mind ever actually does doubt it. The history of Cartesian thought is sufficient to demonstrate, in practice, that this principle, in its strictest form, is wholly unworkable. 'So swift is our progress from the womb to the grave', as Berkeley said, that no one could know much of the world by her own experience (1948: vii. 14). We simply cannot reconstruct anything remotely resembling the body of information by which, perforce, we all live, on the basis of logically self-evident principle, even if we add the immediate deliverances of sense-experience. Nor does anyone make much effort to live by such a rule: indeed, the very idea on which Descartes laid so much stress, that this world might indeed be 'a dream and a delirium' (Marcus Aurelius, *Meditations* 2. 13. 1), is itself one of those wild suggestions that 'moderns' enjoy laughing at, though they have no rational proof that this is not the case.[2]

The refusal to accept another's word or to take for one's basis a theory one cannot oneself demonstrate can only be supposed to be our duty by someone who has quite forgotten what she herself is bound to do in every area of life. We live within a sea of testimony: everything that we ordinarily count upon has been handed on to us; the very possibility of demonstrating anything itself rests on our having been initiated into the techniques and presuppositions of the testifying

[2] I have considered Aurelius' judgement in Clark 1983a, and will do so again in later volumes of *Limits and Renewals*: briefly, the worry that we might be victims of a Cartesian demon or a mad neurological scientist needs to be taken more seriously, and less gloomily, than most epistemologists suppose. It is in fact the necessary context of a belief in personal immortality.

community. 'Most creatures are forced to credit everything long before they are able to prove anything' (Stephens 1982: 25).

I have on earlier occasions labelled the rationalist demand that we believe only what we can ourselves 'prove', Clifford's Principle, after that worthy but misguided opponent of William James's pragmatism, W. K. Clifford: the opposite methodological principle, which maintains that 'we ought to begin by believing everything that is offered to our acceptance [rather] than that it is our duty to doubt of everything' (Newman 1979: 286), I have labelled Chisholm's Principle, but it would be better to call it Newman's, or Yeats's:

I began telling people that one should believe whatever had been believed in all countries and periods and only reject any part of it after much evidence, instead of starting all over afresh and only believing what one could prove. (Yeats 1955: 78.)

The onus of proof, in other words, must in most cases be on those who wish to subvert received wisdom, the testimony of the ages, the principles of consensus reality. Gadamer summarizes the thought of the German (as against the would-be free-thinking English or French) Enlightenment: 'since the human intellect is too weak to manage without prejudices it is at least fortunate to have been educated with true prejudices' (Gadamer 1986: 258)! Fortunate indeed. Burke had said much the same: 'We are afraid to put men to live and trade each on his own private stock of reason; because we suspect that the stock in each man is small, and that the individuals would do better to avail themselves of the general bank and capital of nations and of ages' (Burke 1975: 354). Few philosophers nowadays, even if they still use Descartes's *Meditations* as a first-year text, really think it reasonable to question everything that can logically be denied: what is odd is that so little attention is then paid to the overwhelming predominance of religious thought-forms and religious doctrines in the received body of human knowledge. Vico's view was that 'the common sense that belongs to all nations at all times is composed of those beliefs that correspond to, and are necessary for the maintenance of [the institutions of religion, marriage and burial] . . . the beliefs that there is a provident divinity, that human passions ought to be moderated and that the human soul is immortal' (Pompa 1975: 31). He had a point. Nowadays consensus reality is enthroned as the only available context of rational enquiry, the provider not only of fundamental data but of the very principles of enquiry. But consensus reality is then equated, without any attempt to demonstrate the equation—even in the most straightforward and unquestioning way—with whatever is currently unquestioned by respectably irreligious people, whether of the left or the right.

Critics of any distinctive moral or religious doctrine employ two techniques, without ever—or so it seems—pausing to ask whether they are compatible. On the one hand, they require the believer to produce arguments which would convince 'just anyone', of whatever background, education, or moral character: what would not persuade 'just anyone' cannot be rational advocacy. On the other hand, they suggest that what 'we' (or they) think is normative: the doctrines that they and their friends espouse are obviously right, and need no argument, and whatever contradicts them must be wrong. Students are led to believe that they need not trouble to refute Plato's conclusions if only they can find fault with his arguments, and that the unformed and unproven opinions of their contemporaries must constitute the 'truth'. But, as Gadamer's editor observes, 'it is one thing to find the obvious faults in the deductive logic of Socrates' arguments . . . and quite another to perceive the pedagogical effect of what Socrates is saying' (Gadamer 1980: p. ix). Wiles's claim that 'the truth or otherwise of the [early Church's] doctrines depends upon the validity or otherwise of the reasoning by which they were determined' (Wiles 1967: 40) is simply untrue. Arguments in matters theological are like those in matters mathematical: first we find the solution, and only then attempt to 'prove' it. If our first proofs are poor, that does not disprove the thesis—or refutation would be far easier than in fact it is.

That the onus is on those who dispute received wisdom in no way implies that such disputation is impossible or irrational. 'A state without the means of some change is without the means of its conservation' (Burke 1975: 285). Some moderns or 'post-modernists' who have acknowledged the social context of rational inquiry have gone to the other, irrationalist extreme. In place of the impossible demand that we should 'prove' our beliefs to be logically indisputable, they have set up the claim that all relevant criticism of a thought-world must be internal, that either there is no reality outside consensus reality or at the least we can have no access to it as a criterion against which to measure received opinion. Particular doctrines may be tested for their consistency with other doctrines (though why such consistency should matter is more than we are usually told), but the whole thought-world is beyond criticism. A few theologians have heard this message with relief, and embraced the conclusion that the 'religious form of life' can only be criticized from within. My own judgement, to which I shall return, is that this is itself a profoundly irreligious claim: the essence of piety is that we and our favourite thought-worlds stand under judgement, and that Reality is more than we can, in our own strength, conceive. I share Duerr's opinion that too many of those who have criticized modernist dogma have done so by adopting a limply contrived relativism (Duerr 1985: 103 ff.), forgetting that they thereby make it impossible to criticize the very modernist doctrines they disdain.

Most fashionable anti-realism, however, is dominated by an openly irreligious metaphysic: what seems from the outside like a variety of idealism (that what is the case is constituted solely by what 'we' think is the case) turns out instead to be materialistic. The criteria of identity, for example, that we are assured that we 'must' use, are those of bodily location. Nothing can even be said that cannot be translated into materialistic language, even though it is notorious that current physical theory cannot really be understood in terms of the middle-sized bodies we normally encounter. The complex mathematical symbolism of high physics is exempt, by convention, from the requirement that all consensually meaningful utterances have some simple material translation. This is no doubt because the high physicists are understood to be doing something that our community requires, and the subterfuges they employ to handle the physics of high-energy particles, black holes, or the Big Bang are acceptable even though similar subterfuges in the field of theology would be frowned on. 'That philosopher is not free from bias and prejudice', said Berkeley long before physicists had claimed to be able to transcend ordinary logic as of right, 'who shall maintain the doctrine of force and reject that of grace, who shall admit the abstract idea of a triangle, and at the same ridicule the Holy Trinity!' (*Alciphron* 7. 8: 1948: iii. 296).[3]

In place of the impossible duty of private judgement, irreligious moderns have adopted the second thesis that I anathematized: that no one ought to believe, or ask others to believe (and no 'truly modern person' will believe or ask others to believe), anything that will be believed to be incompatible with 'modern knowledge' or fashionable

---

[3] Physicists and mathematicians alike employ concepts that have been created for mathematical convenience (like the square root of -1, or naked singularities) and then assume that these have 'physical' reality. They may be right. Physicists also suggest that physical experiment can 'disprove' logical laws, as that $p \mathbin{\&} (q \vee r) \equiv (p \mathbin{\&} q) \vee (p \mathbin{\&} r)$. A theologian who made equivalent claims would not be well-regarded.

opinion. Consensus reality is the necessary framework of all claims, and that reality is equated with what is supposed to be 'modern' thought, with what is necessary to sustain the forms of life that are reckoned distinctively modern. Forms of life that fashionable thinkers reckon 'superstitious' or 'anti-human' are to be judged by the strictest possible standards of logic and historical evidence; forms of life that, for whatever reason, are part of the fashionable thought-world are allowed all sorts of useful liberties, sometimes in the unreasoning faith that they will eventually be able to evade their present contradictions. Parochial restrictions on what is to count as consensus reality, prejudicial treatment of persons who have adopted unfashionable forms of life, and highly partial applications of the demand for immediate self-consistency in acceptable theory are all signs of the value-laden character of modern anti-realism, and the thesis that no one ought to believe things apparently at odds with 'modern knowledge'.

A village schoolteacher who makes fun of the curé, and whose attitude dissuades children from going to Mass, derives his persuasive force from the consciousness he possesses of his superiority as a modern individual over a dogma of the Middle Ages, which consciousness is based upon science. . . . In France, people question everything, respect nothing; some show a contempt for justice, property, art, in fact everything under the sun; but their contempt stops short of science. (Weil 1987: 228.)

The value-laden character of all knowledge-claims is something that will engross me in a moment. What is already evident is that such claims, and therefore the study of such claims (epistemology) cannot be clearly distinguished from political philosophy. Who do we allow to 'authorize' belief or action, and on what grounds?

One way of seeming to avoid the trap (of advancing a particular value-system while professing not to have any distinctive 'scientifically indemonstrable values') is the third anathematized dogma, that no one ought to believe any positive doctrine that cannot be verified by 'the scientific method', although it is obligatory to believe all opposing negative doctrines. This is, in origin, an advance upon mere social idealism. In place of the thesis that whatever is consensually—or fashionably—accepted is the unquestionable framework of rational endeavour (so that no one—or no one who was anyone—in seventeenth-century England could meaningfully deny that there were witches), we have the admission that there is a form of rational criticism by which existing claims can be judged and found wanting. This

is not, please note, a return to private judgement: it is as true of 'scientists' as of the rest of us that they cannot possibly prove scientific
theory merely by their individual endeavour. To be a 'scientist', or
more generally a scholar, at all is to swear allegiance to a community of
persons wider than the parochial or national one, a community governed—if only at a verbal level—by stringent moral rules about the
production and use of evidence (see chapter seven). A claim is scientifically verified if it is generally accepted by the relevant scientific community (for in truth there is no one such community, but rather a
complex of interrelated disciplinary groups) as the best (most elegant,
most fertile, least innovative?) available explanation for the data, and as
one without any seriously destructive problems.[4]

So nothing is to be believed by the would-be modern that has not
withstood the competition faced within some branch of the international scientific community. Those who say so, of course, implicitly
exclude a great many propositions. Am I to believe in my wife's fidelity
and virtue, for example, only if those alleged characters have been subjected to destructive testing? Few of us entirely admire folklore heroes
who 'test' their wives! Am I to trust my fellow researcher's veracity only
if I have arranged for her to be tempted into falsifying her results for
financial or professional gain? Am I to believe that there are physical
bodies only if I have seriously tested this claim against the relevant
alternatives (that there are only complexes of sensual qualities, or that
there are communicating spirits for whom such properties are a mode
of discourse)? The very claim that only scientifically validated propositions may legitimately be believed is itself something that lies beyond
scientific validation. If it is false we should obviously not believe it
(there being a primary dictate of reason that we should believe only
what is true); but if it is true we should also not believe it. To live like
that kind of 'scientist' is simply to have adopted a way of life that makes
love, piety, and science itself impossible.

In sum: the rules of scientific method—whatever they may be—no
more define reality than the rules of legal evidence. Many undoubted
truths may not be admitted in court; many equally clear truths cannot
be the object of scientific reason. This is not because they are 'less
true' or 'less reliable' but because they transcend the little provinces of

[4] Notice what socio-political requirements are already implied in this account. If
there is to be 'knowledge', there must be easy and rapid communications, a habit of critical scrutiny on the part of professionals relatively emancipated from immediate political

human meaning that we delimit as scientific. Those who refuse to admit, for example, that non-human animals 'feel pain' because it has not been 'scientifically proved that they do' demonstrate their prejudice by insisting that they are entitled to assume that such animals do *not* feel pain (though that is just as scientifically indemonstrable). That there is a factual question here—rather than a mere difference of socially determined description—is sufficient proof that there are some questions not susceptible of 'scientific' answer. It is true that this is not 'merely' a factual matter (if by 'factual' we mean something that has no evaluative implications). But Rorty's conclusion (Rorty 1979: 188 ff.) that it is not a factual question at all, that 'having feelings' is properly attributed to a being solely on the basis of its expected potential for 'membership in our linguistic community', represents one of those myopic refusals to admit to the existence of a world larger than the social which has poisoned recent humanistic thought (see Dombrowski 1984: 128 ff.). We cannot, therefore, escape the necessity of believing things over and above what is scientifically demonstrable, and of believing that what we believe is really true. Unless all truths are scientifically demonstrable—and we have ample reason to doubt that this is so—we will simply be rendering certain truths inaccessible to us if we restrict ourselves to such beliefs as are scientifically demonstrable.

The Virtues of Prejudice

If we cannot sensibly limit the foundations or criteria of knowledge to those which we might dream up as individuals or as members of some particular historical community, even one self-labelled 'scientific', where are we to begin? Behind the doctrine that we should restrict ourselves to the 'scientifically verified'—a doctrine that unnecessarily restricts our view and that cannot even accommodate itself—lies a more ancient attitude of contempt for the savage or the old-fashioned. 'Pagan' ways, to the urban Christian, were the obsolete doctrines of the countryside. The urban sophisticate regularly mistakes rural life for the 'simple' life, just as the eighteenth century saw sheer savagery in

or financial fears. These must always be seen as 'luxuries' by that sort of self-styled 'practical' person defined by Belloc as one who is ignorant of the principles on which she acts, and careless of the long-term consequences of what she does (Belloc 1927: 131).

what we can now, with an effort, see as just a different culture. But even when we do recognize that 'primitives' are, in their own terms, intensely cultural animals, we are inclined to suppose that the intellectual activity which went to make up their culture ceased long since (see Wiles 1967: 170). What is old, or what is perceived to be old, is no more than a relic of a once-active intellectual life, an attempt to imitate the instinctual, genetically transmitted life-ways of the non-human. Only what is newly minted earns our respect as evidence of intellectual life; only those who have made their stories up for themselves can even think of what they say as true, rather than merely acting out a pattern laid down long before. Maybe so: but are we so sure that *moderns* are self-moving?

It is obvious enough that some long-standing beliefs and practices have, over the years, come to seem false. We can legitimately conclude that not all well-established beliefs are true, and that we must leave ourselves some room for manœuvre not to be tied down to one doctrine merely because people in the past have thought it true. But it does not follow that long-established beliefs and practices have no greater claim on our practical and theoretical allegiance than newly minted ones. They have the signal advantage that they are there, that their ramifications have, to some extent, been explored, that we have some idea of what they really amount to. Old doctrines are not true merely because they are old, any more than new ones are true because they are new: but it is not absurd to suggest that the old ones have our prior allegiance, that they do not need to establish themselves on just the same terms as new theories, that they have, as it were, the benefit of the doubt.

In scientific practice this much is obvious, that old theories are not to be dismissed as obsolete when there is no definite evidence against them, but only if there is some better theory in the running. It is only when the searchlight turns on matters metaphysical, and principally theological, that we are suddenly expected to despise the old merely because it is old, which is to say because it does not fit our current preoccupations or fails to support our current self-images. There have even been some hopelessly ignorant and self-complacent commentators to assert that nothing said about human life and knowledge before, say, the middle of the eighteenth century, is now worth considering: this on the overt ground that 'the scientific method' only took shape in that century, or that only then was, say, the 'true age of the world' established. A little historical sense suggests very strongly that some other excuse would be offered for despising our ancestors' contributions if those were not available. Such fanatical neophiliacs may be the exception, but even humane and reasonable commentators sometimes take their own superiority for granted. Lessing, for example, who elsewhere expresses a proper admiration for the sayings and thoughts of the ancients, suggests (Lessing 1987: 83) that it was only a few hundred years ago that anyone began to think of individuals' having rights against their masters, or the State, as if Nathan the prophet had never rebuked King David, or Pericles never proclaimed that some things were a citizen's own business.

Some ages believe that they inhabit the ruins of greater civilizations; others that they stand at the beginning of a new and glorious world. The latter is the less common view: 'the mass of men always look backwards; and the only corner where they in any sense look forwards is the little continent where Christ has His Church' (Chesterton 1961: 144)! It is likely enough that both these views are, in their measure, right: why should it not be true both that we have lost a great deal of what our predecessors knew, and that we are beginning to find out things that they did not? Which matters more to us depends, again, upon our evaluation of these different fields, upon our view of human life. In an age dominated by myths—I do not say fables—of evolutionary change and a merely material cosmos, it may seem reasonable to think that the best is yet to be, that we progress by shaking off ancient error, that the hope of the world lies in what is new and different from all that went before. But it is in fact fallacious to equate evolutionary change with progress, whether intellectual or any other kind, and wildly optimistic to suppose that in a world ruled only by the laws of decay there will ever be a humanity equipped with all wisdom, all true science. In the world described by moderns we have, as I shall point out at greater length in a moment, no reason at all to expect that we could ever get our cosmological theories right.

So on a modernist view we can have no reasonable ground to expect the later to be better. On a traditional view, on the other hand, we do have some reason to think that existing or pre-existing beliefs and practices do at least contain the truth by which we are to live, however clouded they may be by the slow decay of culture. In past ages every recognizable revolution of the spirit, every occasion when something happened to shake off old complacencies and cruelties, was presented as a revival of the Old Ways, a reminder of some truth long forgotten or distorted.

Whenever I have most carefully revised my moral standards, I am always able to see, upon reviewing my course of thought, that at best I have been finding out, in some new light, the true meaning that was latent in old traditions. . . . Revision does not mean mere destruction. We can often say to tradition: that which thou sowest is not quickened except it die. . . . Let us bury the natural body of tradition. What we want is its glorified body and its immortal soul. (Royce 1908: 11 f.)

What grounds do we have then for imagining that it is an epistemological error to be old-fashioned? Where positive errors can be identified by all means abandon the old. But be very sure that you have not misidentified as error what is only personally or socially offensive or obscure. If something has never been thought of before, or has always before been called an error, the chances are very high that it is an error. Can there really be many serious and important truths about life, the universe and everything that have been noticed literally for the first time in the last hundred years of a thousand million years of growth and exploration? Does it surprise you that I stretch our past so far? But just as it is true that practically all our food-plants or domestic animals were first tamed by palaeolithic or neolithic ancestors, and practically all our socio-political modes were in place two or three thousand years ago, so also our innate responses of affection, aggression, predation, perception were created through evolutionary ages when our ancestors, our 'animal ancestors' (what other kind?) kept records only in their living cells.

> On the backs of the dead,
> see, I am borne, on lost errands led,
> by spent harvests nourished. Forgotten prayers
> to gods forgotten bring blessings upon me.
>
> (Muir 1960: 200.)

Burke's rebuke to the French revolutionists:

You began ill because you began by despising everything that belonged to you. . . . Under a pious predilection for [your] ancestors your imaginings would have realized in them a standard of virtue and wisdom beyond the vulgar practices of the hour and you would have risen with the example to whose imitation you aspired. Respecting your forefathers, you would have been taught to respect yourselves. (Burke 1975: 300.)

Those who despise their ancestors must end by despising most of their ill-educated contemporaries, and exalting the opinions of a liberal élite, 'whilst at the same time they pretend to make [the humbler part of the community] the depositories of all power' (Burke 1975: 321).

It follows, so it seems to me, that we ought to be very wary of dismissing doctrines merely because we can ourselves see little or no reason to believe them, even if we hardly understand them. The claim that no one can be obliged either to do or to believe anything that she herself can at the moment see no reason to do or to believe may at first seem a necessary barrier against tyranny. How deplorable, we may think, to suppose that someone could be obliged or commanded to do or to believe things that she herself does not reckon obligatory. It is one mark of the liberal modernist that she resents commands, especially incomprehensible ones. Every one of us, we pretend, is to be mistress of her own soul. Anything less is heteronomy. But it is worth remembering what the doctrine once was that we now repeat in this sheerly individualistic form. 'No-one can be subjected to the Political Power of another without his own *Consent*', said Locke (1963: 374: 2. 95), but most certainly did not believe that there were no obligations binding on the individual irrespective of her consent to them. The right or duty of self-command was the necessity that one part of the self, composed of desire and temper, bow to the true self, the waking intellect, which was the same in every rational agent. Obedience to the Word of God is not excluded by that duty of self-command, because the duty—precisely— rests on God's command—an issue to which I shall return. Self- command emphatically did not mean doing what one chose to do from within one's normal cloudy and concupiscent individuality: it meant seeking to live in accordance with a higher principle even when one had almost forgotten why. 'You have forgotten what you are', said the Lady Philosophy to the imprisoned Boethius: 'because you are wandering, forgetful of your real self, you grieve that you are an exile and stripped of your goods' (*Consolation* 1. 6. 40). According to the *Brhadaranyaka Upanisad* 4. 3. 7 (cited by West 1971: 183), 'abiding within the senses is a person who consists of understanding, a light within the heart'. Those who think that literally all obligations derive their authority from the agent's own consent cannot reasonably criticize someone who accepts no obligation of autonomy. To say that we do have such an obligation is to admit that not all obligations rest on our consent.

It is that undying light which Kant identified as the centre of the moral life, and Kantian 'autonomy' is not to be identified with egoistic self-determination, the elevation of 'the Ego and its Own' that liberals have, half-heartedly, adopted after Max Stirner. 'Kant almost rediscovers the theory that there is only one intelligence (*nous*) and that it is this unicity which explains why there is one universal rule of truth and goodness' (Merlan 1963: 121). Where moderns see self-determination, a refusal to be bound by anything but one's own decision (and why exactly should successive stages of the human animal be bound by past decisions?), the ancients saw slavery or rebellion, a failure to acknowledge the demands of a higher self. The duty of obedience to the inner light, which has played a significant role in the overthrow of supposed duties of unquestioning obedience to some external authority, does not require us always to disbelieve or even to suspend judgement on all teachings that we do not ourselves understand or appreciate. On the contrary, when I acknowledge that I ought to think and act as that light decrees, I also acknowledge that, being an ignorant, fallible, and appetitive animal I am often likely to be in error. Even on a mundane level so much is obvious: no one thinks the worse of me if I agree to believe that baryons are each made up of three quarks in varying combinations of 'up', 'down', and 'bottom', although I have no understanding of the calculations that have led my betters to this conclusion, and cannot tell what further implications the thesis has. Strictly, perhaps, I do not *believe* this thesis about baryons but only that the sentence, appropriately uttered by high physicists, expresses a truth I neither believe nor disbelieve, but I would still be silly to reject it. Closer to home: I do not understand (i.e. cannot argue for their real truth or draw out their implications) even the simplest assertions about electrical force, but have no particular difficulty in turning on lights or mending fuses. To suppose that everything in religion or metaphysical philosophy in general must be simpler, more transparent than that, is a very strange idea. Why on earth should we suppose that we will immediately grasp and comprehend every true metaphysical or religious claim, and why then should we deny ourselves the right to 'believe' all sorts of things we do not understand, but which we have reason to believe that others, older in wisdom than ourselves, do understand?

Once again, this is not to say that older and immediately obscure assertions lie beyond the reach of criticism. On the contrary, really to believe in the inner light, in a mode of comprehension that transcends our immediate perceptions and likings, is to believe that we may, by lengthy strivings and the grace of the everliving, put aside even the most deeply rooted of our prejudices. But, as Gadamer emphasizes (1986), we cannot do without those prejudices from the start, and we certainly ought not to imagine that our incomprehension is a measure of truth. The Principle of Personal Incredulity, which one recent bio-logist, defending modern evolutionary theory against criticism, has deservedly mocked (Dawkins 1986: 38), has no greater plausibility in matters of religion and socio-political practice. Someone who chose to rewire the plugs on the ground that she could see no intrinsic connec-tion between green-and-yellow wires and the 'earth terminal' or the longer pin, or because she could not grasp the intellectual coherence of current electromagnetic theory, would not be well-regarded. Why is it any more sensible to rewire society or religious doctrine? Corres-pondingly, householders who hire self-styled electricians who profess no belief in traditional wiring practices, or are of an 'experimental' turn of mind, are being rash. An electrician, to be sure, who had no idea at all about why this or that needs to be done would not be an ideal choice either, but—accidents aside—she would be preferable. Why do we not acknowledge the same preference in matters of religion and socio-political practice? Neither ignorant traditionalists nor free-thinking experimentalists are ideal, but the former are more likely to be right than the latter. We ought, accordingly, to strive for understanding, but ought not to dismiss what we do not yet understand.

Facts, Mere Facts, and Values

One response to the argument I have offered for assuming at least as much obedient credulity in the fields of religion and socio-political practice as in the fields of electrical engineering, historical investi-gation, and medicine, has been to say that whereas these last are fac-tual disciplines, there can be no expertise in matters moral or metaphysical, and no higher 'understanding' than the immediate pre-ferences of those compelled to decide. In morals we do not have to decide what is true, but what to do. While we may rightly believe some things, or believe that they express a truth, which we do not under-stand, we cannot even consider deciding to do 'something we know not what'. Our decisions to act must be transparent in a way that our 'decisions to believe or take on trust' do not need to be.

Ancient philosophers would have replied that our decision to act, or to pursue a certain goal, is only a truly moral or human decision if we prefer the action as being *right*, the goal as being *good*. If our preference is merely appetitive, it does not differ in kind from animal, or infantile, or slavish behaviour. They would have added that even in that event people could still be mistaken about what they would truly prefer, and what the likely effects of individual appetitions would be in a world where what we succeed in doing is entangled in what others do. We regularly do things that we would have reason to regret if we saw more of the picture. As Thomas Hobbes well knew, the merely appetitive model of human choice lends no real support to liberalism. The fact, if it is one, that there are no standing obligations laid down from above, and that the body of true propositions entails no particular evaluative judgement, plainly does not support the moral thesis that each human individual ought to do only what she can see reason to do! The idea that moral non-objectivism somehow lends support to liberal values is one of the strangest and most widespread delusions of liberal society. If there are 'objective moral truths' then they may not be what we, as individuals, would prefer. If there are not, then what 'moral' views will dominate any particular community is a matter of historical accident. All of us will, obviously, prefer that it be our own views that triumph; our acceptance of some compromise ruling (e.g. that our own views may determine our 'private' affairs while we bow to pressure in 'public' matters) rests on our perception of the current balance of power. Objectivists with a strong sense of the intrinsic value of each human (or other) experiment may think it right to maintain a society that allows as much liberty to every individual as is compatible with an equal liberty for all. Non-objectivists may have similar preferences, but nothing says that they either should or will.

But though non-objectivism lends no support to liberalism, it may well be true that the passion to be 'free' has lent support to non-objectivism. No really 'modern' person ought to believe that there are any obligations 'laid down from above'. The so-called 'Euthyphro Argument'[5] has persuaded generations of undergraduates that God's

---

[5] This argument, presented by Socrates in Plato's *Euthyphro*, turns on the question whether God or the gods approve of certain actions or characters because they are pious, or whether they are pious because God or the gods approve of them. If the latter, then what is now considered wicked 'might' have been righteous (which is difficult to swallow); if the former, then God's agreement adds nothing to the pre-existing righteousness of those acts or characters. But why should we agree that God 'might' have been quite different or issued quite different commands? And how could we hope to discover any supposedly independent Values if God chose that we should not? The only way in which moral values can sensibly be supposed 'objective' is by reckoning that they are also causally efficacious—which is to say, that they are God. 'When morality is presented as eternal and immutable . . . it is only saying that God Himself is eternal and immutable, and making His nature the high and sacred original of virtue, and the sole fountain of all that is true and good and perfect' (Price 1974: 89; see Clark 1982a, 1987a, 1988b).

commandment cannot be the origin of moral duty, since any duty there is to obey God must be prior to any duty derived from what He tells us to do. If we have no standing obligation to obey God, we solve no moral crux by noticing what it is He tells us; if we do have such an obligation it cannot derive its force simply from His commanding us. I have observed elsewhere how strange an argument this is, how ill-suited to the largely non-objectivist metaphysic of those who place most emphasis on it. What its proponents often do not seem to notice is that it counts quite as much against any form of objective duty as against theocentric ethics. Either there is no moral duty to do what is morally required or there is: if there is, it cannot be one more duty alongside the other duties; if there is not, then we have no duty to do what is our duty. The argument, in this form, is plainly specious: but so is it in the anti-theistical. To be God at all is to be someone who ought to be obeyed, just as clearly as 'being a duty' is being what ought to be fulfilled.

Similarly, the supposedly counter-intuitive suggestion that if the Lord were the sole source of moral duty we might discover that the Lord required, or had come to require, quite different things from what we had supposed, in fact counts quite as much against any form of moral objectivism. We 'might' find out, or it might be true even if we could never find it out, that our 'real' duty was, say, to exterminate the human race. To this we might until recently have replied that the same is true of ordinary non-evaluative truth: we 'might' really be brains in a vat. If this does not render the category of real, objective truth otiose, why should similar emptily sceptical remarks weaken the hold of objective duty? The counter-argument is no longer rhetorically useful, precisely because some thinkers have surrendered so abjectly to anti-realism, and been prepared to abandon even non-moral objectivity—having done so, of course, they must allow a Pickwickian 'objectivity' even to moral utterance (as Lovibond 1983, after MacDowell): 'if men define situations as real, they are real in their consequences' (Schutz 1971: 348). In effect, they make society their God. I should add that in my interpretation of the vat-brain story, the result is not an empty scepticism—but that is because I admit to the possibility of a real and immediate access to reality (which, seeing 'through a glass darkly', we do not now possess).

The other response has been to concede that the 'Euthyphro Argument' does indeed count as strongly against any objective duty. Nothing that would make it even possible for the autonomous individual to be flatly wrong to do what she herself determined to be right can be admitted. 'Being right' cannot then be a fact to be discovered. All truly 'modern' persons must acknowledge that the body of genuinely true propositions is entirely value-free, and that the world is only seen accurately when it is seen without any emotional affect. 'Our highly refined and elegant scientific world picture carries the clear implication that our moralities, art and religions are purely human constructions that are in no way endorsed by the universe at large' (Cupitt 1982: p. viii). This doctrine is often associated with that strange perversion of the scientific spirit, which declares that since science is 'value-free' scientists have no moral duties, and ought never to be forbidden to do what on scientific grounds they think an interesting experiment. That this is itself an evaluative judgement, and one that is wholly and obviously irrational, constantly escapes their attention.

To see the world without emotional or evaluative affect is to be blind to any normative pattern in the world, anything which, irrespective of our present wishes, implies that we would be right or wrong to do this or that. The dogma that no such norm exists owes something of its popularity to the collapse of the medieval cosmological synthesis: in place of obviously evaluative explanations of what goes on (that adult male humans have deeper voices, for example, because this is appropriate to their status as the nobler sex: Aristotle, *De Generatione Animalium* 5, 787[a] 1 f.: see Clark 1982b), the founders of modern science sought out material causes, irrespective of any evaluative judgement about what ought to be the case. I shall in a later volume point out that modern scientific method, both historically and philosophically, owes a lot more to 'normative analysis' than is usually admitted. It is quite usual in fact for high physicists to hypothesize the existence of hitherto unnoticed particles merely because they 'ought' to exist if the theory is to be sufficiently elegant and harmonious. But it is possible, even sensible, to agree that what is the case is not entirely determined by what ought to be. It is at least not a logical truism that what is also ought to be. It is even sensible to add that even human history ought not to be handled in an entirely partisan spirit. The sort of historical writing that amounts to nationalistic hagiography may well be countered by a careful insistence on reporting 'only the facts', as they would be admitted by a witness with no axe to grind, no preference that things go one way rather than another. All this has led us to the conclusion that we ought, in seeking the truth, to describe things as neutrally as possible, and to reserve our moral or aesthetic judgements for our spare time. Things are as they are, whether we like them or not, and what they are can be discovered only if we are prepared to put aside our evaluative prejudices.

This may be a useful, even a vital discipline, but it should not escape our notice that it is itself a heavily evaluative one. It is precisely because we recognize that we ought not to allow parochial or partisan spirit to distort our vision of the Whole, that we seek to calm ouselves in the hope that we shall at last see clearly, and see whole. Juries ought not to let themselves be corrupted by an *idée fixe*, by personal and irrelevant prejudice, by the delusion that what happened must on all occasions have been what ought—in their view—to have happened. It does not follow that the good juryman will forever refrain from passing judgement. Nor does it follow that certain moral dogmas are not rightly entrenched, such as to require no further argument or demonstration. 'People who are puzzled to know whether one ought to honour the gods and love one's parents or not need punishment' (Aristotle, *Topics* 2, 105ᵃ 5 f.).

It has become part of the mental set of moderns that we see things truly only when we deliberately drain them of all emotional affect, as if it were obviously correct to see one's child as merely a collection of animal organs, or a piece of drifting mass-energy, no different in kind from any other heap of protoplasm. Obviously, very few even of those who are most vocal in defence of such indifferentism actually practise what they preach. Why, indeed, should they? If that is what 'truth' is why should we concern ourselves with 'truth'? The ancients, in various ways and differing vocabularies, agreed that the true vision could only come if we put aside parochial desire, and sought to eradicate the recurring delusion that one is oneself more important than any other entity. They did not conclude that the true vision was valueless: on the contrary, it was important that we see aright because what we would then see, the cosmos itself, was supremely worth seeing, and the spirit with which we would see it supremely worth experiencing. A scientist challenged to defend her experimental assaults upon a fellow-creature will usually end by saying, in shocked tones, that 'you can't interfere with a scientist's right to seek new knowledge', although it is axiomatic for indifferentists that there are no real objective rights at all. As I have urged on other occasions, almost *ad nauseam* (Clark 1977a): the wisdom that is worth pursuing is not compatible with such violation of creaturely integrity.

In sum, liberal individualism is a misreading of the ancient demand that we live our lives in obedience to a higher principle, our real Self, the *daimon* that is the donor of *eudaimonia* (see Clark 1975: 146), commonly translated 'happiness'. Just so, modern indifferentism is a perversion of another ancient creed, that the truth is made known to those who approach the world with a kind of love, love purged of concupiscence, and who are moved to admire the real form of things, a form certainly obscured by our particular prejudice and perhaps by real failures to live up to the norm.

Love amid the Ruins

We have forgotten what we are, and what the world is. Draining the world, miscalled 'the environment' as if its only function were to environ us, of emotional affect and professing thereby to see things clearly, we automatically elevate our own personal interests as the only ones worth bothering with. Living in a dead world we warm ourselves by the fires of personal relationships. No truly modern person should think anything more important than those 'personal relationships', and anyone who doubts that it is here alone God lies is thought spiritually deformed. The shock that passes visibly over some commentators' faces if it is suggested that sexual orgasm isn't always ecstasy nor always 'a good thing', is often very funny. Blaspheming Aphrodite is the one obscenity! AIDS has not, so far, killed many people: its peculiar horror is its involvement in what had seemed a safe and happy corner of the human world—though anyone who thought it safe was always self-deceived, and all of us who once imagined ourselves wise should take note that doctrines we once thought absurd have turned out, at the least, to have a point. The equal and opposing error, pointed out by Paris (1986: 102), is to think oneself above such things. Moderns alternate in their attack on old-style piety. On the one hand, piety is at fault in thinking of the universe as a home, a place rightly valued for the life in it: 'mature minds' recognize the alien facticity of things. On the other hand, piety is to blame for disvaluing present personal ties by placing them in the context of eternity. On the one hand, we ought to realize that our species counts for nothing in immensity, that it and its mode of living are an accident, owed no blessing by the alien powers. On the other, we ought to treasure our immediate social pleasures as of immeasurable worth, since there alone we can ever be at home. The position is not wholly incoherent, nor ignoble. But the pious may reasonably respond that this is all pretence, a self-deceived infatuation with something of no real moment. Such moderns pretend to see nothing as sacred, but make a glaring exception in favour of an arbitrarily selected set of hairless primates, and their own wish for physical and social comfort. A truth that matters for the social round will not be the indifferent Void; a society really imbued with nihilism will not be very social. As Plotinus retorted to the Gnostics long ago: 'If God is not in the world He is not in you' (*Enneads* 2. 9. 16). 'If God were dead, so would nature be—and humans could be no more than embattled strangers, doomed to defeat, as we have largely convinced ourselves we in fact are' (Kohak 1984: 5).

Although healthy-minded moderns pretend to a great respect for personal affection and mutual pleasure, usually with the additional claim that 'the pious' have been severely lacking in this area, this can hardly, in consistency, be more than a pretence. In one of Olaf Stapledon's later fables, *Darkness and the Light*, his scientific visionaries uncover the 'real truth of things', that our universe is no more than a snowflake on the battleground of indifferent titans. From that appalling vision we may hide our eyes and forget the truth by giving in to drink, sexual love, or academic infighting. We do not matter to anyone but us, and to us not for very long. If we are to see things truly we must strip our selves and even our best beloveds of their mystery. If we remain enamoured it is with the hidden knowledge that we are willingly forgetful of the truth. The ancients reminded us that even when kissing our child we should remember that she too is mortal, that another child is no different except to us, being misled. That hard advice is now seen as a betrayal of 'love', a refusal to be besotted, as if such love were the only real thing in an empty world.

What are the further implications of living godlessly? For one thing it implies forgetfulness of the encompassing world to which we are so totally bound, both as individuals and as a species. No longer do we feel answerable to this encompassing which is within us, as memory, imagination and consciousness, or without us as soil and sun and air and water. We are forgetful of the fact that these latter are not simply things of our environment but natural powers and fibres of which we are made and which enable us to be sustained in existence every moment . . . Such godless living means for another thing that our species fancies itself to be the purpose and goal of creation perhaps not merely of our tiny earth but also of the inconceivable range and extent of the cosmos. (Gray 1970: p. xviii.)

The belief that this world can only be reckoned valuable as a mechanism

for making people with a special interest in their own personal relationships is so pervasive a mental set that even pious theologians take it
for granted, as they also assume that no modern person should think
anything more important than 'this worldly' ties, or give any credence
to 'dualistic' or 'other worldly' philosophies. Commentators regularly
assert that 'dualism' is no serious philosophical option, 'nowadays',
that it was only a platonizing error that ever suggested that 'God made
not one world, but two' (2 *Esdras* 7: 50). The 'kingdom of heaven' is
now believed to be a 'loving community' of this-worldly beings,
although such modernist theologians very rarely show any expectant
interest in a real historical *parousia*. The dominant style is simultaneously this-worldly and intellectualist, so that the believer can only
ever expect a change in her attitude to this-worldly catastrophe, an
inspired conviction that human love, just as it is, is sufficient glory and
compensation for the ills of this world.

It's really impressive the way modern psycho-analysis has confirmed the
insights of the New Testament. Where two or three are gathered together, you
know. It is an indisputable fact that groups of people, huddled as closely as
possible, do feel much warmer. This is the basis of Group Therapy. It is also
known as the Kingdom of Heaven. (Green 1969: 124.)[6]

---

[6] It is perhaps necessary to point out that Green is not commending this evasion!

2

Ending the Age

Isis Wanderer, by Kathleen Raine's account, sought for the god Osiris, her dead husband, through a landscape drained of meaning, and proclaimed

> This too is an experience of the soul
> the dismembered world that once was the whole god
> whose broken fragments now lie dead.
> This passing of reality itself is real.
>
> (Raine 1981: 21.)

What her first worshippers intended by the search of Isis for the dismembered corpse of Osiris, and its eventual reconstruction, is something outside our knowledge. Perhaps similar experiences, of human loss and seasonal change, lay behind the Greek story of Demeter's search for Persephone. That the stories are now remembered does suggest that they speak to us at some deep level of that state of being which knows itself as loss, deprivation, emptiness. With that loss comes the collapse of ceremonial order, when the sacred spring runs dry,

> the nine men's morris is filled up with mud;
> and the quaint mazes in the wanton green,
> for lack of tread, are indistinguishable.

(Shakespeare, *A Midsummer Night's Dream* 2. 2. 98.)

In Plato's myth the Shepherd of the World periodically allows things to run backward, under their own steam—which is the age of the world that we inhabit. In the other age, he joked, the dead crawl backward from their graves and grow younger as the years pass (Plato, *Politicus* 271 f.). In this age we grow old and die, because the gods have gone.

Plato did not really believe that the God had withdrawn His hand, but the image of loss and departure, of a world that did not fully embody the divine, that reminded us of the divine precisely by not being divine, is deeply Platonic. The gods have gone with the fairies, and 'who of late for cleanliness finds sixpence in her shoe?' Once upon a time, there was a world of love and beauty, ceremony that was never stale, joy that never lost its sense of membership in the whole body of earth and heaven. Once upon a time, things went as they did because they clearly ought to. Our world, the world we now, by habit, think is natural, took its beginning from a death or departure.

There had come into my mind a vague and vast impression that in some way all good was a remnant to be stored and held sacred out of some primordial ruin. Man had saved his good as Crusoe saved his goods: he had saved them from a wreck. (Chesterton 1961: 64.)

Nietzsche's declaration that God is dead occasionally appears on walls, and is, in a sense, well answered by the riposte, 'Nietzsche is dead: (signed) God'. That at least is certain. But there is also a sense in which God's death is as familiar as Queen Anne's. Though I shall have something to say about the Presence of God, and the Practice of the Presence of God, in a later volume, it is important that we should remember that the gods have always 'gone away'. It is of the essence, we might almost conclude, of gods that they are not 'here-now'. Unless we remember that, the story of 'God with Us' loses its mystery. Consider this through the medium of fairy-story for a moment. Modernists convinced of their own virtue may find this move puzzling: surely we all 'know' that fairies are merely fabulous? I doubt that we do, because I doubt that we really know what fairies were supposed to be. Patronizing nonsense about 'gossamer-winged little persons at the bottom of the garden' (as Dawkins 1986: 292) is wholly unhelpful—or rather, it helps us by drawing attention to similar failings in modernist accounts of more obviously religious doctrines. Folk stories, often enough, tell of the fairies' 'flitting': farewell, rewards and fairies. But though the stories put a date on their departure, whether at the Reformation or when the Friars came, this is no more 'historical' than are Greek descriptions of Dionysus as a foreign import. It is of Dionysus' essence that he be 'foreign'; it is the very point of fairies that they are 'once upon a time', and that those who would go to them forswear the present. Tolkien's judgement, as so often, was exact:

[Galadriel] seemed to [Frodo], as by men of later days Elves still at times are seen: present and yet remote, a living vision of that which has already been left far behind by the flowing streams of Time. (Tolkien 1966: i. 389.)

That is the first death, the sheer absence or once-upon-a-time identity of the divine. There is also a second death. Fairies, in the Western tradition, differ from gods or God, because they offer a rival beatitude, something that can be reached only by those who turn aside from the narrow way. They are, it was said, those spirits who fell from Heaven with Lucifer but did not throw in their lot with him. They are almost the anti-gods, the *asuras*, of Hindu tradition, or the Titans of Hellenic—though it does not seem that much religious attention was ever paid to those latter beings. Sometimes a captured human can be restored to present life, baptized, or married into sociality (though thanks to the way time passes in the Hollow Hills they come to us from the past). Captured fairies cannot be finally socialized: brownies take offence at being offered clothes, and fairy wives find some excuse to leave. Fairyland is not the Earthly Paradise, but the Hollow Lands, haven of those who will not take the long loop round through earthly pain and duties. To believe in fairies is to think that possibility is real, and desperately attractive. All order excludes something, and that unorderly life may creep around the corner when we least expect it.

Yeats, one of the most lucid of twentieth-century supporters of 'the Fairy Faith', declared that

We are imperfect, incomplete, and no more like a beautiful woven web, but like a bundle of cords knotted together and flung into a corner. It is said that the world was once all perfect and kindly, and that still the kindly and perfect world existed, but buried like a mass of roses under many spadefuls of earth. The Faeries and the more innocent of the spirits dwelt within it and lamented over our fallen world in the lamentation of the wind-tossed reeds. (Yeats 1959: 104.)[1]

But the beauty of fairies is an illusion that the fairies do not share. The question that Don Quixote raised is a real one: is he deluded, or is it the rest of us who have been deceived by the 'disenchanters', who would have us think that the old glad world is gone (see Schutz 1971: 236 f.)? One common folk-story is of the human midwife, called to assist a fairy birth, who touches her own eye with the ointment meant for the baby. She then sees 'the truth', that the mother 'lay on a bundle of rushes and withered ferns in a large cave', and not in a palace (Briggs 1967: 121). To see the fairies is to see a terrible beauty: to see

---

[1] I have offered a more detailed account, using some of the same material, of how it is that Yeats, and Evans-Wentz (1911), managed to believe in fairies, and why this was not a matter of believing a number of false things about seals or native humans or extraterrestrial visitants, in Clark 1988a. Yeats's philosophical acumen has been neglected even by those who applaud his poetry, and even *because* they applaud his poetry.

with fairy sight is to see (or think you see) the worthlessness, the small-
ness not only of mortal matters but of their own. In a real and horrid
sense those caught up by fairies are not in a dream, but have been 'dis-
illusioned'. They no longer care, and feel no strong passion, though
they infect others.

> Gaze no more in the bitter glass
> the demons, with their subtle guile,
> lift up before us when they pass,
> or only gaze a little while . . .
> for all things turn to barrenness
> in the dim glass the demons hold,
> the glass of outer weariness,
> made when God slept in times of old.
> There, through the broken branches, go
> the ravens of unresting thought;
> flying, crying, to and fro,
> cruel claw and hungry throat.

> (Yeats 1950: 55; see Moore 1954: 179.)

Only those whose ordinary life is structured by ceremonial and human
meaning, who know of their duties and their perils, their friends and
children can clearly conceive that form of life which is fairy. 'That
which she bore has the likeness of a unicorn', said Yeats of the New
Thing whose birth he expected to inaugurate the new age, as Christ
and Helen, respectively, began the Christian and the Hellenic Era,
'and is most unlike man of all living things, being cold, hard and vir-
ginal' (Yeats 1959: 312: 'virginity', for Yeats, is cruel—see Wilson
1958: 74). If fairyland were to enter the very fabric of our lives, we
should not easily attend to it (any more than conceited people know
they're conceited). Those who have despaired of human meaning, who
acknowledge no duties save their momentary whims, who pride themselves on not being charmed or enchanted by the master hypnotists of
piety or affection or moral duty, whose curiosity or greed or lust is both
unlimited and unimportant even to them, are living out the life of fairies. Whether their real human souls are somewhere else or not, what
acts in them here is, in effect, a fairy (see Dante, *Inferno* 33. 142 ff.).
Such fairies are unaware of fairyland: to them it is the ordinary human
heart that is uncanny.

Everyone knows that there are forms of cruelty which can injure a man's life
without injuring his body. They are such as to deprive him of a certain form of
food necessary to the life of the soul. (Weil 1987: 7.)

So perhaps Yeats was right, if not in his occasional worship of the *Sidhe*, yet in his suspicion that the new age dawning would be one in the grip of fairy. 'The knowledge of reality is always in some measure a secret knowledge. It is a kind of death' (Yeats 1955: 482). The death, its gaze 'blank and pitiless as the sun', that 'slouches towards Bethlehem to be born' (Yeats 1950: 211) is something we have cause to acknowledge, and to fear.

We may be about to accept the most implacable authority the world has known. Do I desire it or dread it, loving as I do the gaming table of Nature where many are ruined but none is judged, and where all is fortuitous, unforeseen? (Yeats 1962: 279 f.)

Was Christina Stoddart, the paranoid author of *Light-bearers of Darkness*, a renegade assault upon the Golden Dawn and other such occult groups published in 1930 (Moore 1954: 171; see Harper 1974: 127 ff.), altogether wrong to think that a deadly peril was approaching humankind, even if she was wrong to identify it with secret Illuminati, cabbalistic Jews in league with the Soviets?

In sum, the fairies of Western tradition are in one way gods, ways of speaking of a divine life that lies at the root of things but which has withdrawn or dies away from our everyday existence. In another way they are the enemies of humanity, or the enemies of a dying age. The New Thing, Yeats expected, would be born from

all that our age had rejected, from all that [his] stories symbolize as a harlot, and would take after its mother; because we had worshipped a single god it would worship many or receive from Joachim de Flora's Holy Spirit a multitudinous influx. (Yeats 1962: 393.)

The collapse of ceremonial meaning, of our sense of being 'at home' in a world founded on a divine order, is itself the birth-pang of a new order. Fairyland offers a sweet escape from established duty and the long climb up to heaven, a pretence that we could happily live 'naturally'. But those who seek to live by 'natural' impulse, with the ancient energies of anger, lust, and ignorance, find that the world is drained of affect. Those who follow the fairies away from the human world lose their place in it. The human world, as it has been, is one where different impulses, different energies all lie at the service of ceremony and law. Fairyland, as it takes shape on the common earth, is a land of wars between incommensurable simplicities, where no loyalty is owed forever. The new thing Yeats expected was a disorderly throng of moods, each of which was absolute and all-encompassing. The past age, he thought, had attempted to live by a single rule, an order that gave love, war, and purity each its place. The new age was one where no single spirit would rule, and every spirit would—for that reason—seek an absolute control. A single Deity is only credible when culture can be unified—a goal that pluralism forbids (Cupitt 1982: 68). 'To the extent that society is impoverished and confused in its structure of relations, to that extent is the idea of God poor and unstable in content' (Douglas 1973: 79). Because there is no shared order, no pattern of growth and movement, no one has anything more to rest on than the ferocity of her own passion and any can hope for final victory. When the mood passes (and that is what, in Yeatsian terms, a fairy is) we are left empty.

A fairy, Yeats explicitly declares, is a mood or a mode of conscious being. I have no interest, in this volume, in the ontology of fairies as things existing before or underneath the world of our experience. It is enough that like the Olympian gods (on which see Otto 1954, Vycinas 1972, and Paris 1986) they exist *within* our experience as moods and images and symbols. As Russell remarks of a related topic, 'the Devil is what his concept is, and his concept is the tradition of human views about him' (Russell 1977: 43). Those 'views' are more than opinions: they are themselves modes of experiencing that deadly presence. What Yeats aimed to describe were provinces of human meaning (see Schutz 1971: 340 ff.), irrespective of any theories about their real genesis— though he was in fact (as am I) an objective, Berkeleian idealist (though 'Berkeleian realist' would be less misleading). What he described, pro- phetically, was that collapse of central order which has since issued, in the ethical sphere, in talk of incommensurable, merely subjective ideals, and in the methodological in talk of 'forms of life' or 'language games' or 'finite provinces of human meaning'. Either there is no one such form of life that has any pre-eminence, it is now assumed, or else the world of non-participatory science is paramount. 'God is dead', either because there are many competing gods, all of which have their being in a human experience that is irreducibly and inevitably plural- istic, or because the one 'true' and 'appropriate' attitude is that pre- scribed by Jacques Monod (1972; see Clark 1984: 10, 38 f.), of rejecting any impulse to 'participate' in or empathize with the physical universe, and so to see it as indifferent and without objective or com- pelling value. The doctrines are effectively equivalent: there is no order to which the lesser gods must bow, no divine chain whereby Zeus Father of Gods and Men may control the lesser provinces of human meaning. What Yeats expected was the fulfilment of the sinister prophecy that Apollo would one day supplant Zeus as Zeus had overthrown Cronos. The establishment of Zeus' rule was in the moral and political suppression and control of Titanic forces: Aphrodite Ouranios, for example, was domesticated as the daughter of Dione; Metis, who is crafty wisdom, was born again as Athena; even Dionysus, whose essence is the overthrow of established order, had his place within the realm of Zeus (see Detienne & Vernant 1978: 107 ff.). Shakespeare's image is a similar one: Titania, the Titanid, must be reunited with Oberon so that humankind, whose 'parents and originals' the fairies are, may be at peace (see White 1970: 47). Apollo the Far-shooter, whose nature it is to see clearly from a distance and to turn his loves into mere objects, has no special insight into the real nature of his fellow gods, and no power to establish a just rule.

Pluralism and the Divine Unity

Two of the paradoxes in Yeats's prophecy, and in my statement of what 'God's Death' might mean for us, are as follows:

  (i) 'freedom', or forgetfulness of *Themis*, breeds 'the most implacable authority the world has known';
  (ii) the irreducible diversity of language games, or provinces of meaning, goes hand in hand with an extraordinary dogmatism about the real nature of the world.

To elaborate the second of these: it is simultaneously claimed that there is no right way of thinking and acting, and that the world supposedly revealed by 'science' is the one true world, the 'high ground of fact'. No such world is in fact revealed: the value-neutral, merely factitious universe is simply the object pole of an attitude which is actually incompatible with honest science, quite as much as the familiar figure of Woman the Temptress is the object pole of a concupiscence that is incompatible with honourable love. Apollo's servants—taking 'Apollo' for the moment to name the attitude of non-participatory manipulative science—have as much claim within a purely polytheistic, pluralistic system as Aphrodite's or Artemis'. What they cannot consistently assert within a polytheistic system is that theirs is the only or even the paramount way. If Zeus is overthrown, and *Themis*, Apollo cannot maintain order. In what possible sense is the physical object disclosed in Apolline mood more real than the physical object disclosed in Aphrodisiac or Hermetic mood? Perhaps it constitutes an explanation? But

such a claim is both unwarranted, and inconsistent with the methodological pluralism that is preferred by modernists. The Apolline mood is
ideological: its 'virtue', to those who profess it, that it empties the
world of any meaning which might interfere with their invasive use of it
(on which more below).

True pluralism of the kind advocated most recently, though without
recourse to the Olympian gods, by Goodman (1978) or Putnam (1983)
or Feyerabend (1987), expressly rejects any claim to mastery. All
moods, all methods are correct in their own eyes. The trouble is that,
as I observed in the last chapter, such relativism does not really support
the liberal ideal. Only if there is one world, one order in which each
lesser mood or province has its place, does it make sense for one devo-
tee to allow another cult its place. The more narrowly single-minded
my devotion the less tolerant it can be: precisely because I make no
claim beyond my passionate devotion to some one mood or method my
passion can be unlimited. Because Apolline science has no better claim
than Aphrodisiac devotion to be the one 'appropriate' mood, Apol-
linists may force their way on others. If they think it wrong so to do, it
is only because they secretly acknowledge the rule of Zeus and *Themis*.
Where Zeus does not rule, and all gods are maintained in being only by
the devotion of their worshippers, each cult may hope to create an
overmastering reality to which all others must bow.

The first of the soul's needs, the one which touches most nearly its eternal
destiny is order; that is to say, a texture of social relationships such that no one
is compelled to violate imperative obligations in order to carry out other ones.
(Weil 1987: 9 f.).

What I have called the 'second death' is the process whereby we have
lost our sense of the divine unity, our expectation that truth will, in the
end, prove 'one, without a flaw', that there could be an order in which
each mood may take its proper, partial form, where we can do all our
duties. Blake anticipated Yeats in identifying Shakespeare's fairies and
Chaucer's pilgrims as 'eternal principles or characters of human life'.

The Grecian gods were the Cherubim of Phoenicia; but the Greeks, and since
them the Moderns have neglected to subdue the gods of Priam. These gods
are visions of the eternal attributes, or divine names, which when erected into
gods become destructive of humanity . . . For when separated from man or
humanity, who is Jesus the Saviour, the vine of eternity, they are thieves and
rebels, they are destroyers. (Blake, *Descriptive Catalogue* no. 3: 1966: 570 ff.)

As a matter of practical politics, the different impulses and moods of human life must be woven together. What is lacking in this age of the world is the sense that there is some existing pattern in which each proper impulse finds its place. We have to make up our own pattern, which can only be the result of contemporary power politics, having no moral force to sway the incoming generations. 'The cultures are for-ever seeking to combine peace with prosperity, justice with order, free-dom with welfare, truth with beauty, scientific truth with moral good, technical proficiency with practical wisdom, holiness with life, and all these with all the rest' (Niebuhr 1951: 38 f.). The kingdom of God, the Christ, is another matter.

That our understanding is in its own nature not only very weak and imperfect, but also much obscured by passion and prejudice, is a point too plain to need proof. From all which we may certainly conclude it is not in our true interest to be governed by our own carnal and irregular wills, but rather to square and suit our actions, to the supreme will of him, whose understanding is infinite, com-prehending in one clear view the remotest events and consequences of things. (Berkeley 1948: vii. 135.)

Those who have lost their memory of the one comprehensive order are at the mercy of whatever passion, mood, or fairy chances to drink them up. If Aristotle was wrong to think that there was some one activity, some one ideal, that had the strength and the authority to rule the lesser ideals and activities of human life (and modern commentators often seem to find it obvious that he was), then the different life-ways and preferences of humankind must simply fight it out.

The Deconstruction of Society and the Self[2]

This 'second death' of the divine order is what other commentators intend when they speak of modern society as a 'society of strangers', compelled to live and work together without any shared consciousness of an order within which their different talents, moods and characters can all have a place (as MacIntyre, 1981). That 'God is dead' means simply that there is no established blueprint for our lives together, that existing institutions and schools are only products of past history hav-ing no moral force, no exemplary function. It does not really follow that

[2] 'Deconstructionism' is a philosophical movement of greater influence on English literary critics than on Anglo-Saxon philosophers, but like many such 'Continental' movements, it has its analogues within the analytical tradition. I shall have more to say about it, and about anti-realism in general, in my third volume.

the gods are dead: on the contrary, it is easy to describe our situation in Yeats's terms, precisely as the triumphant return of ancient deities. I repeat that in this context I make no special ontological commitments. Whether the gods 'exist' is not the most important question, even if we altogether understood what it was to 'exist'. The question is, what is conveyed by talk of gods and fairies in the description of our human world—a world, remember, which inevitably includes the 'natural' universe as it exists for us.

'Our present impending danger', Berkeley said, 'is from the setting up of private judgement, or an inward light, in opposition to human and divine laws' (Berkeley 1948: vi. 127). Liberal philosophy in the present century has until recently been able to reply that such individual judgement is the necessary condition of moral and political liberty, and that Berkeley was too pessimistic in believing that individuals could not agree to work together without the goad and guidance of divine command. What Yeats recognized was that the supposed irreducibility of personal identity could not any longer be relied upon: it is true of each of us, as it is true of the world and of the body politic, that it is 'a bundle of cords knotted together and flung into a corner'. Each passion, each mood, each province of meaning has its own weight. If there is no public pattern within which each may find a place there is also no private or personal pattern. The human animal is decomposed into its elements, and those elements are the true immortals, struggling for temporary ascendancy and the life of mortals.

> Eternity is passion, girl or boy
> cry at the onset of their sexual joy
> 'For ever and for ever'; then awake
> ignorant what Dramatis Personae spake.
>
> (Yeats 1950: 332.)

Political philosophers have not quite caught up with the radical dismemberment of personal unity that is occurring nowadays amongst psychologists and philosophers of mind or action. The Ego and its own has for a long time been the solid base on which liberal thinkers have hoped to erect the Great Society. Even if there is no pre-existing pattern, they have thought, it is still possible and obviously desirable for each self-seeking individual to enter into long-term contracts of mutual help and forbearance. Those individuals who are possessed by a spirit that cares less about their 'own' life than some immortal programme can be labelled 'fanatics' and excluded from the clan of calmly self-regarding animals. The hope is that there will be enough of these to maintain a civil life that makes no overweening demands on individual action. Unfortunately, this whole model of individual decision, in which it is taken for granted that there are unified beings who both do and should rationally plan for their whole life together is itself the relic of an ancient era. Max Stirner recognized that Humanity or Reason was only God under another 'name (Stirner 1971; see Carroll 1974, 20 ff.), but imagined that the Ego was immune to deconstruction. But if God is dead, so also is the Self. Philosophers who question Descartes's 'proofs' of God also deny his proof of that lesser god, the spiritual substance that endures through change and illusion, Ego. 'I' is as much a disease of language as 'God'! So much is even recognized, in practice: marriages are not to last beyond the natural enthusiasm of both partners, whatever it was that their 'past selves' may have sworn, and so all oaths are vain. The 'protean self', having no stable or enduring employment or devotion (Lifton 1970), becomes the *The Dice Man* described by Luke Rhinehart, relying on the throw of the dice to determine whether he shall go fishing, wenching, or commit a murder—which is only an exaggerated parable of what must follow from the death of God. How can one moment of a life dictate to others, any more than one person can dictate to others, unless—in either case—the dictation comes from within, from something that is present in every moment or mode of human being?

God's arky, his will for us, is never anything extraneous to ourselves but precisely that which is most germane to our true destiny and being. . . . Rather than a heteronomous imposition, God's arky spells the discovery of that which is truest to myself and my world. (Eller 1987: 3.)

And how, if God is gone away, shall we secure the peace? Hobbes saw that fear of death was the one impulse making for peace when people no longer feared the Lord (see 1968: 188, 200). Moderns now try to escape the fear of death by denying that they have a life to lose. 'He who does not respect his life even in principle cannot be restrained from the most dreadful vices; he recks neither law nor torments' (Kant 1930: 153). Fortunately for the civil peace not everyone who offers verbal deconstructions of the fear of death speaks like one that has the makings of a death-commando!

There is a sense, of course, in which all this talk of 'God's death', and the radical desacralizing and deconstruction of any received order, is merely fashionable chatter. As Feyerabend remarks, 'there is fragmentation; but there are also new and powerful uniformities' (1987: 2). It is easy for bourgeois commentators to pretend that they do not live within an established, peaceable order (whose permanence is admittedly illusory), that there is nothing sacred 'out there in the world', that any evanescent project has as much or as little claim on our attention. It is easy, because it is superficial. Those who claim to believe that there is no such order, and that the truly modern person expects none, are usually pillars of the establishment, or at least find no difficulty about paying their taxes, their mortgages, or their grocer's bills. Those who have made a comfortable living by denouncing sacredness and civil order would be appalled to find themselves among the more impassioned rebels, those who desecrate churches, rob banks, or torture prisoners. Would the egoist, Philo enquired, do away with 'the government of a city, the firm establishment of laws, the guardianship of morals, reverence towards elders, respect for the memory of the departed, fellowship with the living, piety in words and actions towards the Deity?' (Philo, *Posterity of Cain*, 53 (181): 1930: ii. 435). Most theoretical egoists or desacralists would not, even though they mean no more by 'Deity' than the framework of traditional order in which they find themselves. But by proclaiming that there is no sacred significance in human form or consecrated building, that the rules of property are only the record of a power struggle, that no one is to think herself the bearer of a family name or nationhood, that there can be no hope of a real resolution of conflicting preferences, whether within society or the self, and that the self itself is only a disease of language, they do in effect endeavour, as Berkeley said, 'to fill [their] country with highwaymen, housebreakers, murderers, fraudulent dealers, perjured witnesses and every other pest of society' (Berkeley 1948: vi. 219 f.).

It is not only avowed atheists who are likely to resent this charge, which should not be misunderstood. There are those whose 'atheism' merely amounts to self-dedication to a deity who is not of this world, an ideal perfection that influences nothing of what goes on in the world except through its devotees. Their doctrine may be confused—as I believe it to be—but they are not 'atheists' in the sense that I am here discussing. They do not reject all authority over their momentary whim, nor do they despair of civil order.

It is interesting to note, in the context of Berkeley's charge, that moral philosophers have been ready to describe morality as just the sort of rules that might be struck between brigands for their individual profit. So Mackie (1976: 10): 'the truest teachers of moral philosophy are the outlaws and thieves who keep faith and rules of justice with one another . . . as rules of convenience without which they cannot hold together'. But as Donagan (1977: 91 f.) has observed, such rules of convenience, as between desperate ruffians, have no moral force at all: 'it would be absurd to suppose that by promising to commit a murder a member of a criminal gang can place himself under an obligation to commit it, or even to give himself a *prima facie* reason to commit it'.[3]

Theism and Objective Value

There are also avowed theists who have welcomed the 'secularizing' or 'disenchantment' of the world we inhabit, who profess to believe that all material things are at the disposal of human intelligence, that nothing matters but human, personal action in the present day. Their doctrine is, superficially, the same as that with which I began this chapter: namely, that the divine is essentially absent, that the gods have always gone away, precisely so that humankind may be driven back upon itself, and rely no more on something 'out there'. To rely on what is already built into the world is to rely on the old order, which is Satan. The true God is the one who speaks within the heart, who will triumph at the last day but has not yet. The best we can do by contemplation of existing reality is imagine the new world coming.

Consider the following inconsistent triad of propositions:

(i) nothing is real, or really real, that has no effect upon the natural world except through the behaviour of those who act in accordance with a belief in it;

(ii) values have no effect on the natural world save through the behaviour of those who act in accordance with a belief in them;

(iii) values are really real.

It is not necessary to abandon more than one of these. Those who proclaim the second death acknowledge just such values as are natural impulses, War, Lust, and Curiosity (and can therefore, for those values, abandon the second proposition). High-minded atheists

---

[3] I have commented in Clark 1988b on the sort of moral philosophers who have forgotten so completely what it is that Mackie was rejecting that they do not even understand Mackie. The really significant point about Mackie (1976) is that he realized the identity of objective morality and theism, and rejected the former because he disliked the

abandon the first proposition, though without giving any hint of what the metaphysical status of such values may be, or how they could hope to know of them. Some self-styled theists seem to have abandoned the third proposition, agreeing that God is not 'real', but denying the corollary, that there is then no God. My judgement is that this is as much as to say that the human will is God, since an unreal God's authority and power as an abstract ideal lies only in our worship. The old-fashioned theist would have denied the second proposition, without limiting such effective and creative value to the class of 'natural impulse', fairy. Modernist critics of the belief in objective value, and of theism, have mistaken the point. That there are real, objective values actually requires that those values are creative and causally efficacious even apart from our belief in them. In fact it requires that they be God, in the sense described by Price (1974: 89: see above). As Mackie (1976: 232) remarks, 'it matters a lot for moral philosophy whether any such theistic view is correct', for without it we are left alone with our whimsy.

My argument, then, runs as follows.

1. Objective values which we could have no way of identifying as such would be nugatory, and would have to be ignored in any considered life-plan.

2. The only kind of objective values that could be identified as existing apart from the life-plan of particular persons or societies (i.e. existing objectively) would be ones that had an effect upon the world independently of their believers' action.

3. Such causally efficacious values are of the nature of gods, or of God, rather than abstract universals.

4. We must therefore choose, as Mackie realized, between some form of objective theism, and the merely made-up, non-authoritative rules that brigands might adopt.

5. Such made-up rules do not have the force of old-fashioned morality, and do not even constrain people to tell the truth or mind about good reasons.

6. The life of reason therefore requires us to be old-fashioned theists.

But even such old-fashioned theists might agree that God is in hid-

---

latter. Other modern moralists, I suspect, reject theism because they dislike objective morality—i.e. dislike being told what to do. 'The source of ultra-democracy is the petty bourgeoisie's individualistic aversion to discipline' (Mao 1967: 164; see pp. 245 ff.)!

ing, and the here-and-now abandoned to the fairies and the powers of the air. It is that first death which I must now enlarge upon.

Why is it that so many have supposed that God is in hiding, that the present world exists precisely as the relic, residue, or sometime habitation of the Dreamtime powers? A psychological reply might simply be that divine authority is so much a function of the antique, the ancestral, that we are bound to look backwards if we wish to see it. The eldest is most worthy of respect (Aristotle, *Metaphysics* 1, 983^b). What is simply here-and-now is on a level with us, something to be conversed with on more or less equal terms: the gods are not our equals, not accessible, not to be changed by normal human conversation, as any of our contemporaries might be changed. The gods are our authorities, the voices of our parents and guardians as they speak to us from our remembered infancy. They are also the makers, if not of everything, at least of the present order of things. They are the pattern and foundation of present existence, and therefore must have been here before the present, and must now be less 'visible' in their own simplicity than once they were.

But though this goes some way towards explaining the air of ancient days that hangs around divinity, it hardly implies that the gods are gone away. Why is it that the present world exists as if by a divine sacrifice or withdrawal? I do not mean to deny that there are traditions within which this very world is itself the divine, just as it stands, where nothing happens that is not the divine-in-action. Such pantheistic complacency, or life-affirming healthy-mindedness, or paradoxical enlightenment, perhaps contains a real truth. I would certainly not dare to criticize Traherne's judgement that we see the world aright only when we see it as God sees it, as an eternal glory. But even Traherne makes it clear that the vision is one he had in his childhood (or which he now thinks he had in his childhood), one that is not now easy, natural, or the only option. Even that glory has something of the air of fairyland.

All things abided eternally as they were in their proper places. Eternity was manifest in the Light of the Day, and something infinite behind everything appeared. (Traherne 3. 3: 1960: 110.)

What reason is there to think that God has 'gone away'? What reason is there to think that God must go away? That He has (in some sense) gone is difficult not to believe. What ought to be, the pattern that is *Themis*, does not rule the world to any obvious extent, unless *Themis* requires quite different conduct from that which is implanted in our hearts and minds, or unless—which is quite likely—we have a radically incomplete idea of what *does* go on. That the Lord is GOD is a declaration of wild faith, that justice and mercy, wisdom and compassion, will triumph because the LORD stands behind and within every tiny transaction even when we cannot see Him. But it is certain that here-and-now, in any century or province of the world, life as we understand it is not fair and the world is not immediately and obviously governed by the Law we find in our hearts. God, the Lord who should be God, must be gone away, or else the God of this world is not the Lord we know. It is true that if we can manage to live by the injunction not to complain, but rather to see the world in beauty, we shall find life easier. As Berkeley said 'it becomes us with thankfulness to use the good things we receive from the hands of God, and patiently to abide the evil, which when thoroughly considered and understood may perhaps appear to be good, it being no sure sign that a thing is good, because we desire, or evil, because we are displeased with it' (1948: vii. 134). But no one would ever claim that this was easy, and few would claim that it was even decent to think away the evil, say, of a young girl's rape and murder in her parents' house. If the world contains that sort of thing, how can we think it just what the One God wishes? 'We must accept the fact', says Ellul (1970: 166), 'that the powers defeated by Christ are still at work, that they refuse to admit their defeat and are struggling more violently than ever'.

So one important meaning of the first death is simply that the ways of the world are not here-and-now what the God of our hearts requires. Some other principle governs, or at least seems to govern, now. So we may choose between the following three options. Perhaps the God of our worship is in no sense the architect, but something that exists only in our hearts, as an ideal. We know all too well that every goal we achieve will at once be set upon by change and chance. Only what is forever unachieved is pure and free from sin's alloy: so to speak of God is only to outline the permanent challenge to all accomplishment. Without such a challenge we shall at last become those most despicable of men, those who can no longer despise themselves. True piety is the consciously absurd complaint that all things are imperfect because they are less than infinitely perfect—a concept that has, for us, no definable or uncontaminated content. The Great First Light had no part in the founding of temporal existence! Or else, alternatively, the God is not dead, for that principle and pattern which is now in control shall always be: if we see how 'things work' and worship it, we shall have all the kingdoms of this world at our disposal, at the mere price of abandoning unreasonable hopes for 'absolute or infinite perfection'.

These first two options are very alike: Gnostic and Satanist are similar in their disdain for archaic moral rules, and neither partisan would ever expect a traditionally conceived kingdom of heaven to 'materialize'. Nothing will ever be 'satisfactory' by traditionally ethical or pious standards, and our only chance of feeling entirely 'at home' here must be by educating ourselves to like what is. Gnostics and high-minded atheists prefer not to be at home; mere egoists or indifferentists pretend to like the here-and-now—as it reveals itself to the impious and unhopeful eye. The third option, it seems to me, has the epistemological and ethical edge: that the right will triumph can only be a sensible expectation if the right does indeed lie at the roots of the world, if it has, as Ellul says, already triumphed. As the triumphant Baphomet announces in Blish's *Black Easter*, 'Each of the opposing sides in any war always predicts victory. They cannot both be right. It is the final battle that counts, not the propaganda.' If 'God is dead' (as a present reality), then there is no reason to disagree with Blish's inference, that one might be reasonably convinced that 'the Rebellion was in fact going to succeed'. Blish's story is of course a *reductio ad absurdum*: 'God's death', His absolute extinction, cannot be a literal event, but only a way of mentioning the supposed collapse of sacred significance and pious hope that leads to the devil's bargain between black magician and arms-dealer which is his central allegory.[4] We can have no assurance that this will not be so, nor any assurance that things will go on forever in the more or less finitely unsatisfactory way that high-minded atheists presume, unless there is indeed a 'power, not ourselves, that makes for righteousness'. Similarly, in scientific enquiry, we have no rational expectation that we can ever discern the principles on which the world is founded, nor any sensible belief that we shall 'one day' have a complete and final theory of the world (both of which assumptions are necessary postulates of sound science) unless there is something with which we are or may be in some moods united that stands at the base of things.

Reason itself is a matter of faith. It is an act of faith to assert that our thoughts have any relation to reality at all. If you are merely a sceptic you must sooner or

[4] I have discussed the fable's bearing on the covert humanism of such theologians as the later Cupitt in Clark 1988c.

later ask yourself the question, 'Why should anything go right; even observation and deduction? Why should not good logic be as misleading as bad logic?
They are both movements in the brain of a bewildered ape'. . . . In so far as
religion is gone, reason is going. For they are both of the same primary and
authoritative kind. They are both methods of proof which cannot themselves
be proved. And in the act of destroying Divine authority we have largely destroyed the idea of that human authority by which we do a long division sum.
With a long and sustained tug we have attempted to pull the mitre off pontifical
man; and the head has come off with it. (Chesterton 1961: 34.)

The goal or completion of honest thought is that same present reality
that constrains our opinion (Peirce 1931: viii. 12). Either we can't
expect the Lord of our hearts to triumph, or He is indeed the Beginning as He will be the End: not an abstract ideal that can never be
realized without at once ceasing to be ideal—and how then should it be
a goal of ours at all?

According to concrete ideal-realism the ultimate ground of the world is God,
who transcends the world and is more than perfect—a Being that stands above
perfection. The proximate ground of the world, and a component part of it, is
the Kingdom of God, the Kingdom of the Spirit as a realized ideal. Even the
beings that are farthest removed from it may hope to attain it, for that kingdom
really exists, and by the grace of God its rays lighten, if only to a small extent,
each one of us, helping us to endure the sorrows and burdens of the imperfect
life which is our self-chosen doom. (Lossky 1928: 198 f.)

To think that the Lord is not real is destructive of ethical and scientific
hopes. But it would also be destructive to suppose, with indifferentists
and power-worshippers, that what is now is just what ought to be, that
what is owed our absolute obedience and respect is only that pattern
we may see here-now. Actually such a doctrine could not really even
have the effects I have attributed to it: one could not discern the pattern of how one should behave or think simply by seeing how one does
behave or think. Whatever one did or thought would automatically be
the best thing possible. Pantheism has just the same practical disad-
vantages as any deterministic thesis. The point is not that nothing
could be programmed to utter nothing but true sentences (so that the
determinist, believing herself determined, could not rationally believe
that what she said was true). The point is that nothing determined in
that way could have any obligation to believe anything but what, for
whatever cause, it does. There can then be no pattern of rational argument and reasonable theory against which to criticize a programmed
person's actual beliefs and behaviour: on all occasions she does and

believes the best she conceivably can. But that there is such a realizable and obligatory perfection is exactly a necessary postulate of rational argument. Determinists cannot rationally believe that there is any difference between rational argument and effective persuasion of a non-rational kind. All argument is a power play, and all ethics illusory.

So we require the third option, that there is a realizable perfection of argument and action, such that the universe of our present discourse is founded upon it and such that there is no necessity of its being realized here-now. God is 'the final unity which transcends the world's chaos as certainly as it is basic to the world's order' (Niebuhr 1963: 38). There is a pattern, a measure, entrenched in the present nature of things, but not now visible except to the eyes of expectant faith. God is 'dead' only as the seed dies. And we can add that it is only by such a death or withdrawal that any other agent has a place at all: God's 'death' is a condition of our existence as semi-independent agencies. For us to exist at all, He must be withdrawn, or (equivalently) have become 'just one of the boys'. The infinite perfection must become one possibility among many; the original omnipotence must be at the mercy, as far as its realization in this world is concerned, of its own creatures. Creation, in brief, and in anticipation of a much later chapter, is only possible through incarnation and sacrifice.[5] 'God has created, that is, not that He has produced something outside Himself, but that He has withdrawn Himself, permitting a part of being to be other than God' (Weil 1957: 193). The divine glory must, for most of us, most of the time, be only a memory, something glimpsed as we look backward, something that was not quite 'there' for us when we were there. The effort of obedient faith, cordial consent, is to try and see here-now what normally we can only 'remember', the realm that Plotinus meant by 'There'. The thought expressed by talk of the first death is dualist.

And so to end with Raine's Isis once again:

> I piece the divine fragments into the mandala
> whose centre is the lost creative power,
> the sun, the heart of God, the lotus, the electron
> that pulses world upon world, ray upon ray
> that he who lived on the first may rise on the last day.

(Raine 1981: 22.)

[5] This is a point that I have begun to grapple with in my contribution to the Festschrift for John Macquarrie (Clark 1986b), following an insight of his in Macquarrie (1984: 234). I shall be discussing it further in the third volume of *Limits and Renewals*.

3
Society without the State

Gender and the Abstract Agent

In my first chapter I defended a variety of methodological conservatism against the exaggerated demands of liberal modernism. In so doing I may have surprised you: I am, after all, myself a critic of received opinion on how, for example, we should treat beings not of our own species, and my determined use of the feminine instead of the masculine pronoun is certainly a break with the millenial tradition of supposing that it is the male who is the human norm, the 'nobler sex' precisely because the only really human sex. Women, it has been constantly assumed, are beings who cannot be expected to control their own emotions: there is, Aristotle remarked (*Nicomachean Ethics* 7, 1148^b 32, 1150^b 15 f.; see Clark 1982b), no point describing a woman as *akratic*, or weak-willed, since there is nothing else she could be. The point is not that women cannot think clearly, but that their emotions, it was said, are often too powerful for their reason to control. They can see what they should do (unlike natural slaves, who have no conception of moral duty), but are carried away by the passion of the moment. If they act rightly it is because their unreasoning emotions, framed by careful convention and the rule of their husbands, are guided aright. If they act wrongly it is not as a rule a principled and determined wickedness, but their passionate nature. Mother-love is frequently employed as the prime example of a self-sacrificial, absolute devotion: but mothers are not morally commendable for being loving mothers. Because we take it for granted that normal mothers will be filled with passionate devotion for their young we both neglect to make such loving easier when the child is young, and are inclined to want to rescue the unfortunate victim of such absolute and suffocating affection when the child is older. Mother rules within the house, but cannot be altogether trusted in the outside world, or with the care of older and would-be independent children. Female passion, so folk-lore says, is more ungovernable, capricious, callous than the soft and conciliatory male dare suppose.

An older generation of feminists would add at this point, with J. S. Mill, that this is not the only occasion when tyranny uses in self-justification disabilities in its victims that, so far as they are real at all, are products of the tyranny. In a society that expects female children to grow up to be rationally irresponsible, ill-educated, passionate guardians of their little flock and custodians of 'personal emotion', it is hardly surprising that the occasional brave rebel, having to make up her own rules in the face of social contempt or anger, should often have made a botch of it, or should be thought to have done so. The problem was perhaps exacerbated for the Greeks, so Gillian Clark has suggested to me, by their habit of marrying their daughters off so young: pre-pubescent females often do confirm the Greek view of women! But if once we allow all human children to grow up to their full potential we shall find that grown men and women are surprisingly alike, that the 'rational male' and 'passionate female' are only social roles that we have made the children go on playing.

It is not a case that I would wish to contest, except to observe that in the absence of a wholly unconstrained human society, populated entirely by self-aware and saintly persons, we are in no position to know from experience how male and female children would grow up in such an ideal environment. Maybe many male and female differences, disabilities, and personal hang-ups are indeed the product of an 'unnatural' upbringing. But maybe—as good liberal parents confronted by doll-loving daughters and gun-toting sons are often compelled to admit—many of them are just what would be expected anyway: why, after all, has so much of humankind developed just these sex-related genders and social roles if that is not what humans left to themselves would naturally do? We may 'remember' that something else is possible, that it was not so 'in the beginning'. But it is a historical fantasy to suppose that such a different beginning could ever be located in our mundane past, that there were once, for example, happily communistic and permissive matriarchies at one with the natural environment until they were wickedly overthrown by a bunch of murderous rednecks (where from?) who have somehow and unnaturally retained control ever since. If things ever were like that, perhaps (as Paris 1986: 6) the Goddess was overthrown because her rule was perceived as repressive and retrogressive, not simply because the putative invaders had iron swords. But I doubt that this Fall, or any other, was straightforwardly historical. That things now are not what 'naturally' and rightly they would be is a powerful intuition, and one that requires of us an unashamedly dualistic distinction between here-now and There, this world and the Beginning.

Liberal individualists, the product of a wealthy and humane society, like to believe that each human individual could operate precisely as an individual, a free and equal partner in whatever temporary contracts might be going, unconstrained by any physical or economic disability not of her own making. Where there are obstacles to such a care-free life the community should take such necessary steps as will overcome them: that there should be an equal liberty for all is held to require that all be equally relieved of positive and discriminatory obligation. Most of the handicaps faced by women in attempting to live as free and independent agents are believed to be social, mere products of existing prejudice. If there are any merely physical disabilities and obstacles, they should be overcome. The menstrual cycle should be suppressed. Babies should be bottle-fed, and reared in crèches by those individuals of either sex that choose to care for the young. Ideally, women should be relieved even of the need to bear such children as they choose to have: the young should be bred in bottles or in 'host-mothers'—once again, of either original sex. No 'natural' or social restriction of sex-partner should be permitted: if 'racism' is an evil, then such communities as interfere between lovers of different races are anathema; if 'sexism' is an evil of the same kind, then all possible sexual contracts between free and independent agents should be recognized and defended. In such a technophiliac future, sex differences would be as unimportant as the natural colour of one's hair or one's totem. Pronouns like 'he' and 'she' would be as outmoded as the subtle distinctions of rank and relative status embodied in languages of the hierarchical past. Any individual would have before it all the role-models of the human universe.

That such a society is technically possible, let alone desirable, may well be difficult for most of us to think. Versions are described by John Varley in his *Ophiuchi Hotline* series, and Samuel Delany in *Triton*. It seems a very radical answer to the demand that each human individual should be wholly unconstrained in its choices to say that no respect at all is owed to the existing structures that define not only human but all mammalian, and even all animal life. Those who believe that there is a transcendental, asexual Self, incarcerated in a biological organism that drags it down, may be excused for thinking that such a true Self may justifiably remodel the carcass it drags round. Actually such dualists more often urge us to have regard for 'Brother Ass', and teach that the eternal Self hood has a thing or two to learn by playing the part the gods have set for it. Consider Lewis's mythological description of that world 'whom mortals call the Moon':

Half of her orb is turned towards us and shares our curse. . . . On this side the womb is barren and the marriages cold. There dwell an accursed people, full of pride and lust. There when a young man takes a maiden to marriage they do not lie together, but each lies with a cunningly fashioned image of the other, made to move and be warm by devilish arts, for real flesh will not please them, they are so dainty in their dreams of lust. Their real children they fabricate by vile arts in a secret place. (Lewis 1945: 337.)

What is very surprising, or would be to anyone who expected modernists to be consistent, is that this 'revolt against nature' is welcomed precisely by people who think that they are just biological organisms. Why then is it a liberation to be 'relieved' of all one's natural characters? One might as well, as Chesterton remarks (1961: 40), demand that a triangle be liberated from the tyranny of having only three straight sides! Perhaps a radically remodelled being having no permanent or important differences from other human individuals would be a 'happier' being than I, having only such duties as it freely accepted from the whole range of possible human duty. But if all my given nature, whether sexually differentiated or required by any other accident of my creation, is to be wished away, what is left but a Barbie Doll? And on what basis could such a being choose anything, if all its goals are equally provisional?

In the free and equal future 'I' might choose to take on presently 'female' characteristics. But what reason would I have to do so unless I found myself to want what only such a physique could manage, say the experiences of impregnation, child-birth, and lactation? But experiencing such a want is just as much a differentiating and compelling factor as my visible physical nature, just as much something that constrains my groundless independence. If I can also dictate what wants the organism has, on what basis do I choose? Must not all action become gratuitous when I can have it arranged that 'I' should feel comfortable doing literally anything that human beings in general can do? Liberal individualists presumably believe themselves to be clear-headed and tolerant individuals who 'could not' willingly behave with sadistic contempt for human or for animal life, or who 'could not' willingly submerge themselves in tribal forms. But these are limitations on the incorrigible freedom of the individual quite as severe as any imposed by physical or sexual difference. The true and sincere individualist would sometimes have itself made over into a tribalist, or a psychopath: which is the equivalent at a personal level of Plato's description of the democratic state, where no preferences, no policies are allowed to be better than any other.

Pure freedom only begins to make sense if there are indeed the transcendental identities that ancient philosophers supposed—though even they are not wholly without natures. Such beings, like the souls reported by Plato's Er, have chosen their lives, the lives that we live here, on the basis of needs built into their spiritual identity. Perhaps indeed there are occasional seeming errors, when a would-be male is incarcerated in a female body—though it should occur to such a discontented soul that perhaps its task was, exactly, to come to terms with female possibilities, with its own seeming opposite. In the absence of such a metaphysic, undifferentiated freedom and the refusal of all given nature must end in total confusion. Either our choices are entirely gratuitous, since all goals are equally modifiable in a universe devoid of any sacred value, or we must allow a fundamental nature which is not to be altered.

There is a shorter way with individualism of the kind that I have sketched, a way which second-generation feminists may find congenial. Technological interference in the reproductive process, even if it seems to serve the interests of women, has actually been prepared for, and practised, at the expense of women, who have served as ill-informed and often unconsulted experimental subjects. The imagined future, where essentially sexless individuals choose to bear children, is a male fantasy, the attempted realization of the ancient dream of doing without women and the women's mysteries (Corea 1988), freed of the need to accommodate oneself to lovely aliens, or be bound by parental duty. Even LeGuin's imagined world of Winter, in *The Left Hand of Darkness*, is not genuinely whole and hermaphrodite, but, as Gwyneth Jones has observed (*Foundation* 42 (1988), 93), a male, ambisexual society. More generally, the idea of careless and unfettered freedom that individualism embodies, after all, is a flattering self-portrait of the rich, adolescent human male. If that is the highest form of life available, then anyone who cannot or is not allowed to live it may resent the restriction, and seek ways of escaping from the harem, the sewing party, or the suburban dream. If freedom is doing just exactly what you choose, unfettered by social expectation, *geis*, or unsought duty (which Locke, of course, expressly denied: *2nd Treatise* 22: 1963: 324), and freedom is a good, or the sole condition under which one can oneself achieve a good, it is understandable that all of us should want it. The fantastic collapse of human motivation that I have described, adumbrated in adolescent existentialism, is—we may thank our gods—too distant a disaster to impinge on us. And of course, even as adolescents, we do not really mean it. Individualists of the kind I have described would all, of logical necessity, be anarchists: by which I do not mean that they would be the self-styled anarchists who seek the overthrow of capitalist society in favour of some ill-conceived Soviet experiment. They would, on the contrary, be capitalists of a fervour and intensity to make the present government blush. Anarchistical individualism, which denies the force of any external obligation, or even in some cases any individual contract, must make all social organization purely and immediately voluntary. No one is bound by laws she did not make, or does not now agree with;[1] no one can have any standing, natural obligation to care for the weak or comfort the oppressed; no one need even follow the merest counsels of prudence, not to excite such hatred in the hearts of others as will make one's own life hell. It is, after all, the art of the 'free' mind to make a heaven of hell.

My own view is Weil's: 'Those who are lacking in goodwill and remain adolescent are never free under any form of society' (1987: 13). Locke's liberty under the Law of Nature is not that sort of irresponsibility. What duties there may be to obey what kind of ruler is the topic of my next chapter. Here I wish to draw attention to another, weirdly neglected aspect of our life together, the first obstacle to fall in the way of the free male, and the point from which real feminism starts. I refer of course to families, and to friends.

Family Duties and the Adolescent Male

It is entirely understandable that the first efforts of members of an oppressed class, or of a class that believes itself oppressed, will be to obtain the acknowledged right to behave as members of the oppressive class already do, or as they are seen to. The drawback is that master and slave class are, as Aristotle saw long before Hegel, an inseparable pair. If there are to be masters there must be slaves, and if those who were slaves become masters in their turn they too will require a subject population. Democracy has similarly 'tended only to limit the power of rulers, without changing the fundamental relationship between those

---

[1] A doctrine that, as Chesterton observes (1961: 121), 'would not only ruin morality but spoil sport . . . If I bet I must be made to pay, or there is no poetry in betting.'

who rule and those who are ruled' (Thayer 1973: 44). If there are to be free and independent individuals happily about their self-chosen business, it is necessary that someone look after those same individuals before they are free and independent. If there are to be persons who can afford to neglect their natural ties and duties there must be others who will pick up the pieces. The assumption is readily made that there will be someone whose nature and satisfaction it is to care for children, facilitate the wild adventures of the individualist, and make a house a home—even though the dominant rhetoric of liberal individualism suggests that all such care and duty is a burden on the free spirit, such that no one of a proud temper could be bound to it. All that happens, in other words, when some few women join the ranks of the liberated individuals is that those—of either sex—who don't get even less consideration than they did before. Sheer individualism must reject past chivalry as romantic folly: 'On this [enlightenment] scheme of things a king is but a man, a queen is but a woman, a woman is but an animal—and an animal not of the highest order. All homage paid to the sex in general as such . . . is to be regarded as romance and folly' (Burke 1975: 344). To be a 'woman' is to be excluded from the main body of decision-makers, and human beings who happen to be female may well respond, given the chance, by turning against 'womanhood'. But perhaps it is not wholly foolish to think that males owe women some respect, and that there are better ways to reform the system than to abuse our ancestors as knaves and our ancestresses as fools. It is easy enough, no doubt, to destroy impulses to chivalrous respect: are we so confident that we can destroy jealous possessiveness, lust, and hatred?

Immanuel Kant believed that although a 'society' of uncaring individualists could be conceived, it could not be willed by any rational agent, since to do so would be to will that one was oneself uncared for when in need and some great trouble (*Groundwork* 56: Paton 1948: 86). The attempt to deduce real duties from purely formal or from such semi-empirical premisses is not, perhaps, entirely convincing. But the central observation stands: we cannot all, or any of us all the time, expect to be self-sufficient individuals. The core of human society is not, except in the most outlandish circumstances, an accidental crowd of unfamiliar and competing individuals. If it were, and if we had no prospect of discovering or sympathizing with each other's special aims, we might have no choice but war, or some enforced agreement to leave well enough alone. But as Aristotle said (*Politics* 1, 1252ª 24 ff.), we are the sort of animal that forms couples and family groupings, that makes friends, and is faced by duties not of our own contrivance.

Liberal ideology contrasts the truly 'human' life of the irresponsible male adolescent, set free by the care of others from any fact of life that interferes with his own momentarily chosen projects, with the heteronomous, emotionally confined existence of a woman too feeble to resist the biological imperative to care for her newborn. The liberal ideologue, in short, is the exact pontificating replica of the Greek patriarchalist: women are too feeble to be free, unless they are liberated from their biological nature and encouraged to play the games of irresponsibility. What both varieties of ideologue implicitly accept is the presumption that true freedom lies in being free of any obligation—even in some cases any obligation to abide by word once given—and that such freedom is incompatible with 'emotional domination' by the needs of another. We know that mothers—and indeed fathers—must be found from somewhere, and somehow manage to believe that they will turn up—by nature—even if we make it clear that they will not be role-models for a 'free spirit'. To state the obvious, one cannot be a mother—or a decent father—just when and how one chooses. To become a parent is to be duty-bound in ways not of one's choosing, even if one did deliberately do that act which has resulted in the fact of parenthood. Only those of a corrupt mind can suppose that if they did not 'intend' to procreate, but only to 'have sex', they have no obligation of care for mother or 'accidental' child.

Real feminists at this point, if not earlier, should ask why the preferred behaviour of rich adolescent males should define the better life for us. Old style patriarchalists at least acknowledged duties no easier for the male than for the female. The irresponsible can only exist by courtesy of those who take responsibility. What is the core of human life if not adolescent gaming? The answer, obviously, lies in the making of friends and the care of children. The real life of humankind, from long before it was a human kind, is in the delicate relationship of lineage and alliance.[2] That evolutionary beginning—which I do not mean to identify with the divine Beginning—will occupy me in a moment. Before I give a more detailed account of it, I must sum up what I take to be the lessons of our non-adolescent experience of life together. It is quite understandable that adolescents, of either sex, often rebel against

---

[2] These are terms of ethological art: 'lineage' signifies the ongoing line of mothers and children; 'alliance' the continually renewed assembly of adolescent males evicted from the central group.

what they suppose to be the crushing weight of convention. Their elders after all are rarely shining examples of what humankind could be, and it may often seem that almost anything is better! It is not only understandable but right that we should believe perfection possible, and think it withheld from us only by the ignorance or malevolence of impious spirits, though it is unwise as well as uncharitable to identify those spirits too closely with one's relatives. The charge of hypocrisy or unenlightened selfishness comes easily to the lips of rebels who rarely trouble themselves to do the washing up. It is also understandable that adolescent rebels should begin to doubt even their own natures and inner conviction, if they believe them to be wished on them by their depraved forebears. But the normal processes of finding friends and founding new families are not a retreat to slavery. It is exactly in the development of those new bonds that we come to ourselves, and can look back on our unshaped and would-be rebellious past with the tolerant recognition that it was then that we were slaves, not now. Instead of thinking of freedom as something enjoyed by the unobligated, 'feckless' male, we can see it without paradox and quite traditionally as the recognition of necessity. It is in finding what one ought to do, and seeking to do it, that we begin to exist as social individuals. Freedom is not a condition outside society, that we feebly surrender for the sake of security: as Aristotle said, someone who willingly abandons all society, all social obligation, is not an especially free man, but a wild beast or a god (*Politics* 1, 1253^a 29). Freedom, the free society, is one where true friendship is possible, is not socially forbidden or prevented, between any members, where differences of rank or social role—if they exist—can still allow us to meet as friends, where what we do and are is not laid down quite independently of what each individual comes to find as his or her vocation and love-liking.

Those who still wish to insist that we can have no real obligations but those of our own choosing, who yet agree that anyone with family and friends has obligations to them, may say that we have 'chosen' such ties, that their moral force rests only in our consent. Even this much implies that we might now have duties that we may not now much care for, that we would not choose if we had our time again— and the consistent rebel will reject such self-chosen bonds, and so all real human freedom. But the fact is that we do not choose our friends: they are forced upon us as we slowly realize that what we are and have come to be is bound up with what they are. Gadamer's exposition of Plato's *Lysis*: friendship is where one feels at home (Gadamer 1980:

18). In seeking to live up to the bonds of friendship we are obeying a vocation and so discovering a self. The deconstruction of the self that is advocated by some moderns[3] is not as unexpected as they think: my experience suggests that students often hardly know what it is that they are being asked not to believe in. They have not yet 'found themselves', and are therefore unshaken by the suggestion that there is nothing there to find. That is why the young are often—to an older eye—incredibly reckless and self-destructive. It is only as we acquire fresh obligations that we have a clear view of the self we then desire to preserve.

> The bachelor he fights for one
> as joyful as can be;
> but the married man don't call it fun,
> because he fights for three—
> for Him and Her and It
> (and Two and One make Three)
> he wants to finish his little bit,
> and he wants to go home to his tea.

(Kipling 1927: 466.)

It is in line with this judgement that a properly informed socio-political theory can say that the real units of society are not voluntarily contracting strangers, but 'face to face communit[ies] in which unlimited commitments are the rule and in which every aspect of every self's existence is conditioned by membership in the interpersonal group' (Niebuhr 1963: 71 f.: see Thayer 1973: 124). Is this an offence to liberty? If liberty requires, in Overton's expression, that 'every man by nature be a King, Priest and Prophet in his own naturall circuite and compasse, whereof no second may partake, but by deputation, commission and free consent from him whose naturall right and freedom it is' ('Arrow against all Tyrants': cited by Macpherson 1962: 14), then the answer must be yes. Overton's vision, of course, was of human liberty under God: he did not suppose that the 'self propriety' whereby

---

[3] Parfit (1986), for example, has argued that we should not trouble with strict identity, and that psychological continuity (usually, but not necessarily, grounded in the brain) is all that could rationally matter to us: such continuity, of course, is not an all or nothing affair. Some of my 'future selves' will be very unlike me, and only distantly related to me: why then should I mind about 'my own survival' or 'my own future prosperity' rather than about the existence and well-being of others? Parfit is not the only recent thinker to deconstruct the self, and I shall attempt to put the argument in a wider context in the second volume of *Limits and Renewals*.

every individual was himself, was something that could exist without the co-operation of heaven and earth. His individualism was not that of Lucifer. But it is noticeable even so that he has Kings in mind, as though the only true individuals were male, like the Cyclopes that rule their households solely by their own will (see Aristotle, *Politics* 1, 1252[b] 22 f.).

The historical reality, not merely for the human species but for the higher primates in general, anthropoids and cercopithecoids, is that society has never been made up of independently existing strangers. Human individuals are not even strongly territorial, despite popularizing misuse of ethological research. We do not, that is, strongly resent and resist the incursion of other human individuals into our self-claimed property and rule as monarchs from a suitable perch. The common form of primate society is a group of females with their young, existing in some delicate relationship with a throng of males. Young males are characteristically pushed out to the fringes of the group, where they make such alliances and friendships as will enable them at last to be received back into the central mother–daughter group as protectors, impregnators, or pets. Other strategies for eventually creating a viable male–female grouping include the male hamadryad's technique of kidnapping and rearing young females, co-operative endeavours to evict an existing male from what ethologists confusingly call his harem (and kill his young), and pair-bonding. In all these cases the young come to maturity by finding that there are things that they must do if they are to be complete. They survive their immaturity only if others accept responsibility for them.

This balance of largely female lineage and male alliance conditions us. In the past young males would serve as the troop's first line of defence, its sacrifice to passing predators—including other human troops. Such security as they had lay in their making friends—if only formally—with their fellows, in finding relatively harmless ways of discovering their individual powers and prospects. Those friendships are at once a necessary part of the young male's initiation rites and a dreadful danger to the welfare of all if the alliance grows too far away from the lineage it exists to serve. It is hardly surprising that the *ephebeia* is a common feature of quite different and historically unconnected cultures, nor that the ephebes commonly quarrel with those males who have already moved into the lineage. The success, and stability, of a culture will depend in part on its ability to guide ephebes into full membership of the economical and political club. Sheer individualism, and the demand that every (male) individual have his own king-dom, is simply to delay that process.

Parenthood and Natural Duties

That children below the age of reason 'have no rights' in their own right is a necessary consequence of any doctrine that limits the class of rights-holders to the class of recognizably and actually rational entities.[4] If there were, so Hume remarked, a race of creatures inter-mingled with ours that could never make us feel the impact of their displeasure, and could never be expected to keep any bargain that we thought to strike, we should not owe them justice, even if we owed them compassion (Hume 1902: 190: *Principles* 3. 1. 152). Hume placed no restriction on the sort of laws a legislative body might enact: on his terms, child-welfare legislation or even laws protecting a child's 'rights' (or the rights that would or might be hers when she was adult) would be perfectly proper. What mattered was the usefulness of such laws, for the general utility. Later liberals have often denied that the Law has any business between a man and his morals, that present rights were all that the state might intervene to defend. It must follow that children should not be protected against their owners, however much we may, morally, disapprove of the treatment they are getting. Alternatively, some device must be invented to allow that children do indeed 'have rights', if not in their own right, yet as members of a com-munity which 'rationally must' treat all its members with respect. Chil-dren, in any event, are classified as 'marginal' entities: the main work of state legislation is to protect the perceived interests of rational adults. Since 'children' do keep growing up, and may hold grudges, they may get some protection from the law, but not as much as fully paid-up members do.

That morality and the law are bargains between desperate brigands is of course a distortion of the ancient idea that 'rational' beings should and will respect each other's rational humanity. Stoics who decreed that animals, not being rational, lay outside the bounds of justice, spoke out of respect for rational humanity, not simple selfishness. And there always was another motif in Stoic thought:

---

[4] I argue in greater detail for the centrality of children and the natural duties of parents in Clark 1988g.

In the whole moral sphere there is nothing more glorious nor of a wider range than the solidarity of mankind, that species of alliance and partnership of interests and that actual affection which exists between man and man, which coming into being immediately upon our birth, owing to the fact that children are loved by their parents and the family as a whole, is bound together by the ties of marriage and parenthood, gradually spreads its influence beyond the home, first by blood relationships, then by connections through marriage, later by friendships, afterwards by the bonds of neighbourhood, then to fellow citizens and political allies and friends, and lastly by embracing the whole of the human race. (Cicero, *De Finibus* 5. 65.)[5]

The origin of moral and political bonds lies with those immediate natural relationships, and care for children is not marginal, but central. That is why contemporary discussion of the 'rights' of future generations must strike traditionalists as scholastic. The issue is not about their rights, but about our duties.

As we feel it wicked and inhuman for men to declare that they care not if when they themselves are dead, the universal conflagration ensues, it is undoubtedly true that we are bound to study the interest of posterity also for its own sake. (Cicero, *De Finibus* 3. 64.)

Our duties are defined for us by what it would be wicked and inhuman to do or not to do. Vervet monkeys, so it appears, can recognize whose cub it is that is crying, and expect that cub's mother to respond. The special gift of humankind is that we can (and usually do) enforce on others the demands of nature, to care for our offspring and the social bond. This gift, in its turn, is forced on us by the fact that there are those who would otherwise fail to live up to the demands of natural law. Briefly: the more we care for others, the wider the circles of our carefulness, the greater the chance that free-loaders will be benefited by our care, and the greater the need to invent further social and cultural constraints on individual behaviour. Positive law and abstract morality have their place, but they are not the roots of humane endeavour. I do not treat my children decently because there is a law requiring me to treat children in general, or human beings in general, or sentient creatures in general, as I would have them treat me. The force of those larger obligations is derived from the particular felt duties of parenthood and friendship. Just so, my concern for particular regions or buildings that were important to me is not the consequence but the

---

[5] As I shall point out in a later chapter, humankind is not the final circle of companionship: the whole world is to be the beloved community.

source of any wider commitment to 'conservation': why should I think it worth conserving 'old buildings' in general if none of them already mattered to me 'in their own right' (see Clark 1986d, 1988e)? How could we be social creatures at all if affection for our children were not natural (Epictetus, *Discourses* 1. 23. 3)? Even the Hobbesian state of nature included groups bound together by the 'natural lusts and affections'. Impulses to mutual aid, enjoyment of each other's company, shared interests in offspring are the context within which a concept of oneself develops. Why then should we seek to restrict ourselves to a consideration of what we 'would' have decided, if we had been rationally self-serving individuals ignorant of our age, class, or competence (as Blustein 1982: 123 ff. after Rawls 1971: 249)? Being what we are we already have a natural commitment to preserve and nourish more things than 'ourselves'.

It is worth adding that even those commentators who have acknowledged the importance and 'moral considerableness' of the young sometimes ignore them when it comes to formulating theories of society. The point is not simply that human beings, like other mammals, characteristically respond affectionately to the young. That is certainly true, and that is why it was always silly to suggest that children were only 'marginally' rights-holders. On the contrary, even hardened criminals generally think ill of child abusers, and it is the death or hardship of children that most moves us to compassionate action. Practically speaking children have far more 'rights' (that is, lay far more duties on the rest of us) than do the self-serving adults of mainstream political theory. But children are not merely passive, and 'we human beings' are not only adult. What needs to be remembered is that human beings are not merely (as adults) susceptible to infantile appeal, but also very adept (as children and as other 'powerless' individuals) at manipulating those who would otherwise exercise power over us. Too much popularizing ethology has given the impression that the dominant males are the leaders of an animal society. Better observation suggests that such dominants are mostly those who could be expected to win any dispute over territory and possession. They do not necessarily 'lead'. On the contrary it may often be the youngest of the group that literally leads, or works out the innovative technique: the young chimpanzee that clatters empty oil-drums round the clearing to attract attentive deference; the young macaque who learns to separate sand and grain by tossing handfuls into the water. Curious and playful behaviour, conciliatory tactics in lieu of confrontational, distancing manœuvres, are the province of the young. Because there are such creatures, who control their protectors by being 'charming' and desirable, and their environment by locating new techniques that are not needed by the dominant few, the tribe and species of which they are a part can survive as a sociable and innovative one.

It is a familiar enough thought that human beings, as a species, are neotenic apes. We resemble the young of other mammalian or primate species more than we do their adult forms, and can remain happily 'impractical' and 'playful' for far longer than our more serious cousins. It is also a familiar thought that great poets and scientists retain that capacity for play and for irreverent affection longer than the mass of humanity. Two morals are forgotten: first that literal children may perhaps have something to teach the rest of us, just as they are; and second, that we should seek to order our society to give such playful, 'childish' types a better chance. Philosophers have usually followed Aristotle in supposing that no serious person would take 'childish amusement' as the goal of her life (*Nicomachean Ethics* 10, 1176^b 32 f.), even though Epictetus acknowledged the strong temptation 'to join in the sports of attractive and wideawake children and crawl on all fours and talk baby talk' (*Discourses* 2. 24. 18). There are times and places where the advice to put aside childish things does seem appropriate: 'for God's sake, grow up!', as the Divine Boy of Stapledon's imagined future Patagonia insists to followers who have misunderstood his earlier plea for youthfulness (Stapledon 1972: 109). But there are also times and places when a real maturity can only come by putting the false masks of 'adulthood' aside: we have sinned and grown old, and our Father is younger than we (Chesterton 1961: 59)! Most human beings are very young, and the leading edge of humankind is likely to be found amongst that number.

Personal Friendship and Position[6]

'There are as many different kinds of claim upon our neighbourly charity as there are different kinds of relationship', said Ælred of Rievaulx in his discussion of friendship (Squire 1969: 46). Family and 'personal friends', colleagues and fellow-professionals, townsfolk and fellow citizens all have some claim upon us. All will usually be judged

---

[6] See Clark & Clark (1988) for a further study of friendship in Christian tradition, and of the alleged disparity between Christian and Hellenic notions.

to have stronger claims than any unrelated, unknown person. Christians, as well as those post-Christian moralists who seek to act upon a universal law of charitable action, may be inclined to disregard such claims, and thereby to deny that they can ever really have friends at all:

> He who loves his Enemies betrays his Friends;
> This surely is not what Jesus intends.
>
> (Blake 1966: 751.)

Universal love of humankind, however praiseworthy, is not obviously what we wish to see in those around us, nor do we unfailingly praise those who give their money to the desperately poor at the expense of their own family, friends, and fellow-citizens.

All friendship is preferring the interest of a friend to the neglect or perhaps against the interest of others; so that the old Greek said, 'He that has friends, has no friend'. Now Christianity recommends universal benevolence, to consider all men as our brethren; which is contrary to the virtue of friendship, as described by the ancient philosophers. (Johnson: Boswell 1953: 945 f.)

It is one of the few occasions when Johnson actually conceded defeat in an argument: his opponent, Mrs Knowles, pointed out that 'the household of faith' had, on occasion, preference, and that Jesus himself had one disciple whom especially he loved. She might also have observed that 'the ancient philosophers' did not in fact advocate an undiscriminating universalism. Philosophical pagans sought to find friends among the wise, of whatever culture, race, or age, but expressly denied that wise and foolish people could ever quite be friends, or the wise wish for fools what the fools wished for themselves (Clark 1987c). Augustine seems more plausible:

All men are to be loved equally. But since you cannot do good to all, you are to pay special regard to those who, by the accidents of time, or place or circumstance, are brought into closer connection with you . . . as by a sort of lottery. (*On Christian Doctrine* 1. 28: Meilaender 1981: 19.)

Not to do good to our 'nearest and dearest' on the pretext that we must 'love' those far away may actually be sinful even in the eyes of those who profess to praise a 'universal charity' supposedly superior to the friendship ties of pagan humanity (as Peschke 1978: ii. 186). Misplaced partiality, the satisfaction of trivial desires in a closer circle of friends at the deliberate expense of vital interests in a wider circle, may be 'unwise' (and sinful), but it does not seem that we can do without the thought that we have particular and positive obligations to our friends. I ought not to rob anyone: it does not follow that I therefore have a positive obligation to give to everyone or anyone. 'An ethics of undifferentiated love which allowed of no application to proximate relations could have little relevance for embodied human beings who can only be in one place at a time and must needs be closer to some people than others' (O'Donovan 1986: 240).

In saying this I have no wish to deny that the real and pressing dangers of people I have never met, or whales that I have never met, may require a response from me, even at some cost to my friends. But such a universal charity rests first upon the perception that they are someone's friends, that the networks of responsibility reach out beyond my personal horizon. Loyalty to nation, civilization, species, biosphere, or the imagined city of the wise (whose membership, for all we know, extends into the heavens), all start out from the simple loyalties of 'kith and kin'. Those who would easily betray their brothers or their colleagues or their fellow citizens in the name of some abstract good can never be trusted, even by their co-conspirators. Contrariwise: those who betray their nations, civilizations, and the rest upon the plea that they must be loyal only to their 'friends' mistake their place. 'Every real Friendship is a sort of secession, even a rebellion' (Lewis 1960: 45). Christians before Constantine were accused of opting out, of living in little societies of friends, showing a praiseworthy concern for each other and for other cases of need, but forgetting that they also belonged to cities, to an empire, to the human race. Politicians nowadays quite often think that Christians should restrict themselves and not express inconvenient moral judgements on wider issues. But that restriction is another instance of being too much concerned with those who immediately 'belonged', and forgetting that friendship extends to link individuals and groups into communities. *Pace* E. M. Forster (and Meilaender 1981: 81) Dante did not put Brutus and Cassius into the lowest circle of Hell because they had betrayed their personal friend rather than their country, but because they had betrayed their sworn duty to a divinely endorsed emperor. Only when a country has ceased to be a community, linked by interconnected networks of friendship and by a shared vision—as I shall argue—of the good, do the smaller circles of friendship become the 'true country'.

And that is perhaps the point where our usual modern understanding of 'friendship' requires to be corrected. We tend to think of 'friends' as 'personal friends', people who know and like each other, but do not conceive that they have any special duties to or about each other. Our friends are not our kinsfolk or our fellow citizens, but special individuals united to us by love-liking or a shared taste in books, games, food, and drink. 'Real friends', perhaps, are intimates, and actually seek to share each other's troubles: 'it is indeed a consolation in this life to have someone to whom to open your heart, with whom you can share your secrets, to whom you can commit the privacy of your mind, a consolation to choose for yourself a faithful man to congratulate you when things go well, sympathize in your sadness, encourage you under opposition' (Ambrose, *De Officiis Ministrorum* 3. 22)—or, of course, oppose your favourite follies without disowning you (since 'opposition is true friendship': Blake 1966: 157)! Ambrose apparently shared the notion that we somehow 'choose' our friends, or at least our intimates: a different look at life suggests that they are chosen, let us say 'destined', for us. At any rate we cannot 'unchoose' them, though we can betray.

Most of our friends are only people we are glad enough to see, and happy to help or even be helped by if the chance arrives. But the ancient conception has a greater strength to it: friends are those with whom we are at home, with whom we belong, by whom we can be made ashamed, or glad. Not all of those with whom we are united in a kind of 'civil *philia*' are people that we know, or maybe even like. Some must be, or else the community of which we are a part will fall apart, and it is doubtless those who are the real and paradigmatic friends. But friendship is a civil relationship even when we speak of intimate and real friends, wishing those real goods for each other that they wish for themselves. And other forms of civil relationship are rightly called a kind of friendship.[7] The actions of my friends are not the sort of thing that I can be indifferent to: for good or ill, because they 'belong to me', their acts can make me happy or ashamed. The same is true of fellow-professionals, fellow-townsfolk, fellow-citizens. This is not to say that I can sensibly feel guilty if a fellow-citizen does ill: but her wrongdoing brings shame on all her kin. The thought should not be unfamiliar, any more than the experience. Anti-racists charge whites, especially, for the crimes of their ancestors and cousins (strangely, no doubt, if they also deny the moral relevance of race). Feminists regularly charge all men with complicity for the sins of rapists and domestic tyrants. Their

---

[7] My thoughts on this point were greatly assisted by a paper of John Cooper's, read to the Southern Association for Classical Philosophy in 1987.

error is in saying all men are guilty in the sense familiar in an individualistic system: what I myself did not do, nor ever intend to, cannot
be my crime—but it can be something for which I variously feel
ashamed. Our complicity in the sins of those who are of 'our kind',
'one of us', 'belonging'—and our corresponding pride in their achieve-
ments—is an essential feature of our human life. As in Adam all die, so
in Christ are all made alive . . .

Such solidarity may serve evil ends, but it makes little sense to reject
it. When Royce praised loyalty, he was not infrequently challenged by
those who claimed that humankind had 'outgrown loyalty', that it was
'one of humanity's most disastrous failings and weaknesses'. But
Royce could respond that his opponent's 'earnestness, his passion for
the universal triumph of individual freedom, his plainness of speech,
his hatred of oppression, were themselves symptoms of a very loyal
spirit' (Royce 1908: 60 f.). His loyalty, his solidarity, was with the
oppressed; his rage at evil-doing was itself evidence of his proper
shame. Nobody rages about the evil-doings of wolves (supposing they
do evil)—because we do not usually think of ourselves as fellow mammals, fellow predators, their crimes do not reflect on us. Because
Royce's opponent feels himself human he is indignant and ashamed,
emotions impossible for one who really stood 'alone', without kin to
comfort or deplore.

A burning sense of shame at the deeds of his government and the acts of horror committed by German soldiers and police was the mark of a conscientious
German at the close of the war. 'I am ashamed to be a German' was a not
infrequent remark when friend was speaking to friend as the revelations of
what the Third Reich had done became generally known. (Gray 1970: 202.)

And as Gray makes clear, non-Germans too had to feel shame, at what
was done in wartime: 'when the news of the atomic bombing of Hiroshima and Nagasaki came, many an American soldier felt shocked and
ashamed. . . . No human power could atone for the injustice, suffering
and degradation of spirit of a single day of warfare. . . . What bitter
cruelty all of us exercise! Nothing that happens to me in future will I
ever feel unjust and unmerited' (Gray 1970: 200, 203). One may react
to this by coming to see all other associations than the strictly voluntary
as 'external and accidental', but this is no real solution. On the one
hand those other, larger associations are not 'inessential': we are members of them in our very historical essence, not abstract intelligences
gazing impartially at a world-at-war. On the other, no association at all

is entirely voluntary, not even the idyllic intimacy of a Damon and Pythias.

We do not wholly 'choose' our personal friends, let alone the friendships of our nation, class, or creed. But we can distinguish communities whose only approved friendships are made by rule from those that allow chance acquaintance (or the will of the gods) to blossom into a novel solidarity, where people from quite different walks of life can recognize each other as 'of a kind' or 'belonging' to a household that did not exist before. Leonard Williams's community of woolly monkeys looks like a free and really liberal society precisely because two females widely separate in rank can still be friends (Williams 1967: 85 f.). Ours, despite its many virtues and its patent superiority to the Third Reich (a superiority which is not to be despised, nor taken for granted), does not quite qualify.

The Domestic Net

Not all human beings live in nation-states, with governments that claim a monopoly of force within some historically created boundaries. Such states, and their governments, are the topic of my next chapter. It is an important one, but too great a concentration on that aspect of socio-political existence distorts the record. Most such governments have been male governments. We have, as I remarked before, no record of any consistently matriarchal states and no historical reason to believe in them.[8] But all human beings live within family and friendship groupings, such that somewhat different behaviour is expected of young and old, male and female, organizers and dependents. Some such groups are rigorously divided against themselves, isolating each subgroup from all the others. Other such groups seem at first to allow a promiscuous mingling of age, caste, character, and gender, but it appears that there will always be some rules, forged in the daily experience of having to get on together despite 'natural' differences, and providing—often enough—the sources of a growing individual's dignity as someone who can be trusted now to take his seat among the

[8] Anyone who thinks that evidence of Goddess-worship is evidence of political matriarchy should ask herself what some future archaeologist could deduce about the politics of Spain or Italy from the prevalence of statues of the Virgin Mary! What is interesting is not that there really were once matriarchies, but that so many writers should wish to believe there were. We project our image of the Real Beginning, the Unfallen World, into the historical past—an impulse I shall discuss in a later volume.

men, her seat among the women. Where we see oppression—and I do not wish to deny that there will sometimes genuinely be oppression—native speakers of the cultural language see their maturity: at last they are old enough to be bound tight by adult ceremonial. Oppression may sometimes even consist in a general refusal to think that members of one subclass could ever be obligated to obey the group's chief rules, the rules that define them as The People. Not to be asked to obey the law is often the deepest insult—an insult that merely individualistic liberalism can hardly understand. The 'freedom' of a tramp or an itinerant labourer, having no obligations and sometimes earning a contemptuous pardon for conduct that is normally outlawed, is not obviously a liberty we should desire: the condition of being a free man or woman, in the sense approved by the ancients, is one defined by acknowledged duties. Free people do their duty. That is why Aristotle denied that slaves, or natural slaves, could be *eudaimones*, could have lives well-lived (see Clark 1985b). Their 'happiness' could only be 'the serenity of the slave, who has no difficult responsibilities, no high aims, and to whom nothing, past or future, is of greater value than the present' (Nietzsche 1956: 72). That there is a possible transvaluation of the life of itinerant labourer, or slave, is a topic to which I shall return in chapter eight.

It may also often be true that initiation comes with pain: the shared experience of having been marked as one of the People guarantees a fundamental equality in adult society (Clastres 1977: 153 f.). We should, I fear, at least consider the possibility that it is the absence of common, painful initiation rites that permits the radical inequality of our own society, the overwhelming barriers to free friendship that are erected by differences of temperament, education, and locale. Women at any rate must share the experience of menstruation, and many of them have shared experience of childbirth and demanding babies: Dame Nature is no respecter of persons! Men can usually persuade themselves more easily that they have nothing in common: perhaps that is one reason why they more readily go to war, in order that they may make real to themselves their shared vulnerability (on which I shall say more in a later chapter).

What—you may be asking—are the religious dimensions of all this? Am I about to reassert traditional values to the extent of asking women to accept their primary role as wives and mothers, men their roles as husbands, soldiers, and fathers? Is my careful use of the feminine pronoun, and my acknowledgement of the absolutely and literally central role of the lineage, of women and children, in human evolution, merely a cloak for my male chauvinism? I may be extolling the importance of the family, the value of sex-differentiated ritual and duty, with the secret, or even the subconscious, wish to get women back in their place. It is, after all, uncomfortably obvious that the mainstream Churches—or at least their most active laity and most consciously orthodox clergy—are by now the chief proponents of sex-inequality. The more sophisticated opponents of women's ordination may speak simply of the need for general consent before one embattled fragment of the Universal Church can take so great a step, or say that they have important aesthetic or symbolical objections to a woman's standing in for Christ at the altar but none at all to her playing a proper and important part in the life of the Church, or that they have themselves no idea at all why women should not be priests, but bow to universal tradition as good methodological conservatives. But it is difficult to escape the conviction that behind these—relatively rational—points, there lies an attitude of profound contempt for the abilities and personal character of women. Women are held to be naturally bossy, unreliable gossips who must be kept in order by their menfolk; their symbolical affinity is with darkness, earth, and passion, whereas men may symbolize the light, heaven, and reason. In short, the worst and most obviously male-invented aspects of ancient misogyny are with us still: Mother is the being we must escape if we are to follow the Father out into a wider world.

To the personal charge of sexism—if anyone wishes to make it—I can obviously have no final answer. Sexism, like racism or the charge of child abuse, is now as indefeasible an accusation in some circles as witchcraft once was. Merely to be accused is proof of guilt. But I do have one abstract response. I am indeed suggesting that the 'pre-political' life of human society, the network of families, baby-sitting circles, residents' associations, parents' associations, children's gangs, church guilds, business and informal friendships, colleges and choirs and grocers' shops and pubs, is the most important part of human society. It is this network of 'voluntary associations' and their corresponding obligations—obligations which are not simply what any individual chooses that they should be—which continues to provide us all with a sense of who and what we are. This pre-political level, in almost all its septs, is structured and maintained by women and by children. Even all-male groupings within the network, one can guarantee, will have attendant womenfolk. The 'humanizing' of the young male (and of the young female) is almost entirely a function of his (and her) adoption into the network. It is actually as true of us as of the Tupi-Guarani Indians studied by Clastres that we are 'exogamic demes made up of a few extended families, joined by matrilineal and patrilineal ties' (Clastres 1977: 48). We simply have other ties as well. I do not actually need to say that disaster would follow if any substantial number of women abandoned their duty to preserve the network: I do not need to say it because there is no chance at all of its happening. What I do propose, and thereby look backward to an older and wider tradition than our parochial conviction that males should stand above or alongside the network of merely 'personal' or 'pre-political' life, is that human society is vitally dependent on the proper companionship of all kinds and conditions at the pre-political level. It matters less that women should join the 'ruling classes' than that men and women together should learn that friendship matters more than rank or symbol.

In speaking of this network, this 'bundle of cords', as pre-political, I may be countenancing error. Ogilvy's term, the 'para-political' (Ogilvy 1978: 306 f.), is perhaps a better one. It is in one sense pre-political: it precedes and underlies the formal structure of state-power. Statist politicians may take steps to destroy it precisely because it offers an alternative context for human action. Family and local loyalties, casual friendships, and craft-associations may all compete for the human soul: statists may want us all to identify ourselves solely as citizens of the one state, and use monotheistic language precisely to encourage that purity of motive. But the network is not 'pre-political' in the original sense: on the contrary a *polis* is a lot more like an association of clubs, and its governing sept a lot more like the Athenaeum, than it is like a single, unitary nation-state (see Clark 1988h). Not all political life is statist.

Revolutionary statists and the mere passing chances of history constantly shake up and seek to unravel the net. Any of its bonds can be unloosed, but we can be reasonably confident that the net will reshape itself, that afterwards there will again be families and friends and clubs and craft-associations.

If feral children could survive and breed despite their isolation from the influences of culture, we can be reasonably sure that they would do a predictable variety of things: they would spawn a society with laws about incest and whom to marry; rules about property; habits of taboo and ritual avoidance. They would defer to the supernatural and try to control it in some regular fashion. They would have their initiations; they would foment courtship ceremonies and fuss elaborately about the adornment of young females. . . . Our biogrammarian would be sure to find the following: myths and legends, dancing, psychosis and neurosis, adultery, homosexuality, homicide, suicide, loyalty, desertion, juvenile delinquents, senile fools and various shrewd practitioners to cure or take advantage of the various ills from which communities and people suffer. (Tiger & Fox 1974: 31 f.)

This claim is not one that can readily be checked, but it has an overwhelming plausibility, which should not be confused with the much more parochial conviction of David Hume, that all human beings everywhere—unless corrupted by monkish superstition—would think just like a Hanoverian gentleman! There is a natural base of human existence, and that is why the exaggeratedly pessimistic view of our situation is never quite correct. The ceremony of innocence may be drowning, and the blood-dimmed tide be loosed, but we are never wholly abandoned to the Titans or fairies described in the last chapters. Anger, lust, and ignorance are perpetually trapped by the network of acknowledged duty and affection, shared skills, and experiences. It is natural law, the ancients said, that parents—and not just human parents—care for their children; they could add that we also care for our clan-mates, our teachers, and our pupils, and that we locate ourselves precisely by our gradually discovered place in the constantly reforming net of pre-state, or para-state, life.

In sum: we do not experience ourselves as isolated individuals but as nodes within a shifting network of relationships. When the nets of which we are elements are highly congruent, so that the very same people are related to us in many different ways, our self-concept is relatively rigid. When the nets are more diverse, and we find ourselves in very different groupings (at work, at home, at worship), our self-concept is itself at once more confused and likely to be more 'individualistic'. We are forced to remember what it is that lies behind or within our multiple roles or personalities—unless, that is, we read a little too much modern philosophy and forget that inner self again! Because this network constantly reforms, all assertions that we live in a radically desacralized world are bound to be exaggerated: order is not lost, nor the sense that some bonds are sacred. That indeed was the essence of Zeus' power: he was the god of hospitality, and of word once given. These are values that do affect the world, and without our consent: it is not only lust, anger, and ignorance that shape the world, but also those tenuous and constantly recreated links of loyalty, craft devotion, and obedient love.

It obviously does not follow that women ought to be regarded as 'inferior partners' in the enterprise of human life, nor that 'we' (who?) should take steps to return women to the confines of the patriarchal house. On the contrary, it seems clear to me that humanity is shaped as male and female both, and that human living will constantly recreate institutions that allow such different sorts of creature to be friends.

> The rituals surrounding Hestia do not, perhaps, symbolize the patriarchal order only . . . but may also have symbolized the importance of the powers conferred on the mistress of the house. . . . Such a power is not negligible, and even today a great number of women do not wish to 'leave the house', for it is their only place of real and significant power . . . (Paris 1986: 185.)

Let us not be too eager to throw overboard the rituals and meanings even of our patriarchal past. Exactly what shape the network takes in any age is not predictable. I doubt if it is even possible to insist that monogamous relationships must always be the norm—after all, they have not always been. It may be, as some have speculated, that we are witnessing the emergence of a somewhat different sort of institution, the marital club or group companionship which Engels thought was attested amongst Australian aboriginals (Engels 1985: 75 f.; see Clark 1983c). Natural law does not allow us to decree that just one sort of pattern is rationally required, as if we could work out in the abstract what 'abstract intelligences' would prescribe for themselves. It is implicit in the historicist, flexible, Burkean approach that I have been advocating that there can be no such abstract intelligences. How the net forms, and how we form within it, is a function of our actual past and prospects, not of self-evident principle. 'Reason exists for us only in concrete, historical terms, i.e. it is not its own master' (Gadamer 1986: 260). The pious conservative can welcome the diversity of life-forms shaped at this pre-state level by the experience of those who seek to meet their obligations. In fact, only the pious conservative can do so: we have no idea of what would be required in the abstract, and can only trust that what is finally borne in upon us as we go about our lives in the honest intention of doing good will be the right way for us to walk. If human history is just a drunkard's walk through possibility, our hopes are few. If God has not left us without witnesses, then we can have a reasonable assurance that the gates of hell will not quite prevail.

4

The Irrelevance of Consent

Government, Banditry, and Taboo

When the emperor Justinian commissioned a body of Byzantine law-
yers to codify the civil law (a task they completed in AD 534), they included sundry definitions of Law, amongst them Ulpian's. That there
is a difference between local, civil law and international or natural law
they all agreed. Ulpian's contribution was to distinguish 'natural law'
from 'international': the former is 'that which nature has taught all
animals . . . From this law spring the union of male and female,
which we call matrimony, the procreation of children and their education' (as d'Entreves 1951: 29). He might reasonably have added that
friendships, clans, trails, and territories are equally natural. The institutions that come under the *ius gentium*, by contrast, are 'wars, the separation of nations, the foundation of kingdoms, the division of
property, in short all those legal and political institutions which have
developed out of the growing complexity of human intercourse and
life' (d'Entreves 1951: 30). You will recognize that what I addressed in
my last chapter was 'natural law', and deduce from the list of titles that
in my next I shall speak of the *ius gentium*. The topic of this chapter, by
elimination, is the *ius civile*, or more precisely the authority of states to
make their own laws, and what sort of laws it is right that they should
make.

Despotism, by Kant's definition, 'prevails in a State if the laws are
made and arbitrarily executed by one and the same power' (1970:
101)—from which he infers that plebiscite democracies are necessarily despotic. A republican constitution is one that imposes a legislative check upon the executive, where the legislature does not
merely exist to license what the executive wants to do. 'Government
without or beyond law is despotism, and it is nonetheless despotism
because it is benevolent . . . As Lord Bacon said, judges ought to
remember that their office is *ius dicere* and not *ius dare*' (McIlwain
1939: 270). Just, or republican, rulers differ from brigands to the
extent that they obey a law greater than their own will—and not just
any such wider law.

St Augustine says: 'There is no law unless it be just'. So the validity of law depends upon its justice. But in human affairs a thing is said to be just when it accords with the rule of reason: and as we have seen, the first rule of reason is the Natural law. Thus all humanly enacted laws are in accord with reason to the extent that they derive from the Natural law. And if a human law is at variance in any particular with the Natural law, it is no longer law, but rather a corruption of law. (Aquinas *Summa Theologica*, 1a 2ae, 95, 2: d'Entreves 1951: 46.)

The content of that natural law as I have already expounded it is given by the constantly renewed experience of friendly and familial confrontation, where individuals find their dignity in the fulfilment of particular and local duty. Purported laws which seek to prevent the natural development of friendly association and moral dignity are not real laws at all, not '*ius*' because not '*iustum*'.

Kipling, in the persona of the revolutionary MacDonough:

> Whether the State can loose and bind
>   in heaven as well as on Earth;
> if it be wiser to kill mankind
>   before or after the birth—
> these are matters of high concern
>   where State-kept schoolmen are;
> but Holy State (we have lived to learn)
>   endeth in Holy War . . .
> Whatsoever for any cause
>   seeketh to take or give,
> power above or beyond the Laws,
>   suffer it not to live!
> Holy State or Holy King—
>   or Holy People's Will—
> have no truck with the senseless thing.
>   Order the guns and kill!

>   (Kipling 1927: 546 f.)

I remark in passing that anyone who criticizes Kipling for his supposedly imperialist or 'jingoist' tendencies forgets to see that the law of his admiration was the law of freedom, that his enemies were those who set a trap for the innocent, and that he well knew the mortality of all imperial power. It is perhaps precisely because he was suspicious of all self-complacent authority that liberals conscious of their own rectitude insist on misrepresenting him. Weil justly observes that Hitler achieved 'exactly the sort of greatness . . . before which we all bow down in servile admiration as soon as our eyes are turned toward the past' (Weil 1987: 216), namely that of Sulla, or Caesar, or Tamerlane, or Al Capone: but Kipling did not bow down before 'the Old King, under any name' (Kipling 1927: 294).

The law of freedom, in Lysander Spooner's words, dictates that 'the right of every man to do anything and everything which justice does not forbid him to do is a natural, inherent, inalienable right' (Spooner 1972: 'Letter to Grover Cleveland', 7). Lawmakers, accordingly, 'can add nothing to [justice, the supreme law] nor take anything from it. Therefore all the laws of their own making have no colour of authority or obligation' (1972: ibid. 3). In Hayek's terminology, '*thesis*', modern legislative action, has usurped the functions of '*nomos*', the laws of spontaneous social order (Gray 1986: 71).

The great part of that order which reigns among mankind is not the effect of government. It has its origins in the principles of society and the natural constitution of men . . . Common interest regulates their concerns and forms their law; and the laws which common usage ordains have a greater influence than the laws of government. (Paine 1987: ii. 1: see Tivey 1981: 183.)

Spooner concluded that the American federal government, and of course all others, violated right with conscription, taxation, appropriation of wilderness, and the federal monopoly of postal services and minting ('Letter to Grover Cleveland', 31 f.). 'I have evidence satisfactory to myself', he reported sardonically, 'that there exists scattered throughout the country, a band of men having a tacit understanding with each other, and calling themselves the people of the United States, whose general purposes are to control and plunder each other and all other people in the country and so far as they can even in neighboring countries, and to kill every man who shall attempt to defend his person and property against their scheme of plunder and domination' ('No Treason', 34).

Though Spooner is now a hero of the right-wing anarchist, or anarcho-individualist,[1] his rejection of state law rests on the same perception as Kropotkin's, a hero of the left, or anarcho-communist. Kropotkin's judgement:

The law's origin is the desire of the ruling class to give permanence to customs imposed by themselves for their own advantage. Its character is the skilful commingling of customs useful to society, customs which have no need of law to ensure respect, with other customs useful only to rulers, injurious to the

---

[1] Martin (1970) and Schuster (1970) offer histories of individualist anarchism in America. Later anarcho-individualists are discussed by Machan (1975).

mass of the people and maintained only by the fear of punishment. (Capouya & Tompkins 1976: 34.)

Kropotkin, conversely, shared the anarcho-individualists' distrust of state subsidy: 'it is to be the state that will give alms to him who is willing to recognize his inferiority. From thence to the Poor Law and the Workhouse is but a stone's throw' (Capouya & Tompkins 1976: 106). Both thinkers were unlike later partisan revolutionaries, or minimalists such as Benjamin Tucker or Ayn Rand, in that they drew their support from a theory of natural law, rather than from Max Stirner's egoistic principles. Spooner's concern was not simply to reject the supposed right of any person to command him, but to resist the spoliation and degradation of the earth's inhabitants, 'as savages, barbarians and wage laborers', whom the prevailing ethos of state government, he believed, prevented from working together in free—which is not to say lawless— association. Government claims to seek the positive welfare of the governed he regarded as at once *ultra vires* and hypocritical. The genuine welfare of the governed would be best served by getting off their backs, not by taxing, conscripting, and regulating their doings in accordance with some vision of a higher good which they had not themselves endorsed. Governments are protection rackets. The suggestion—still to be found in some political theorists—that real consent can be inferred from the victim's participation in some political processes (like casting a vote, or even campaigning), let alone from her simply forbearing to revolt, he treated with well-merited disdain: 'to take a man's property without his consent, and then to infer his consent because he attempts by voting to prevent that property being used to his injury is a very insufficient proof of his consent to support the Constitution' ('No Treason', 14). That a conscript soldier—once in the ranks—will fight to save his life does not of itself justify his original conscription.

Tucker eventually believed that anyone had an absolute right to act as he chose to preserve his own life and purposes, adding only that a rational man would seek out friends and allies against the storm, not engage in villainy. He sought to avoid the force of Chesterton's comment that 'to preach egoism is to practice altruism' (1961: 38) by explaining that he too would profit if everyone else acted in their own interests. His opposition to Hobbes, in the last resort, was tactical, as he believed that passing strangers would elect to keep the necessary peace without any threat from Leviathan. Hobbes on the one hand gave greater credit to natural affection than did Tucker, and on the other thought that strangers would be duty-bound to distrust each other. Spooner, I think, was of an older and in some respects sounder tradition than either, holding that we all have a right to live in that way which allows others to live freely: we have no right to expropriate or kill, and hence no 'right to do these things' which we can hand over to a government on our behalf. 'No man can by agreement pass over to another that which he hath not in himself', said Locke (2. 24: 1963: 326), and people can give their government 'no power to do an unjust thing such as it is to make an unjust war (for they never had such a Power in themselves' (2. 179: 1963: 435). If I should not take your labour, time, or money on the plea that I know better what to do with it, by what right does a government do just that?

Sheerly egoistic individualism, holding that I can have no obligation to do what—in my present judgement—does me no good, allows no state authority at all. The pretence that state authority can do me good against my will, can do to me what I do not think good, convinces few of us. Even if I could be wrong about what 'does me good', or what I will one day think good (which may indeed be so, as I have argued in an earlier chapter), what evidence have I that actual rulers mean me well, or anyone? Most actual states require their citizens to pay for services they do not use, for the sake of 'the common good'. If family and local loyalties are real, and residents in consequence have far more obligations than to their 'own' survival, those duties at any rate may rightly be enforced. But what right has the state to require of me new duties, ones I would not have in nature, even when that 'nature' is understood to include the pre-political network of family and friends?

The distinction between rights of liberty and rights of welfare is crucial to liberal and libertarian debate. Modern liberals believe, unlike their forebears, that governments may rightly take our money and our lives to defend the realm, to care for the needy, to equalize resources, to alter moral attitudes, to finance social services or support failing businesses: in fact, to do whatever the rulers—or their schoolmen—think fit to do. Some of those who endorse a conception of 'children's rights', for example, do not mean by this that children, as such, should be encouraged to take responsibility for their own lives: they mean rather that state officials should decide what is good for them regardless of their parents' or natural guardians' opinion. Amongst recent horror stories emanating from the States (and I emphasize that I do not know how the story really ends) is one of a judge who gave custody of an orphaned child to the child-minder originally hired by the child's grandmother, even though nothing could be said against the, still-living, grandmother. The story is symptomatic of what appears to be a deliberate attack on 'natural' as against state-sponsored ties, and of a wholly unfounded trust in 'experts' and State officials to be better informed and more benevolent than common humanity. No major competitor for political power is likely to object too much to the principle: the exact nature of the expenditure may be opposed, but not the government's right to do as it please with our own. In the words of one anthropologist describing the Polynesian institution of taboo—which is occasionally mentioned as an example of superstition by good moderns:

Taboo provided the means of relating a person to his superiors and inferiors. One can imagine a Chancellor of the Exchequer declaring eight or nine shillings in every twenty taboo as a measure of the power conferred on him. . . . In the Polynesian system this power could have been conferred on him only by someone exercising an even more awful taboo, and that the Polynesian Chancellor would use the same term for his share in your pound and for the rights of his superiors, because these rights would concern him only as infringements of his own rights, just as taking eight shillings is a restriction on your use of twenty shillings. The measure of a person's political authority is the taboos he can impose, and they can be rendered invalid and overruled only by the taboo of a higher official. (Steiner 1967: 39.)

If the fundamental units of society are individuals, and government has no authority that is not conferred on it by those individuals that must endure its sway, then it can have no rights that they have not granted, and no rights that they themselves have got no right to grant. Thomas Jefferson himself—and it is not without reason that anarchists sometimes claim simply to be unafraid Jeffersonian democrats—suggested that the American Constitution would need to be unanimously ratified all over again in each generation: 'Nineteen years is the term beyond which neither the representatives of a nation, nor even the whole nation itself assembled can validly extend a debt' (cited by Wills 1978: 124). Locke (2. 12: 1963: 316) similarly thought that statute laws were null and void after a century. Or is it supposed in practice that parents have the right to command even their adult children to obey? If I have no right to take your money, I cannot confer such a right on a third party. A merely individualistic egoist might suggest that, 'in nature', I do have just such a right (in that there is nothing at all to stop me), but one whose universal exercise would amount to an unending war. If my analysis (and Locke's) of 'pre-political society' is correct I would not have such a right 'in nature', even before the establishment of state authority.

Liberalism began with the entirely reasonable wish to restrict the power of princes, to lay it down that their authority came only from the consent of the governed—and not merely from the notional consent of those too frightened to rebel, or too little troubled by their chains. From that position, so it seems to me, one can only go on to anarchism. Laslett's remark that 'there was really no stopping place between the ground . . . Locke occupied and logical individualism, final democracy, the sharing of political power with women, children and servants' (Locke 1963: 82 f.) is actually too weak. Even a wider electorate would have no right to demand of me what I did not agree to give, or had no right to give. It was the American anarchist, the anarcho-capitalists, who also carried Mill's requirement to its fateful conclusion: I can be forbidden to do nothing save what directly harms my neighbour. I cannot be required to live in some purportedly righteous or well-meaning fashion against my will, nor contribute to schemes I think half-baked, unjust, or simply not my scene. Political right-wingers in this country profess to believe this much about some schemes of social action; political left-wingers demand the same right of conscientious objection when it comes to weaponry. Only the anarchists denied at once the state's right to fund either weapons of mass destruction or 'gay rights groups' and the like. Modern liberals are now defenders of the massive collectivizing of economic and social power, but without any convincing account of how a state could acquire such authority and not be Leviathan. If governments are to be subject to a law not of their own making, if they are to be decently republican, then either they derive their authority from the real assent of the governed (who are presumed to have a natural right to govern themselves, and not to be a slave), or (having more authority than that—including, in the last resort, the right to license homicide) they derive it not from the real and direct consent of self-governing individuals but from some higher authority, some superior tabooer.

Binding the King

There is an institution closer to home than is taboo, though it is likely to be even less familiar: namely, the ancient Irish system of *gessa* (of which the singular is *geis*: Rees & Rees 1961: 327 ff.). Obligations are laid, chiefly on great chieftains and warriors, to do or forbear, with the mythological sanction that a violation of *gessa* will lead immediately to death, and the psychological that such violation precisely violates the individual's own sense of self-worth, courage, identity. A chief is known to be doomed if his weird leads him into situations where one *geis* or other must be violated: he must refuse to share a meal with a chance-met companion—which is forbidden him—or else eat the flesh of an animal that is forbidden him. 'It is a wretched man that violates his *gessa*', because he has violated the bargain under which he holds a place in life. Our identities, remember, are discovered or created precisely in our acceptance of objective obligation. There were doubtless always those who saw no sense in petty restrictions on their will to power, as there were also those—at a higher level—who believed themselves relieved of their enslavement to the angels of their rank and place. A special *geis*, incidentally, may be imposed on individuals, not in virtue of their rank or descent, but by the mere will of others: so Gráinne demanded that Diarmaid elope with her by laying a *geis* on him, as we might say, 'a spell' or, better still, 'a dare'. She dared him to do it, so that he would be thought a coward or 'not a gentleman' if he did not, even though he might well have truly said that there was a *geis* upon him not to betray his captain. Torn between conflicting *gessa*, or faced by spell-binders of differing powers, Diarmaid was lost (Rees & Rees 1961: 281 ff.).

We grow up among such *gessa*, such obligations, spells, and dares. So far from being a literal 'superstition', something left over from a metaphysical or religious system that gave it sense, it is the *geis* which gives birth to the system, or to many systems! Cartesian attempts to found human knowledge on self-evident principle have failed: it has proved simply impossible to demonstrate what we all experience and believe to be the case. It is similarly impossible to justify the everyday moral and legal practices of our society on the basis of liberal intuition, the doctrine that we can only be obliged to obey those authorities that we have consented to obey or that we ourselves see present reason to obey (if those). All moral systems that rest upon a supposedly self-evident right of self-ownership by independent individuals must deny all rights of taxation, conscription, expropriation, and moral regulation. Still worse: if I am obliged to do only what I now see good reason to do (independently of my being ordered to do it), how should I even obey such 'simple little rules and few' as not making U-turns on motorways? We can all be glad that most of us, most of the time, do obey such rules unthinkingly, and do not entertain the option of making such a turn 'when it seems safe'! As in epistemology, so in politics: our actual historical and personal experience is not one in which authority is accorded to our rulers or our dogmas after lengthy thought and by indefeasible argument. Things work the other way: we find ourselves believing, and reverencing, all manner of things, and then slowly find reasons (internal to the system in which we live) for abandoning or modifying some constraints upon belief or action. The self-owning individual does not stand at the beginning of political society, but—as MacIntyre has it—near its end.

Do [the revolutionary theorists] mean to invalidate, annul, or to call into question, together with the titles of the whole line of our kings, that great body of our statute law which passed under those whom they treat as usurpers? to annul laws of inestimable value to our liberties? (Burke 1975: 287.)

If past kings, ruling without the express consent of all, had no authority, then all the laws they promulgated are without authority. But it is those same laws, or some of them, that define and defend our freedoms. Either they must be discarded (and mere anarchy prevail), or else their authority rests not on our or our ancestors' express consent, but on the value of the liberties they define, or the moral weight of their authors.

What I am suggesting is almost a return to Filmer, a political theorist whose only fame is now in the fact that Locke sought to refute him—though Locke himself was more like Filmer than we usually remember. Where Locke founded political society in an original contract less absolute—and to that extent more fragile—than Hobbes's, Filmer had suggested that all kings and princes (as distinct from brigands) held their authority as heirs of Adam, inheritors of his primordial paternal clout. Locke mocked the theory, as an ignoble and ultimately ridiculous attempt to deny man's 'natural freedom', and assert an absolute monarchy quite out of line with tradition. Filmer himself probably merited the mockery. But it is not, as far as I can see, absurd to suggest (i) that kings, princes, and governors are in fact given reverence by virtue of their being presented as natural authorities of the same kind as parents or heroes, magical figures on whom our attention is focused quite apart from any choice of ours, and (ii) that the attempt to think away all such *gessa* leads straight to anarchistic individualism of an even more extreme sort than Spooner's. Locke himself denied that liberty was license (2. 22: 1963: 324), but that was precisely because he saw that we all lived under Law.

Historically, our 'natural state' was never an accidental congress of unobligated strangers who must somehow create for themselves the possibility of mutual trust and respect for law. Locke can adduce a few such examples (2. 101: 1963: 378 f.), but they are, precisely, gatherings of deracinated, exiled bandits, 'a handful of adventurers brought together by necessity', and so lacking any sense of obedience to sacred law (Weil 1987: 261). What is natural to us is to live in families, alliances, and clans where particular figures stand out as our authorities and are themselves laid under *gessa* not of their contrivance to take care of their subjects. If there were no such experienced obligations our obedience could only ever be a forced obedience, a laying down of arms for fear of the stronger sword. Political authority would always rest—where it does often rest—simply with the most powerful group—a group, of course, which is in historical fact itself likely to be one governed by *gessa* and experienced obligations. Whatever Filmer's intentions in this, it does not follow that we must accept an 'absolute' or 'unlimited' authority in our present rulers, although it may well be true that rulers in the past have sometimes been accorded such an absolute respect, and that all parents, even now, can count upon an astonishing degree of deference from their young. But the limitations on princely or parental authority are themselves taboos, *gessa*, obligations which do not rest on any explicit contract. The undoubted success of Lockean liberalism in unleashing the productive capacities of the West and eroding ancient tyrannies is itself evidence of the existence of the human capacity to lay and to acknowledge *gessa*. The king's subjects have laid a *geis* on him, or reminded him of a *geis* laid by a superior. Traditional rulers, with the Mandate of Heaven, served as the gate between this world and the divine precisely because they were constrained by ritual observances (see Eaton 1977: 90 f.).

> All we have of freedom,
>   all we use or know—
> this our fathers bought for us
>   long and long ago.
> Ancient Right unnoticed
>   as the breath we draw—
> leave to live by no man's leave,
>   underneath the Law—
> lance and torch and tumult,
>   steel and grey-goose wing,

wrenched it, inch and ell and all,
    slowly from the King.
Till our fathers 'stablished,
    after bloody years,
how our King is one with us,
    first among his peers.
So they bought us freedom
    —not at little cost—
wherefore must we watch the King,
    lest our gain be lost

           (Kipling 1927: 294.)

The liberty of freeborn Britons, as constitutionalists affirmed long before Burke, is a function of the network of historically established rights and privileges, duties and permissions that make it impossible for any one man, any one government, to gather all the threads into its own grasp. This is not to say that they will not continue to try, even while they pretend to value local freedoms. If they ever succeeded they would have destroyed the environment within which their subjects learn what it is to be obligated, and will have to resort to mere force to compel obedience.

Obedience being a necessary food of the soul, whoever is definitely deprived of it is ill. Thus any body politic governed by a sovereign ruler accountable to nobody is in the hands of a sick man. (Weil 1987: 14.)

The Tupi-Guarani seem to have turned aside from that development which led their kinsmen to the unitary state of the Incas' Peru: 'Tupi-Guarani prophetism is the heroic attempt of primitive society to put an end to unhappiness by means of a radical refusal of the One, as the universal essence of the state' (Clastres 1977: 182). They preferred, as Yeats might have said, the 'multitudinous influx of fairy' to the 'single god' of the age just past. Liberal pluralism is polytheistic, resentful of the dead hand of a tyrant power. The problem for such liberals is that they do not really wish to do away with the state. Statists, on the other hand, may often use the vocabulary of monotheism to justify their centralizing vision. The state, the central government, claims to embody the One spirit or command that rises superior to all lesser obligation, or contains them all. T. H. Green's judgement:

The ultimate moving force which inspires and controls political action is a spiritual force, a common conviction that makes for righteousness, a common conscience that alone can arm the ministers and agents of the community with power. That conviction or conscience at once creates rights, creates the law or system of rules by which those rights are maintained, and creates the sovereign whose mission it is to enunciate and enforce that law, and to sustain in complete harmony with one another all the living institutions which are the concrete embodiment of rights and of law. (Barker 1915: 38.)

Such a sacred purpose is usually associated with consciously illiberal authority, but even a liberal state could be described like this. In fact, Locke's own rhetoric of liberalism, unlike that of his successors, rests on just such a conviction. The state's right of command is given by its duty to maintain the natural system of friendly association between human beings who know they hold the land from God. Such a government has more duties and fewer rights than would be easily agreed by just any bunch of 'self-owners'. It exists to serve a law that precedes it. But the more obvious embodiment of a simply theocratic state may well seem quite opposed to liberal ideals, and most of my readers will by now be suspecting that I intend to force on them—if only in theory—a choice between anarcho-capitalism and the sort of polity that we in the West identify with Islamic fundamentalism or the Bible Belt. They are, of course, essentially correct! Either the state can have no authority beyond that of a simple police force (if it has that much), or else it must be supposed to embody a sacred, moral purpose that constrains or contains all lesser purposes within society. To be loved, the state, like anything else, must be lovable. But there are at least two ways of seeking to serve that kind of ideal, two kinds of patriotism: if we can feel neither, let us relapse on anarchistic pluralism.

One can either love France for the glory which would seem to ensure for her a prolonged existence in time and space; or else one can love her as something which, being earthly, can be destroyed, and is all the more precious on that account. (Weil 1987: 164.)

It is not necessary, indeed it is fatal, for patriots to identify the state with God.

The State is sacred, not in the way an idol is sacred, but in the way common objects serving a religious purpose, like the altar, the baptismal water or anything else of the kind are sacred. Everybody knows they are only material objects; but material objects which are regarded as sacred because they serve a sacred purpose. That is the sort of majesty appropriate for the State. (Weil 1987: 174.)

Not all 'sacred statists' look forward to the time when their own state is a world state: they may prefer to think that their own national spirit, embodied in the laws and institutions of a nation state, is messianic, an example or saviour for the whole world of nations. That was Luto-slawski's view of Poland (Lutoslawski 1930: 147 ff.) and maybe Yeats's hope for Ireland, once its hatreds had been purged[2] and its people re-united in ritual service of the spirits he put on display in the theatre and in his poems. Such nationalists do not rule out the possibility that some other people might, as devotedly and piously as they, embody some quite different image. The 'Napoleon of Notting Hill' (mis-called) proclaims the victory of his vision when his opponents begin to feel as deeply and morally for the spirit of Bayswater, and knows his failure when Notting Hill at last grows rich and insolent enough to deny other folk their vision.

'Notting Hill is a nation: why should it condescend to be a mere Empire? You wish to pull down the statue of General Wilson, which the men of Bayswater have so rightly erected in Westbourne Grove. Fools! Who erected that statue? Did Bayswater erect it? No. Notting Hill erected it. Do you not see that it is the glory of our achievement that we have infected the other cities with the ideal-ism of Notting Hill?' (Chesterton 1946: 143.)

Good modern liberals, as well they might, find Chesterton's fable faintly disgusting (it is, by the way, the original '1984'): the very idea that people should kill or die for a 'rise or high ground of the common earth on which men have built houses to live, in which they are born, fall in love, pray, marry and die', or that they can make what would otherwise be a joke into a terrible beauty by shedding blood for it, is something that we would wish to forget. I fear that it is because we have put it out of our minds that we are so taken aback when others act on it. But if a people should never be filled with a willingness to die or kill for their national idea, and the land in which it is embodied, that is as much as to say that the governing body of such a people has no authority to claim the lives of its subjects. If we are not to live and die for such an embodied, or partly embodied, vision, then the role of the state can only be what minimalists or anarchists propose. If it demands more than it justly may, and it may never justly demand of us a loyalty to death, transcending any individual or local goals we have, it is no more than any band of brigands when it pretends to lay commands on us 'of its own making'. It may be that we cannot rid ourselves of bri-gands, and that our best hope is slowly to tame and humanize the crew,

---

[2] 'G— said that he has always thought that the bad luck of Ireland comes from hatred being the foundation of our politics' (Yeats 1955: 486).

until they cease to pretend that they have rights to what we do and make and are. Revolution, on the historical evidence, rarely does more than substitute untamed brigands (of another class or tribe) for the semi-civilized kind. But minimalists, once again, seem to have the edge: the obvious moral of liberal doctrine is that a land and nation that is not worth dying for has no authority to command the least obedience of those who chance to be within its borders. If the empire of Notting Hill is comic or disgusting, because no 'modern man' should think anything worth more than the carefree fulfilment of whatever goals she chances to have, and because the only acceptable laws are those required to keep the 'peace' between competing individuals and warring factions—then any empire, any state is just as bad.

So Holy State does end in Holy War? At the least, if we shrink back from the idea that people may be called upon to die or kill in the name of the state, we must believe that the state is no more than a convenience, or something worse than that. 'The State's duty is to make the country, in the highest possible degree, a reality' (Weil 1987: 157): that can be our duty only if that country is or will be one to which the people 'really feel they belong' (Weil 1987: 160), one that is worth dying for. Pure egoists, of course, can think nothing at all worth dying for—which is why Hobbes himself denied that we could ever have a duty to die for Leviathan (1968: 268 f.: Book 2, ch. 21). Most of us, having come to ourselves through the recognition of objective duty and of unities wider and more long-lasting than our fragile flesh, will more readily agree that there are some things for which we would, in the last resort, be prepared to die or even to kill. Our distaste or moral repugnance for the vision that Chesterton, at times, presents perhaps rests in our failure to see what it was that he thought worth defending. He allows his characters to suggest, sometimes, that mere violence can hallow any cause, but that was not his true opinion. What Adam Wayne was defending in Notting Hill was what Alfred defended against the invading Dane: the homes and hopes and memories of the poor against the brigands who would enslave and rob them of the works of their hands and the imaginations of their hearts. What he describes is a society that has lost any common moral purpose of such force and authority that can oblige its victims to serve a wider good than theirs alone. His opponents simultaneously assert that the poor of Notting Hill ought to allow their own lives and purposes to be lived by the wider unity that was once Britain, and deny them the right to be lived by the unity of which they really feel themselves a part. Bluntly: why should a local community, knit together by shared obligations and memories, be sacrificed to the mere convenience of a state—or its complacent oligarchs—that no longer even pretends to embody a high moral purpose, the shape into which all members of its commonwealth will hope to grow? Either the state is to be no more than the guardian of existing property rights and common law institutions or it is to embody a high purpose that takes precedence over local rights and duties. In neither case can it simply deny those local ties without being revealed as a pirate-crew, a band of brigands. If it is to be a minimal watchman-state, it can claim no right to regulate its clients' lives except to insist that they forego violent expropriation as a tool of policy. A mere police authority of that kind has no right to my unlimited obedience over and above my law-abidingness. Not even every aspect of *nomos* is enforceable by state action; *theses*—supposed laws that depend for their authority solely on the will of state officers—are not justly enforceable at all. 'The rights of the State over us and its claims upon us diminish in proportion to its loss of traditional legitimacy. When it no longer acknowledges any transcendent authority, it must become our servant, providing protection and certain amenities—a kind of glorified Water and Sewerage Authority' (Eaton 1977: 98)—and who would die for the Water Board? If we think that the state and its officers do have more authority than that, an authority that permits them to alter lawfully established practices and traditional norms of conduct at their will, to redistribute wealth, and to call their unconsenting subjects out to war, we must be acting on the assumption that the state embodies a sacred value, higher than that embodied in the mere common ordering of society. 'Even the Romans understood that their sometimes clownish Emperors must be "deified" if they were to merit obedience—for who but a slave would obey a merely human master?' (Eaton 1977: 90).

The essence of the institution of the parochial state is the custom that calls on its citizens to give their lives for it in war, and this demand is psychologically possible so long as their country fills the whole of their mental horizon and appears to embrace the sum of things human and divine. This pretension of a state to be the Universe, preposterous though it be, only ceases to command assent and obedience when the last of the contending parochial states of a disintegrating society have been annihilated and replaced by a single universal state which, at the beginning, commands the loyalty of no more than that fraction of its population that constitutes the imperial people, and when concurrently the people's religious devotion is transferred from cults with local roots to higher religions with a message for all Humanity. (Toynbee 1954: 395 f.: on which more below.)

The Land we Live by

In the sixteenth century an anonymous Welshman[3] lamented the cutting of Glyn Cynon:

> Many a birch tree green of cloak
> (I'd like to choke the Saxon)
> is now a flaming heap of fire
> where iron-workers blacken.
> For cutting the branch and bearing away
> the wild birds' habitation
> may misfortune quickly reach
> Rowenna's treacherous children!
>
> (Jones 1977: 71.)

The poet's complaint is not that an abstract principle of justice has been violated, that the wild birds have been robbed of what is theirs by abstract right, but that the particular meanings that the wood had for him and for his people have been overwritten, a new *Gestalt* formed. Glyn Cynon was sanctuary and trysting place, a land of happy memory. He cursed the invader because his identity was bound up with the land he lived in and by. But the English have their happy places too, the visible record of their personal and national past, their own account of property and proper use. Even those things that once 'desecrated' the landscape may become elements in that ancestral *Gestalt*: Cromwell's soldiers fired arrows at the angels of Mildenhall church, and the arrow-heads themselves are now a part of history, something that it would be wrong to remove (an example taken from Frank Harrison's paper in BANC 1987: 13 ff.). In a hundred years or so, no doubt, the ruins of air-bases will be the subject of a conservation order! Environmentalists lay themselves open to easy mockery if they preach that we should not interfere with 'wilderness areas': few areas that we really admire are all that wild, and almost none will survive in their present health and beauty unless we take steps to help them—in which case they will not be really wild any longer (as Clark 1983b). Antiquarians make a similar error if they appeal only to what what is original or ancient: many of the buildings and landscapes they admire have been

---

[3] Some of the material in this section was presented to a meeting of the British Association of Nature Conservationists in May 1986 and printed together with other such papers as 'The Ecological Conscience' (BANC 1987: 7–12); see also Clark 1988f on the importance of 'concrete' rather than 'abstract' value.

extensively modified by succeeding generations, and any attempt to return to the 'original' will involve 'skinning the church [as it might be] alive' (as Ruskin and his followers would put it: Clifton-Taylor 1974: 13).

It is not unreasonable to preserve things of the very same kind as we should now think it right to prevent: to keep the arrowheads *in situ*, but to prevent similar acts of high-principled vandalism. It is not unreasonable because what we are preserving is a great mnemonic, the externalized history of our tribe. The sense of history, the way in which we can read our real or imagined past from the landscape we inhabit is a vital ingredient in the ethic of conservation, and of patriotism itself. 'People will not look forward to posterity, who never look backward to their ancestors' (Burke 1975: 298). Whether we seek to conserve wetlands and the whooping crane, or Ely cathedral and its surrounding buildings, what matters is the vast sweep of our past, and the pledges it offers to the future. The value such things represent is more than aesthetic, which is one reason why a farmer who chops down a longstanding hedgerow and then claims to have 'replanted it', as if it were no more than a row of nursery bred wallflowers, is deceiving himself. Another reason, of course, is that it takes a long time to establish any such thriving hedgerow. A hedgerow is more than a hawthorn!

More even than the work of the great architects, [Ryder] loved buildings that grew silently with the centuries, catching and keeping the best of each generation, while time curbed the artist's pride and the Philistine's vulgarity, and repaired the clumsiness of the dull workman. (Waugh 1962: 214: ch. 3. 1).

For one cleric of Tunbridge Wells the preservation or otherwise of old churches is 'a straight fight between Christians and conservationists' (cited by Binney 1977). When the Chicago Stock Exchange Building was under threat in 1972, *Time* magazine described the contest as one between 'the practical necessities of change' and 'impractical, even sentimental preservation' (Costonis 1974: 4). Both *Time* magazine and churchman, while speaking of the 'practical needs' of the community, wholly ignored those needs which rest on our identities as something more than business or sociable secularists. On what grounds do they discount our need of beauty, remembered history, sacred space?

The proper ethical view sees man as a part of nature, and man's role as one of living together with other species in some reciprocal relationship, concerned for them, helping them and the entire ecological system to change and develop in some selective direction. (Lynch 1972: 106.)

By the same token, the proper religious view sees us as custodians under God of aesthetic, historical, and sacred value (see Clark 1986d). 'The soil of our country exercises over us a power that is both magical and mystical. We look upon it as a "relic" of heroic ancestors, and it inspires us to emulate them, and to strive to make our earth more like the sun—a shining abode of genius and sanctity, a true paradise of boundless happiness' (Lutoslawski 1930: 88). If there is a government anywhere that really deserves our loyalty it will be one that seeks to preserve the land we live by, and that encapsulates the very historical tradition that has made us a people. When we no longer find that land worth living by, that royalty worth honouring, we shall be condemned to live by transitory bargains among deracinated strangers. The danger may be imminent, but the barbarians are perhaps not quite as powerful as MacIntyre has suggested (1981: 245). Toynbee's comment seems an apt one:

An eighteenth-century English Whig landowner, who had put his treasure into the founding of a family, would plant avenues which even his grandchildren would not live to see with the eye of the flesh in the glory of the timber's full-grown stature. A twentieth-century Ministry of Agriculture planted soft wood to replace the hard wood that it felled; and in this greediness for quick returns, it was advertising its disbelief in its own immortality. (Toynbee 1954: 518.)

The Pivot of the Four Quarters

The competing models of the state that I have sketched are very familiar ones. The first is as follows: state officials are at best barely civilized brigands who may serve to protect us against still worse brigands, but who have no shadow of right to our obedience outside the narrow realm of enforceable justice. They can demand, as may anyone else, that I not assault or rob my neighbour; they may even demand that I look after those for whom I have, by *nomos*, special obligation. They may not require my financial or personal support for schemes of their contrivance that supposedly bring some benefit to creatures for whom I have no special responsibility. Nor may they demand that I lend my support to breaches of the natural law—as it might be, the financing of weapons of mass destruction. If they claim power above or beyond the laws of freedom they are usurpers—which is not to say that I therefore have a right or duty to organize a campaign to withhold such tax as would, I calculate, be used in schemes which I think wicked. The money I pay belongs to Caesar, and must be a matter of indifference to faith-holders (see Eller 1987: 165 f., 195 f.; and chapter six below).

There is no moral and ceremonial system that is willingly agreed by literally all members of any modern state, nor any that can be shown even to be the one that they would agree to 'if only they were rational enough'. It has accordingly been very widely suggested that the laws of the state must not embody any one particular moral order: the state can only 'hold the ring'. What is strange to me is that those who say so draw back from the minimalist or anarchist conclusion, that the officers of the state are profoundly ill-qualified to be moral educators, and have no more business than any other private citizen interfering in established folk-ways that involve no direct, dangerous, and obvious injustice. Consider the following contradiction entertained by really modern minds: on the one hand, the state has no right to require women to display heroic virtue, or even what would once have been called decency, by forbidding them to have their offspring aborted. On the other, the state apparently does have the right to compel us all to care for friendless beggars, or the unfamiliar old, or anyone at all who does not choose to work. To care for beggars is a duty indeed, in any of the great traditions: a duty of humanity, and not of justice, because the beggar has no enforceable right to help. But it might equally be thought a duty of humanity not to abort one's young. If 'Good Samaritan' legislation cannot be endorsed by 'liberals' (as Thomson 1971 has it), then all 'welfare rights' must fall. If such a duty is enforceable by rulers with the Mandate of Heaven we cannot rule out the possibility that they might rightly require such service to the unborn.

The alternative and ill-regarded thought is this. The state and its officers hold their authority from above: not from the consent of the governed, which may be wholly unreal, but as embodiments of a sacred order that needs the visible unity of the state, not just the flexible and decentralized networks of society. Although I have in part endorsed the thought that 'para-political' order is that which women and children have in fact sustained, and that too much of statist government has simply been a male conspiracy, it must needs be added that those Cyclopes were real, and that 'the state' has sometimes been a saviour. In Mill's words, 'the domestic life of domestic tyrants is one of the things which it is the most imperative for the law to interfere with' (1848: 5. 11. 9; see Goodin 1985: 181). Perhaps the visible unity of state control does not merely serve to lead its subjects in the one right way by issuing such commands as they grow into real virtue by obeying:

perhaps it gives them a veritable image of psychological unity—where there is no such central command the people may exist like Plato's democrats, swerving from one life pattern to another as the fancy takes them.

All past states, making no pretence of 'secularity' or 'value-neutral law', have consciously sought to embody or represent a god. By showing Athena to the sometime members of Attic clans and patronal fellowships, Athenian politicians forged a unity out of families, clans, craft-associations, clubs. In *A Midsummer Night's Dream*, so White (1970: 45 f.) observes, it takes the reconciliation of our 'parents and originals' before Theseus can muster the energy to withstand the patriarchal cruelty of Egeus. Only a state that can convince its subjects that it speaks for a god they know, or will come to know, can hope to claim authority beyond the minimal. The question then is: what god can we locate and represent in something like the forms we have inherited? If there is none, then the choice will indeed in the end lie between anarchism and the consciously theocratic politics of Islam or the Marxist. My own judgement here cannot be fully expressed until a later chapter, when I have sketched out some details of the law of nations, war, and ecological morality, but it is possible to make a beginning.

I have suggested already that patriarchalism is a corruption or misunderstanding of those natural institutions, parenthood and matrimony and the *ephebeia*. It occurs when men claim for themselves the sacred authority that they can really only serve. In the same way, I suggest that 'state authority' is what emerges when households, clans, and crafts first recognize a 'sacred centre' in their lives together, and then forget whence the centre gets its authority. A sacred centre, with the acknowledged right of judgement and the sword, arises to challenge the complacent properties of familial and friendly association, when it is realized that there are moral duties that cannot be fulfilled or even wholly understood at a 'pre-political' or 'para-political' level. The sacred centre speaks for the gods of a higher devotion: where the institutions of the 'natural' level all too easily imagine that the land they farm, the animals they hunt or train, the servants whom they patronize are 'theirs', the voice of the High God reminds us that the land is His, and the cattle on a thousand hills, that the poor require justice and not simply alms.

When rights and duties exist which go beyond the lineage then Allah is the one who imposes them and guarantees them. He is the promoter of the *giwar* by which the natural circle of the community is widened and supplemented in a fashion which benefits above all the client and the guest. (Wellhausen: cited by Wheatley 1971: 287.)

Zeus Xenios offered a similar guarantee in archaic Greece. Such a sacred centre or nascent state can easily itself become corrupt, substituting the words of men for the word of the High God. Historically conditioned Reason arises in the conversation of friends and equals: would-be abstract Reason, isolated from the human form, turns out to be an ideology of control.

Faced by that danger, prophets may arise—as they did among the Tupi-Guarani as well as in Israel—to lead their people back into the 'pre-political', and away from the One. If the people then survive, as a people, it will be because they have found another way of representing the High God, in the songs of the prophets or the laws of the scholars. That may be the better way, but it is not impossible to suppose that here and there a state exists which really serves to focus the pious and moral aspirations of a people, to embody the demands of a higher authority clothed in images drawn from experience of our 'natural' authorities, the king who emerges as 'father' of his people (who were not wholly one people till they had that father) precisely because he demands a higher justice than is afforded by the natural network of fathers, teachers, and friends. A king who no longer embodies such a recognizably higher order, and seeks to rule by his own whim, must at the last be reabsorbed. That our present 'king' is the notional product of the manifold wills of competing interest groups in no way proves that this collapse of state authority is not upon us. Only a state that embodies a higher moral order, a higher sacredness than can be embodied in the 'economic' network has a *right* to our obedience. The king is given for the realm, not the realm for the king (Aquinas: Voegelin 1952: 42), even if the realm in question is something that did not quite exist until the king. Other states may get obedience—from fear of state officials or of what worse brigands lie in wait, or else from loyalty to the One who has placed us here for His own purposes. Only sacred centres can deserve obedience, and only they while they acknowledge the source of their own authority, a moral vision that can convincingly command the economic net. 'The pre-nineteenth century State did not serve nations; it did not even serve communities. It served God, the Heavenly Mandate, the Law of Allah' (Tivey 1981: 13). Anything less than that had best be replaced by the minimal night-watchman state, or by the familiar net of friendly association.

Either there is a moral or religious demand that transcends our own individual wills or there is not. If there is not, and individual consent alone is the root of any authority another may exercise over us, then no existing state government has any such authority. But even if there is, it cannot easily be identified with just any state, or any state at all. God-fearing peoples may honour the king appointed to them, but they dare not equate God and the king. There is no social or political order, present or to come upon this earth, which can be unequivocally and eternally endorsed. Plato's point, by Gadamer's interpretation (1981: 80), is that 'genuine community, authentic solidarity should be realized': but any attempt to realize it in the here-and-now will last only as long as the world's winds blow fair. A final gesture: it is likelier that such a vision will remain intact, and relatively uncorrupted, if it is the vocation of a social organ that is not itself an executive power. As Kant said: the executive must not be tempted into bending law to its own passing purposes. The best kind of state, if there is a best kind of what must always be a deeply suspect organization, is one where *Brahmin* and *Kshatriya*, priest and king, are separate (see Rees & Rees 1961: 112). Somewhere in Heaven, maybe, those two powers meet: in the here-now which we inhabit they had best be separate pointers to an infinitely distant There.

5

Civilizations as World Orders

Rulers as Incarnate Law

I have been suggesting, in effect, that the only sort of state ruler that could claim our obedience as of right would be one that embodied, or at the least obeyed, a law higher than is given either by the natural law or by the sword. 'Natural' institutions of humanity, the ones that Paine thought were of more importance than any government whatsoever, can—in the view of anarchists—give us as good a chance of civil peace as any brigand can, and—in the view of minimalists—need only to be defended by the civil power. Anything more than that, any attempt to embody a sacred order that might in the end demand our lives and livelihood, or direct our attention away from natural goods, requires the Mandate of Heaven.

In short, man has no right to legislation [i.e. no right to make laws]. Whatever law he formulates will be nothing but an academic exercise. Reason dictates that man is subject to no command except that of God who possesses the universe and the creatures within it. (Ruhollah Khomeyni, *Kashf Asrar* (1943), 289: cited in Rajaee 1983: 54.)

Rulers, in the ancient phrase, must ideally be a '*nomos empsuchos*', an incarnate Law—not in the sense that any whim of theirs is law, but in that they act always and entirely under Law when they act as rulers. 'The king . . . should have no man over him, but he should have over him the law' (McIlwain 1939: 21, after Bracton). 'The last modern illustration of this type of ruler', remarked Goodenough (1967: 45), 'is the Roman Pontiff, who is a man, yet by virtue of his office is believed to be filled with the Spirit in so unique a way that his official pronouncements are the immediate formulation of divine truth.' Even if the Pope were less reliable he might serve well enough as a symbol of that sacredness which must rest upon or bless a genuine king—though you will perhaps observe that, like Dante, I prefer to distinguish king and pontiff, and that, in the end, my image of the '*nomos empsuchos*' is neither.

I have no wish to deny the judgement that many of my readers must be making: namely, that we have no convincing examples of such a *nomos empsuchos* to hand, least of all amongst statesmen and 'state-kept schoolmen'! We do not only feel a mild distrust of anyone who purports to have found such a leader, or such a sacred order: we feel an entirely well-merited alarm. When Philo asserts that no gentile laws are true embodiments of the heavenly *Logos*, but that the Mosaic Law, and Moses himself, give us just what we need, we can acknowledge his bias with a tolerant nod. Philo, after all, lived a long time ago, and was in no real danger of finding that the world had begun to obey Moses. Dante's impassioned praise of the world-monarch as one 'who of all mortals can be the purest incarnation of justice' (1954: 17) is understandable, even commendable, as a response to the cupidity of lesser princes with something to gain from rivalry. When Khomeyni is thought to say this sort of thing about Islamic law, Muhammed, the Imams, or the religious intelligentsia, the *ulama*, any of us unbelievers may begin to panic. Better a minimal or 'convenient state' than rulers who think they have the Mandate of Heaven to flog, stone, mutilate, and kill. 'Holy State, we have lived to learn, endeth in Holy War.'

Reason can never accept that a man who is no different from others in physical or spiritual accomplishments, and even perhaps inferior to them . . . should have his dictates considered proper and just and his government legitimate. (Khomeyni, *Kashf Asrar*, 222: Rajaee 1983: 59.)

What is faintly surprising is that the very people who are most exercised by the actual or potential corruption and self-righteous wickedness of rulers, who are most scornful of the absolute moral pretensions of the believing few, the fanatics, are often also those who wish officers of the state to take responsibility for yet more aspects of our lives together. Rulers who cannot claim a divine Mandate without being suspected of evil or insanity are expected to take all manner of decisions about the education and medical treatment of children, the deployment of resources, the availability of this drug or that, the proper mode of interpersonal relationship, and so on. A government that had really abandoned all claim to know 'better', and that stood out of the way of the natural, 'pre-political' life, except insofar as action was needed to enable every individual or natural grouping to join the net, would be denounced precisely for failing in its duty to impose a moral vision on society by correcting the natural prejudices of the *fellahin*. Liberals who say they distrust all claims to be embodiments of sacred law are, in effect, behaving just like Philo, or Khomeyni. 'Their' vision is so much the truth that they demand that everyone be made to behave or think like that, although they never offer any credible justification for the rights of their favourite state. '[The populace] is almost never given sufficient reason to respect the claims of its political superiors to possess superior cognitive authority, and . . . the latter no longer dare to acknowledge openly their lack of any such authority' (Dunn 1986: 152). And neither is it given any reason to respect the claims of its would-be superiors, armchair radicals, or bomb-throwing rebels. Government is illegitimate, maybe: but so, in that case, is organized rebellion, and for just the same reason (see Eller 1987: 215 f.). At least Khomeyni, in claiming God-givenness for the Islamic law, does not simultaneously deny that there is a God! He at least can admit the fallibility of all merely human lords, and at the same time give due respect to their application of the *Shari'a*, the God-given laws of Islam.

On the one hand, man is seen [in Shiite Islam] as God's representative on earth whose mission it is to realize God's revealed truth (the *Shari'a*), but on the other hand, man is a wicked creature who would corrupt the earth if left on his own. To control the dark and wicked side of man's existence God has extended his benevolence by appointing his representative on earth to guide the people and serve as a noble paradigm for them. They are the prophets and in particular a few infallible leaders. (Rajaee 1983: 11 f.)[1]

The doctrine is not as unfamiliar in the West as Rajaee perhaps supposes: it is in fact an orthodox Christian sentiment—apart of course from the not-entirely-trivial substitution of the *Logos* for the *Shari'a* (see Paternoster 1976).

What good liberals really have to offer should be an alternative vision of the Law, of what it is to be great, not a cynical rejection of all imaginable claims to greatness, all imaginable claims upon our loyalty.

Was it [Hitler's] fault if he was unable to perceive any form of greatness except the criminal form? . . . People talk about punishing Hitler. But he cannot be punished. He desired one thing alone, and he has it: to play a part in History. . . . The only punishment capable of punishing Hitler, and deterring small boys thirsting for greatness in coming centuries from following his example, is such a total transformation of the meaning attached to greatness that he should thereby be excluded from it. (Weil 1987: 217.)

Either there is a form of state which embodies a moral and sacred

[1] Shiites differ from the Sunni majority in their belief that authority rests with particular religious leaders rather than with the whole congregation of the faithful. The Shiite Imamate is 'a universal authority in the things of religion and the world' (Rajaee

demand whose authority does not rest upon its subjects' real consent, or we must quietly revert to the merely convenient and minimal (perhaps ultra-minimal) state. 'That governs best that governs least: that governs least that governs not at all.' Anything else is brigandage, however polite. 'The worship of God is: Honouring his gifts in other men, each according to his genius, and loving the greatest men best; those who envy and calumniate great men hate God; for there is no other God' (Blake 1966: 158). How then shall we define the demands of the sacred, and true greatness, for our time and place?

Everyone realizes sometime that our national angel, the spirit that informs and is embodied in the institutions of our common life, is not the only candidate for Godhead, and cannot prove its divinity to anyone who is not ready to accept it. 'The precept which enjoins obedience to civil laws cannot itself, with any propriety, be accounted a civil law' (Berkeley 1948: vi. 31), any more than the Bible itself can justify our taking the Bible to be the Word of God. The realization that we need an external justification, if we are to have one at all, is brought on by the discovery of a tribe next door, who 'look upon We as a quite impossible They' (Kipling 1927: 710), and who sometimes seem to have right on their side. The only tests we have as a species yet discovered for resolving such contradictions are called War and Peace. Either we kill and enslave the foreign devils, or we notice that they too are born, marry, build houses, get children, pray, sing, laugh, and die. Somehow, through whatever layers of mutual misunderstanding and disgust, we get to like at least a few foreigners. War, whatever its sometime successes, is not now an option save for the terminally suicidal or in the shape of a temporary, temporizing police action (though see below).

Human beings today, accordingly, are forced willy nilly to interact internationally. But in the absence of a plausible medium for fair exchange or any clear and rational basis for mutual trust to expect them to appreciate this enforced fellowship is wholly unreasonable. Nations, perhaps, are merely the largest demographic units over which the fantasy of enjoying such a medium of exchange or of possessing a sound basis for mutual trust has as yet been successfully synthesised, even fitfully. (Dunn 1986: 115 f.)

The overwhelming practical issue for political philosophers in this present day is to look out for an image of international order that can

---

1983: 11). 'Twelvers' (see Watt 1968: 111) believe that in the absence of a visibly appointed representative, the Twelfth or Hidden Imam, the religious intelligentsia serve as his deputies.

plausibly claim the loyalties of any sufficient number. In older days the image of Christendom served as well as the *Umma*, the people united under Islamic law, to provide a context for mutual comprehension, mutual trust between different nationals, and simultaneously defined the acceptable duties of princes.

This explains why two guides have been appointed for man to lead him to his twofold goal: there is the Supreme Pontiff who is to lead mankind to eternal life in accordance with revelation; and there is the Emperor who, in accordance with philosophical teaching, is to lead mankind to temporal happiness. None would reach this harbour—or at least few would do so, and only with the greatest difficulty—unless the waves of alluring cupidity were assuaged and mankind were freed from them so as to rest in the tranquillity of peace; and this is the task to which that protector of the world must devote his energies who is called the Roman Prince. (Dante 1954: 93.)

Later attempts to provide such a context, whether it be socialism, market capitalism, or Buddhism, have so far been profoundly unsuccessful. It is astonishing that political philosophers have had so little to say in this, preferring to debate the nature of welfare rights within the state, redistributive justice within the state, civil disobedience within the state, and so on, as though all humankind even lived, of their own will and spirit, in such states, and as though the international scene were of no moment, and the world itself—by which I do not mean the socio-political world—were not at stake.

It is clear enough how much must have changed when the primary political value becomes the preservation of the species [and, I would add, the world] itself and when the political agencies available for securing this value are as bizarrely unsuited to their task as those which we now possess. (Dunn 1986: 186.)

Our predecessors were not so naive. 'The problem of establishing a perfect civil constitution is subordinate to the problem of a law-governed external relationship with other States, and cannot be solved unless the latter is also solved' (Kant 1970: 47). Civil law—the law of our life in any single state—is pressed between the 'pre-political' law of nature, and international law. It is to that wider law, the *ius gentium*, that I now turn.

International Orders

The original—and notional—contract that defines just conduct within a lawfully governed state has nothing to say about foreigners. They are, by definition, outside the social contract which supposedly licenses that state's rulers to demand obedience unto death from its citizens.

America, the negro countries, the Spice Islands, the Cape, etc. were looked upon at the time of their discovery [*sic*] as ownerless territories; for the native inhabitants were counted as nothing. In East India foreign troops were brought in under the pretext of merely setting up trading posts. This led to oppression of the natives, incitement of the various Indian States to widespread wars, famine, insurrection, treachery, and the whole litany of evils which can afflict the human race. (Kant 1970: 106.)

Kant believed that, by the cunning dispensation of providence, even human selfishness at last compelled or will compel commercial nations to acknowledge the humanity of their victims. 'For the spirit of commerce sooner or later takes hold of every people, and it cannot exist side by side with war' (Kant 1970: 114). As we are forced into ever more complicated commercial alliances with each other the Peace of Dives takes hold:

> With gold and fear and hate
> I have harnessed State to State,
> and by hate and fear and gold their hates are tied . . .
> So I make a jest of Wonder, and a mock of Time and Space,
> the roofless seas an hostel and the Earth a market-place,
> where the anxious traders know
> each is surety for his foe,
> and none may thrive without his fellows' grace

> (Kipling 1927: 277 f.)

It is unfortunate, of course, that Kipling wrote this poem in 1903: our 'Master in the Pit' was not as unsuccessful in the troubling of Dives's Peace as Dives expected. But Kant and Kipling—and neither was as confident as Dives—did have a point. What troubled the peace was a reversion to the political—which is to say the military—means, and a consequent forgetfulness of where our economic interests lay. Each nation-state, each village, now lives in inextricable association with its neighbours.

Even in the furthest recesses of the Ghanaian rain forest today illiterate cocoa labourers know quite well that the social causality within which their lives must be lived out is bounded not by the hamlets in which they reside nor by the forest itself nor even the territorial borders of the State of Ghana (which many of them have crossed in order to secure a cash income at all) but rather by the world cocoa market and the consuming tastes and habits and capacities of the

populations of very distant and alien countries. No doubt most of them understand this vast and intricate causal field very poorly indeed . . . What matters is
that even in the depths of rural Africa modern selves, the selves of today, must
incorporate into their amateur social theories in however gingerly a fashion, a
conception of how global social and economic causality bears upon their own
lives. (Dunn 1986: 128.)

'Primitives' are not ignorant.

Faced by alien and by definition untrustworthy peoples we have
formed ourselves into armed camps, into states (see Kant 1970: 112).
But the economic and pre-political means constantly undermine the
walls we build. The peace of Dives is not absolute, because other
selves—or demons—than the merely economic are at work. But those
same economic and pre-political ties are now reinforced by the knowledge that it is the whole earth that is at stake in our dealings.

The problems we have to confront are increasingly the worldwide crises of a
global organism: not pollution of a stream, but pollution of the atmosphere and
of the ocean. Increasingly the death that occupies each human's imagination is
not his own, but that of the entire life cycle of the planet earth, to which each of
us is as but a cell to a body. (Stone 1974: 53.)

The purely ecological aspects of that millennial expectation will occupy
me in a later chapter. The merely sociological inquiry as to why political, and religious, philosophers have had so little to say on the subject
is a matter on which I would welcome enlightenment. My suspicion is
that the questions are simply too uncomfortable, as well as very difficult.

　1. Have our commercial dependence, and our mutual fear of that
Great Day when the kingdoms of the earth shall be o'erthrown and the
rocks melt in the sun, now brought us willy nilly to the point when each
of us must conceive herself as a citizen of the world, a cell in the
earth's body, and not primarily as a subject of state authority? Must we
indeed accept Khomeyni's implicit dictum that no one can serve both
God and the Great Satan?

　2. If so, what are the duties of this new estate, and how are they to
be met?

　3. What sacred vision is it that can give such citizens a necessary
solidarity, a sense of belonging to a socio-political community larger
even than Christendom, let alone our local state?

　4. Must such a world community take shape as a world state or
Empire, Pax Americana, Sovietica, Islamica, or Sinica?

Nothing I say here in answer to those questions is likely to have much effect: like Kant himself I can fairly claim the licence of an academic, abstract theorist, at whose broadsides 'the worldly-wise Statesman need not turn a hair' (Kant 1970: 39). Unless, that is, the theorist happens to express a spirit that is moving more widely in the world. It is the job of writers to give voices to the wind.

Must we acknowledge a higher loyalty than that owed the nation-state? To give an affirmative answer and to agree, for example, with Khomeyni that one who 'claims to be an Iranian first and a Muslim second is practising polytheism' (Sermon 1979: Rajaee 1983: 69), is not to denigrate the very real importance of national spirit in our lives, nor to deny that the complex institutions of our national or our local heritage may be such as to awaken a fierce and unrepentant love. God has set a principle of mutual attraction in our hearts, analogous to the natural principle of gravitation, that draws us 'together in communities, clubs, friendships and all the various species of society' (Berkeley 1948: vii. 226; see Leary 1977). The one good thing that even the least advantaged subjects may enjoy is love of the land, including urban land, they live in. Town and country, church and monument and housing estate are great mnemonics, embodying the memory of our own personal lives and of the people of which we are a part (see Rykwert 1976: 189; Lynch 1972). Those who can easily think that such things are commodities or obstacles to a truly international intelligence are much to be pitied, or to be feared. Perhaps, as Philo said before St Paul, we should consider ourselves tourists in this earthly region: our true home is the heavens (Goodenough 1967: 84). But how—to borrow a phrase—can we love Heaven which we have not seen, if we do not love the land we have? 'That man is little to be envied, whose patriotism would not gain force upon the plain of Marathon, or whose piety would not grow warmer among the ruins of Iona' (Johnson 1924: 385). How for that matter can we even begin to understand the feelings of those who only have the land when that too is stripped from them if we do not ourselves know what it is to love such things?

This is to emphasize that there are at least two very different sorts of internationalism, best defined by Berkeley's aphorism: 'The patriot aims at his private good in the public. The knave makes the public subservient to his private interest. The former considers himself as part of the whole, the latter considers himself as the whole' (Berkeley 1948: vi. 254). Knaves pretend even to themselves that their 'internationalism', which demands that primitive peoples be expelled from their homelands for 'the public good', rests on the insight that it is better to love the whole earth than just one segment of it. Patriots experiencing themselves as part of a wider whole, may—as they grow in imaginative sympathy—see that aboriginals elsewhere have their own loves, not to be stripped from them on a specious plea of achieving 'public goods' which are not good except to deracinated intellectuals and commercial travellers. Duties of conservation are real and important ones, but we should not overlook the damage done to local communities by the demands of tourist boards and ecomystics while fervently denouncing multinational companies. Who broke the Ik (see Turnbull 1973)? Multinationals, or a National Park?[2]

The internationalism I advocate, in brief, is not that of Kipling's Cat, to whom all places are alike, but something more like Chesterton's, or Lutoslawski's:

> The unity of mankind cannot be achieved otherwise than by certain instruments, or organs, which are *true nations* . . . which unite many races in voluntary assimilation, as happened for centuries in Poland, in obvious contrast with the Germanisation and Russification recommended by Pan-Germanists and Pan-Slavists. A true nation is the home of liberty. (Lutoslawski 1930: 155.)

My sort of internationalist would seek to preserve the rights and splendours of each little tribe, and so to defend nationalism or tribalism against the spuriously international exploiters, whether they call themselves business men or missionaries or sophisticated tourists: 'A sense of identity with his ancestral land [is] the core of Aboriginal life' (Coombs 1978: 8)—to which a traditionalist like myself must respond that 'aboriginals' do not sound very different from the rest of us.

> The Arapest Indians conceive of themselves as belonging to the land, in the way that flora and fauna belong to it. They cultivate the land by the grace of the immanent spirits, but they cannot dispose of it, and cannot conceive of doing so. (Lee 1959: 169.)

And even that attitude is more familiar than contemporary moral theorists suppose, as Lutoslawski testified.

A sound internationalism respects the 'gods of the country', instead of dismissing them as antique superstitions of no 'modern'

---

[2] The Ik are a tribe of hunter-gatherers, displaced from their ancestral hunting grounds. By Turnbull's account they have become callous or cruel egoists, revealing (so he thinks) the 'real nature' of the savage beneath the skin. My own view is that some of what Turnbull describes is not callous behaviour, but the gallows humour of a people on the edge of destruction.

significance. At the same time it allows them a voice in the international community itself: one perverse interpretation of the principle of respect that I have just enunciated, after all, is called apartheid:

a form of separation of peoples, which may have an appearance of autonomy or independence for them. . . . But it is an imposed separation, in contradiction of the principles of self-determination; it excludes the Bantu peoples from any effective participation in the government of South Africa, in which as enclaves they must at least economically have great concern. (Fawcett 1979: 5.)[3]

There is an obvious Hobbesian argument, acknowledged by Kant, for the creation of a world state to which all existing authorities should surrender their supposed sovereign rights of exploitation and pre-emptive strike. But this, as he says, is 'not the will of the nations, according to their present conception of international right' (Kant 1970: 105). The larger such a state, in any case, the greater the distance between government and people and the likelier the government is to be despotic. In practice all we can have, and already have in embryo, is not a world republic, but a federation, a network very like that of pre-political life, which can secure the necessary conditions of economic community and civil peace. The socio-political world of which we are to reckon ourselves 'citizens'—but maybe 'denizens' would be a better term—is not a state in competition with our national or local spirit (nor one that embodies it at an imperial level) but a framework within which we can learn to live. One of its principles is a respect for the gods of the country—but that is not to say that it adopts or could adopt a liberal neutrality. We have to admit that there are at present several competing visions of the international order: one of them, for obvious and not wholly ignoble reasons, is the rule of non-interference in any state's 'internal affairs', an analogue of liberal belief in a region of merely 'private' morality. Just as there is no satisfactory formulation of that latter principle, so in international life—it cannot be a matter of indifference to us that people with whom we are inextricably involved at economic and personal levels are practising iniquity. The very demand that local gods be honoured is a demand that governments honour them even

---

[3] At the risk of alienating many I would rather have as friends: I do not mean to denounce South Africa as uniquely evil. There are plenty of governments, and peoples, that behave as badly, and I see nothing but scholasticism in the claim that South Africa is 'wicked in principle', and the others only 'wicked in practice'. The South African government, no doubt, displays a deplorable intransigence, a refusal to recognize the common humanity of its black subjects or really listen to what its opponents say, a willingness to break the law to achieve its ends: but organizers of boycotts and supporters of

when their worshippers are a subordinate element in the state. Neighbouring peoples have no duty to refrain forever from the defence of embattled minorities in other states. Even the *Jihad*, the holy war, cannot be ruled out for ever.

The idea underlying the treaties for the protection of minorities is to secure for certain elements incorporated in a State the population of which differs from them in race, language or religion the possibility of living peaceably alongside that population and cooperating amicably with it, while at the same time preserving the characteristics which distinguish them from the majority, and satisfying the ensuing special needs. (*Permanent Court of International Justice* 1938: Fawcett 1979: 7.)

Minorities, I should add, are not always well protected by invoking, or even by protecting, 'individual rights'. Tribal peoples in India, for example, may never have registered any land-claims as individual owners, although they have cultivated the land for generations as co-owners and members of the collectivity. This is not to endorse a Marxist analysis of right, though it is to agree with their criticism of merely (and speciously) individualistic liberalism. It is the whole community, existing through time, that has interests that should be protected, not merely the individuals who may never—until infected by modernism—have imagined that they had any right to possess land for their own use, or alienate it from their fellows. Such collectivities, of course, are not necessarily egalitarian or communistic. Different groups within the larger group may have different offices, and different rewards; there may be individuals with special rights of command. But it does not make sense to suppose that even those lords actually 'own' the land, or should wish to. The land is entailed.

Notoriously, and even rightly, there is no one organization with the acknowledged right or duty to mobilize military force to enforce such international law. There is no Hobbesian world state. But world opinion and the complex of economic and military transactions have their own coercive power. The international order is an anarchical society, but not necessarily a chaotic one. The better it works, of course, the easier it may eventually be to dispense with state authority even at a local level. If states do remain, as convenient and domesticated spokesmen for our national characters and local lands, or as

armed revolution show just the same traits. In so far as the legitimacy of a government rests upon the civilization of which it is a part, the present government of South Africa is, strictly, illegitimate: but so are others, and so also would be a government of the ANC.

merely local arbitration agencies, they will at last be seen to get their licence from the international, moral order, whatever that may prove to be. Those who continue to defend and recognize mere bandit states are in danger of losing what moral authority they had.

The crimes of the [Pol Pot] regime proved no barrier to continued participation in the General Assembly of the United Nations. In September 1979 a majority of 71 (against 35, with 34 abstentions), voted to continue the assignment of the Cambodian seat to the ousted government. Among nations supporting the resolution were governments that had previously denounced the regime before the Commission on Human Rights—Australia, the UK and the USA. (Kuper 1982: 11.)

Kuper goes on to remark that 'given the many failures of the UN to act against regimes engaging in continuous massacres of their subjects, it seems to me that there is great need for individual nations, or preferably groups of nations, to reassert, under carefully defined conditions, the right of humanitarian intervention against genocide, and other gross, consistent and murderous violations of human rights' (Kuper 1982: 11; see p. 14).

If genocide is 'an odious scourge' so also is famine. The two conditions, indeed, are almost one, since modern famines are so often the product of military endeavour and imperialistic agrobusiness, whose officers are psychologically protected from the pains of personal responsibility by the delusion that it is not they, but their organization, that acts in such situations, while the organization just as such is not a moral agent at all. The individuals are not responsible, and neither is the corporate body of which they are a part! It would be better, as O'Neill points out (1986: 32 ff.), to admit that such corporate bodies are moral agents, agencies that can be, and should be, held to account for their doings. Businesses and nations alike can commit crimes—but of course this judgement carries with it the implication that it is not only their 'own' misdeeds for which individuals should pay. Sometimes it is right that they should pay for the misdeeds of the group of which they have been all-too-compliant parts.

One complex way of neglecting the gods of the country is by importing inappropriate agricultural techniques and ignoring the pre-political network—very often of female agriculturalists—in favour of an ersatz and soon-to-be-slavish system of cash-crops planted by men in order to get foreign exchange to buy consumer non-durables. On top of that gross error comes the military interventionist in pursuit of her non-national dream, the imposition of a new order that invariably turns out to be an old despotism.

States exist within the international order partly to make life bearable: if we were really and readily aware of what is going on elsewhere on this globe our ordinary lives would be impossible. So they are, for some of us: some individuals, some groups may find it quite impossible to go on sharing in the life of a wealthy nation, geared to complain if trains don't run on time or the streets aren't clean or there's a shortage of fresh cabbages. Any of us, on special occasions, may be induced to act or seek to act on behalf of our violated, starved, and desperate cousins. Almost all of us relapse—and not wholly without reason, if we suspect that existing governmental and quasi-governmental bodies do more harm than good. Our flimsy hopes of happiness, as Powys pointed out (1974), depend on not allowing ourselves to know what we know very well. Saints are those who truly experience the world's agony and act on it: the rest of us, lacking such supernatural joy and courage, only do our best not to allow the agony elsewhere to contaminate what little happiness we have. State boundaries help.

They also help to slow down messianic fervour, and other all-too-rapid infections. 'The role of the State is to act as a filter of [transactions] in order to ensure that change is within the capacity of systems to absorb without destruction of social values' (Burton 1968: 33). A world state, no doubt, would be an asset if it were a genuinely just one, one embodying the highest of our mortal dreams or serving the one God: what if it had been, as more likely it would be, such a monster as the Reich, the Turkish Empire or Democratic Kampuchea? Even a state of war, uninfluenced by a federal union,

is still to be preferred to an amalgamation of the separate nations under a single power which has overruled the rest and created a universal monarchy [Lutoslawski's *false* nationalism]. For the laws progressively lose their impact as the government increases its range, and a soulless despotism, after crushing the germs of goodness, will finally lapse into anarchy. It is nonetheless the desire of every State (or its ruler) to achieve lasting peace by thus dominating the whole world, if at all possible. But nature wills it otherwise. (Kant 1970: 133.)

Kant believed that it was by a merciful dispensation of providence that linguistic and religious differences made the world state a fantasy. He placed, perhaps, a little too much trust in both the commercial spirit as an antidote to war, and the willingness of human beings, 'as culture

grows and [they] gradually move to greater agreement over their principles', to act according to those maxims they could will to be universal
law. It is none the less possible to consider the forms of world-
federation, and hence the structure within which the gods of the country
and the great gods of mood and happenstance can find their place.

Sacred Checks on Power

What I am after, though the analogy is not exact, is an account of
Sacerdotium, as a check on *Regnum*. The long medieval dispute
between the spiritual and temporal authority ended, in effect, with a
victory for state power. The right of the Church to excommunicate and
so depose a king had rested upon a general perception that kings had
their authority from God, the sword of the Lord against the wicked. If
they used their power wickedly, as the Church defined wickedness,
their right also lapsed. Popular history suggests quite falsely that the
West has moved smoothly away from tyranny into the well-lit uplands
of liberal democracy. The fact is that even the most liberal of modern
states claim a degree of authority over their subjects that past kings
never envisaged, and it was with Renaissance and Reformation that the
notion of mere national sovereignty took shape. Till then there were
many authorities, subject to external judgement, and without any
acknowledged right to anyone's, let alone everyone's, obedience, or
power to enforce it. This is hardly the time, and neither am I the man,
to resurrect the papal plenitude of power—a phrase first used by St
Bernard to describe the Pope's ecclesiastical authority. But there was,
it seems, another model of the *Sacerdotium*: 'as being composed of
various corporations, each with its own carefully articulated organization and representative officials' (Morrall 1958: 66). Sacerdotal
power, in the end, rests with the entire community of the faithful, communicating through local synod and general council. So also elsewhere:

In the Islamic world . . . the men with actual political power never had control
of ideas. . . . The theory was everywhere accepted among Sunnites that the
most powerful sultan is subject to the *Shari'a* just like the humblest Muslim. If
the sultan disobeys God's commands, he may escape punishment in this life,
but will have to pay in the world to come. Thus no sultan or other ruler of Sun-
nite Muslims has anything like the power over men's thinking possessed by the

occidental totalitarian dictator. (Watt 1968: 122; see also p. 127 on *ijma'*, consensus, as the Sunni criterion of judgement.)

But who are the faithful? What community, however diffuse and decentralized, can serve as the context—as once Christendom and the *Umma* almost did—for local lords and states? The economic nexus has contributed some laws (as 'bargains are to be kept: *pacta sunt servanda*'); the fear and fury of the nations at genocide begin to lay down expectations about how far any state's ruler will be allowed to go. Kant's principles for 'Perpetual Peace' are mostly practical responses to otherwise overwhelming dangers. But we hardly gain if we replace the wars of nation-states by wars of world religions, competing images of the wider community within which we have to find an earthly peace. A world community composed of Aztec States, or organized according to the rules of those New Guinea cultures that found their identities in the service of war, would not be to our taste, and would inevitably be opposed by the Kantian federalists. Indeed, we do not need to resort to fantasy to find just such competing internationalisms; the federated West, the Soviet bloc, resurgent Islam all proclaim themselves the type of a future commonwealth, all implicitly demand the right to judge all local lords and treaties in the name of the one God—and the fact that neither Westerners nor Soviets will normally admit to having such sacerdotal ambitions is beside the point.

Toynbee's suggestion was that the 'churches', those communities more or less united by bonds of faith rather than bonds of law or local loyalty, were to be the butterflies that would emerge from the chrysalises of agro-industrial, military civilizations (Toynbee 1954: 420 ff.). He may have been correct: but such a company of faithful people must not wholly abandon the gods of the city and the country, ties of historical community, rights bought for us by our ancestors. Nor can we hope for a merely 'value-neutral' consensus, the sort of minimal international rules of non-interference and respect for national boundaries. We cannot hope for it, both because most of us would not indefinitely allow state leaders to have things all their way just across an arbitrary stream, and because (even if the thing were achievable) it would not be worth having or dying for. A true world civilization must be one, like any decent national order, that is worth dying for, in which we can hope to have continued being. 'There can be no unity of Mankind without the participation of God; and conversely, when the heavenly pilot is dropped by an insensately self-confident human crew, Society inevitably falls into a Time of Troubles.' (Toynbee 1954: 511.)

Kant's own, optimistic answer is explicit. There are in the end no different religions, but only different confessions, different books, whose differences have nothing to do with religion itself: they are only 'the vehicles of religion' (Kant 1970: 114). As we grow to know and understand each other, and to follow through the implications of our historic creeds, we can expect a real convergence on the image of a divine humanity. Each local variant, each little distorted image, will be corrected by its own internal logic and the pressure of circumstances till every enclave of the global society can see and respect itself and others as cells within a wider whole whose essence is in the respect for all embodiments of universal reason (see Toynbee 1954: 513 f.). Such a hope, of course, can only be remotely realistic if the God of our devotion is indeed in charge, and not simply a name for those ideals that human beings might converge upon, or not. And even in the context of a realistic theism, it is not entirely obvious that there can only be one form of commonwealth. The traditional expectation, after all, has been that it is the form of iniquity, the Kingdom of Darkness, that will be consolidated on the earth, and the faithful remnant 'caught up to the clouds'. The Last World Community, despite Kant, may yet be the world state that he feared, the rule of unrepentant will unchecked by any common sense of what is sacred in the land and laws, the 'Great Satan' that Khomeyni sees, from his particular vantage point, in the USA (Rajaee 1983: 76), and Reagan, from his, in the USSR!

In such an age, 'a wolf-age, an axe-age before the world's ruin', our only hope will be coming of the true Husbandman (Goodenough 1967: 24), the Man who is indeed a *'nomos empsuchos'*, the Incarnate Word come down to judge the nations. That expectation, which has its own political moral, I shall consider in a later chapter. I end here with a gesture toward the wider world, the accidental commonwealth of struggling clans and nations, the laws of whose being we already know a little. What are the gods whose glowing forms are already taking shape in this our human universe? The 'multitudinous influx of fairy' need not be simply the re-emergence of undisciplined Titanic shapes, owing no respect to *Themis*: some of them, at any rate, are gods worthy of our partial worship, our respect. A new pantheon, or newly perceived aspects of the one immortal *Logos*, can be traced. We are no longer allowed to let ourselves believe that what occurs beyond our national borders is of no importance, that foreigners have nothing to contribute to the commonwealth, that only states or only individuals have rights, that bargains need not be kept nor the weak protected.

And it has always been possible to see the messianic expectation as a prophecy not of one man's coming, but of the growth and splendour of the beloved community of those from every nation who have come to see that point to which the whole creation moves and in which each local tradition finds its fulfilment. 'These boundaries drawn around [territories of] the world to designate a country or a homeland are the product of the deficient human mind. . . . The world is the homeland of humanity. All people should reach the salvation of both worlds here. This will happen only by the implementation of God's divine laws' (Khomeyni, *Kashf Asrar*, 167: Rajaee 1983: 77).

It may be that what moves them, what judges the nations by its mere being, is as simple a thing as the image of a human child faced by unspeakable and institutionalized wickedness: a Jewish boy, perhaps, hands raised in surrender to a Nazi soldier, or a Vietnamese girl running naked and screaming down a road. Nothing in the world deserves our loyalty, in the last resort, that does not stand by those children. The world order which we may have some hope of seeing is one that seeks—amongst other things—to give any child the chance to grow into a free and equal friend. Justice, civilization, is not the bargain of godless brigands that modern moralists have suggested: it is the service of the divine in human and defenceless form.

Which is what our forebears thought. Although the bargain of godless brigands is one that some philosophers thought crucial to the formation of civil society, it was also recognized—as I pointed out in an earlier chapter—that children, so far from being 'marginal' people with fewer or less securely grounded rights than adults had, were precisely what civil society was for. That is our best image of the Living Law.

6

The Laws of War

The God of Battles

We have so far devised two ways of resolving those conflicts to which humankind is heir, namely War and Peace. The paths of peace are those of productive exchange and ritualized aggression, pathways very like those that other creatures have devised to avoid violence. Most intra-species aggression is carefully controlled: animals may compete with each other for dominance within their group, for territorial advantage, and for mating rights, but they do not usually do so 'to the death'. Their displays are usually in lieu of combat, and even in their battles they do not treat each other merely as prey. The explanation for this is simple enough: not that they are much concerned with the good of their species or even their tribes, but that individuals who regularly fight to the bitter end are likelier to be killed themselves. It is better not to press displays to the point of battle, or battles to a fatal conclusion (Tinbergen 1968). There is little evidence that human beings, at a pre-political level, behave very differently. It is not particularly surprising that human beings do kill each other sometimes: so do other animals. There is nothing absolute or impregnably given about species-boundaries, as though it were very much odder to kill one of one's own species than one of another. A conspecific could be a close relation, and will usually be rather like us (though not necessarily more like us than any member of some other species): whether we notice or care about this conspecificity depends on circumstances. It is absurd to suppose—as Lorenz and his imitators seem to do—that there would be no murders, no intra-specific killings, if there were no weapons, or that humankind carries any special, ancestral taint from its 'killer-ape' origin (for which there is vanishingly little evidence). That we sometimes kill each other requires no special explanation; that we have invented war perhaps does. War is a social institution, with its own style, morality, and spirit, its own special devotees. Soldiers do not go out to fight because they cannot control their tempers, nor yet (at a different level of explanation) simply because their bosses tell them to. We go to war to achieve or to defend things that seem good to us when the ways of peace have failed, but we do not always prefer those ways of peace even if they have not failed. War is a possibility because human beings can be excited, 'taken out of themselves', enlivened by the prospect of battle. Ares may be—along with Aphrodite—the most hateful of the Olympians, but it is obvious that human beings get an almost sexual frisson from his proximity. Aphrodite regularly prefers the bloody god of battles to the industrious Hephaistos (a god, according to Homer (*Iliad* 1. 599 f.), whose own particular way of dealing with quarrels is to get the gods laughing). Wars may be initiated by old men for their personal or political advantage: they are actually fought by young men and nations who welcome such excitement. The god of battles, whether god or devil, is at least Olympian, and the human soul has often deliberately turned away from peaceful industry to follow him.

> Nor law, nor duty bade me fight
> nor public men, nor cheering crowds,
> a lonely impulse of delight
> drove to this tumult in the clouds;
> I balanced all, brought all to mind,
> the years to come seemed waste of breath,
> a waste of breath the years behind
> in balance with this life, this death.

> (Yeats 1950: 152.)

Or—since what the non-soldier said is perhaps not evidence—consider J. Glenn Gray's quotation from the diary of a German soldier in World War I, and his succeeding comment:

'With a mixture of feelings, evoked by bloodthirstiness, rage, and intoxication, we moved in step, ponderously but irresistibly towards the enemy lines . . . I was boiling with a mad rage, which had taken hold of me and all the others in an incomprehensible fashion. The overwhelming wish to kill gave wings to my feet. . . . The monstrous desire for annihilation, which hovered over the battlefield thickened the brains of the men and submerged them in a red fog. We called to each other in sobs and stammered disconnected sentences. A neutral observer might have perhaps believed that we were seized by an excess of happiness'. . . . When soldiers step over the line that separates self-defense from fighting for its own sake, as it is so easy for them to do, they experience something that stirs deep chords in their being. The soldier-killer is learning to serve a different deity, and his concern is with death and not life, destruction and not construction. (Gray 1970: 52 f.)

If human beings were not addicted to this sort of excitement we would have that much less need of states. If states did not exist we would have that much less need of wars. Some forms of international order, as I remarked before, depend upon and are designed for war: the Aztecs' 'flowery war' was directed to no clear economic or even dictatorial end, but to maintaining a supply of sacrificial victims for Huitzilopochtli or Tezcatlipoca, and so to enthral his peoples (see Aho 1981: 47). Even in less explicitly murderous orders the virtues of the soldier are those by which men at least are judged. In relatively civil orders all may agree, in principle, that soldiers exist to defend the peaceable interests of their kin, that 'war is for the sake of peace' and soldierly virtue different from berserk rage. But that is like saying that racing-car drivers exist to test new motor-cars, that no one races, or watches races, for their deadly excitement.

Human infatuation with war, or with danger in general, can be given an evolutionary explanation, and a biochemical. Doubtless our ancestry has ensured that young males in particular, who must serve as the tribe's first defence against marauding predators, will actively enjoy banding together to see off the raiders. Doubtless the release of adrenalin is linked with a sudden brightness in the air, by comparison with which one's ordinary life is dull. That latter shift in consciousness is something that some can engineer in other and less violent ways, but it is simply silly to deny to others the dangers that they crave without giving them any hint that there are other routes to joy. As William James recognized, if the war-system must be judged to have outlived its usefulness (because it is now too dangerous to indulge on the scale that it will, almost inevitably, be indulged if given half a chance) we have to find a moral equivalent for war, a system that will encourage necessary virtues, channel energies, and awaken happiness in more of the populace (James 1970; see Royce 1908).

Merely negative propaganda against war is likely to be worse than useless. There are those who insist that there is never anything worse than going to war, that any number of treaties should be violated without reprisal and any number of our friends betrayed, rather than that we should have recourse to military action. Those who say so, and at the same time demonstrate their own willingness to suffer and to act, by any other means, on behalf of those whom we ought to defend, play no ignoble role. I have certainly no wish to suggest that pacifism in its strict sense is either logically absurd or ethically null. But the usual propaganda for peace is insulting, in so far as the propagandists assume that nothing matters more to any of us than our own comfortable life, and that those prepared to fight and die can only be crazed dupes. 'There is nothing so characteristic of narrowness and littleness of soul as the love of riches . . . [whereas] in defence of liberty [which is *not* to say, the chance to do exactly as one pleases] a high-souled man should stake everything' (Cicero, *De Officiis* 1. 68). When the only reasons for keeping the peace that are offered are ignoble ones, it is hardly surprising that some people turn to war to awaken themselves from torpor.

To preach against war is to seek to tame an Olympian, just as surely as to preach against sexual indulgence. Both Olympians regularly ruin lives, but neither is easily excluded. It is pointless to claim that nobody ever wants war, or that peace is always morally superior. People sometimes want to have a war, either a particular war against an identifiable foe or a mere occasion to prove their virtue. It is now a fixed assumption of the liberal conscience that the First World War at least was an unnecessary war. Perhaps it was, and no one ever supposed that it was not horrific: but it is worth remembering with what fervour the chance to put one's life on the line was greeted, and against what enemy they fought. Recall the words of Kipling that I cited in chapter three:

> All we have of freedom, all we use or know—
> this our fathers bought for us long and long ago . . .
> Give no heed to bondsmen masking war with peace.
> Suffer not the old King, here or overseas.
> They that beg us barter—wait his yielding mood—
> pledge the years we hold in trust—pawn our brother's blood—
> howso' great their clamour, whatsoe'er their claim,
> suffer not the old King under any name!
>
> (Kipling 1927: 294.)

Kipling's genius, of course, was to give shape and words to many moods, including ones that we loathe to acknowledge. I would not have any of us forget the contrary: consider the 'Common Form' of epitaph for those slain in battle—

> If any question why we died,
> tell them, because our fathers lied
>
> (Kipling 1927: 383.)

> They shall not return to us, the resolute, the young,
> the eager and whole-hearted whom we gave:
> but the men who left them thriftily to die in their own dung,
> shall they come with years and honour to the grave?
>
> (Kipling 1927: 297.)

I have no settled opinion on the rights and wrongs of 1914, and sympathy for pacifist and combatant alike. My point here is simply to insist that we gain no more by pontificating against war than we do by announcing self-righteously, and ignorantly, that good Christian people do not catch Aids, or legislating against drink. James followed H. G. Wells in insisting that 'the conceptions of order and discipline, the tradition of service and devotion, of physical fitness, unstinted exertion and universal responsibility, which universal military duty is now [1908] teaching European nations will remain a permanent acquisition when the last ammunition has been used in the fireworks that celebrate the final peace' (James 1970: 14). This now seems over-optimistic.

We cannot control war by announcing simply that we shall never fight a war, nor ever wish to. Dwelling on the undoubted horrors of war will do no good: sometimes those horrors will be less than the horrors of a dishonourable peace; sometimes they will be relished even if there is a chance of peace with honour. If we refuse to think how wars should be conducted, on the excuse that they never should be anyway, we ensure that they will be even worse, and do not diminish their likelihood in the slightest.

> When the Cambrian measures were forming,
> They promised perpetual peace.
> They swore if we gave them our weapons,
> that the wars of the tribes would cease.
> And when we disarmed They sold us
> and delivered us bound to our foe,
> and the Gods of the Copybook Headings said:
> 'Stick to the devil you know'.
>
> (Kipling 1927: 718.)

Or in the words of the car sticker: 'Disarm Today—Dat Arm Tomorrow'.

The Nature of Olympians

Those who fight for killing's sake, the servants of Ares, are as dangerous to us all as the followers of Ouranian Aphrodite, the Titanic power that acknowledges no pledge of loyalty or friendship. But Aphrodite cannot be ignored, and must be enlisted in the service of good order, *Themis*, if our kind is to endure. Even in the heyday of anti-eroticism, when good Christian couples would not mate (or would not admit to doing so) except to produce children (and stopped doing so when they had had their regulation pair), they could not have done the act at all without Aphrodite. Even if wars should be fought only for the sake of a just peace, and not for the joy of battle, it is difficult to see how anyone could stand to fight unless Ares were allowed a place. Our problem, as it has always been, is to require the gods to take their proper place as 'servants of the infinite and eternal of the human form'.

But before I try to lay out the traditional understanding of what a just war might be, and how it might be justly fought, I should explain again what I intend by 'gods', 'Olympians', 'Titans', and the like. Gods are moods and modes of personal being, such that they may be re-encountered in one's own life and in the life of others. It is the same thing that arises in Phaedra and the besotted Catullus, the same world-look that willy nilly they inhabit. We figure aphrodisiac obsession and the air's brightness as a goddess, an immortal essence. Whereas the particular existents which moderns have learnt to think of as the ulti-mate bearers of all properties, the subjects of all well-formed proposi-tions, may change their qualities and certainly will perish, gods do neither, because they are themselves the natures, world-looks, powers that particular things sometimes display. We mistake the meaning of mythology as long as we suppose that story-tellers think of gods and goddesses as just another species of particular thing. Their imagined attributes and forms are symbols of the world-looks, forms of life, provinces of meaning, moods, modes of being that arise within the universal mother.

When the ancients spoke, or contemporary religious speak, of Mother Earth as the matrix within which such gods take shape (see Vycinas 1972) they are not talking about the planetary globe inspected by geologists in the service of Apollo: that globe may or may not be the causal origin of all our lives. There are, in my view, serious reasons to doubt the popular materialism of our day. But whatever causal story we eventually tell, the matrix of all world-looks, mother of gods and men, is the whole phenomenal scene, the experienced place of all epiphan-ies, all alterations of mood and circumstance. Our worlds, in Heideg-ger's evocative expression, are clearings within the forest. It is that richly experienced Earth, not 'the false appearance which appears to the reasoner as of a Globe rolling thro' Voidness' (Blake 1966: 516), that is intended. 'In an honest polytheism Apollo has a right to his place and the honors belonging to him' (Paris 1986: 179), but for us here-now the living earth, Hestia, is the civilized centre of the universe, not a dump to be abandoned or rebuilt. Mythologians express the truths of experience in stories that, taken 'literally', lead those ignorant of the language of symbolism to expect to find Kryptonian supermen on a mountain peak in northern Greece, and to jeer when no such organisms are locatable. But the truths of Olympian religion are constantly confirmable as long as we remember that they are not reports upon the fauna of a geological Olympus. The Loch Ness Monster was once, I suspect, just such another inhabitant of dream or nightmare, a figure for the panic terror of the lonely places. Those who now go dredging for the thing are being as silly as the proverbial Wise Fools of Gotham, trying to fish the moon up from their pond.

The moods and modes of human and more than human experience take shape for us in images and stories that provide a map of possible experience. What makes them demonic is their disruptive effect, their failure to allow for other moods, or to acknowledge their origin. Titans, in the Olympian story, are those vast powers that shake the earth before—I do not mean chronologically—there is any hope of an order not founded upon force, on sheer brute strength. What Zeus provided was just such an order. In another tradition the rainbow served as a visible sign of the God's covenant with His people, of a new order that forbids oppression. In Olympianism the physical lightning became a concrete symbol of the illuminating realization of one's small place in the world: the overweening, God delights to humble. The Titans are imprisoned, or reborn within the Olympian family, constantly itching to have things their own way, and constantly caught back to serve the proper order of things.

Ares and Aphrodite, as I have mentioned, are the most hated of Olympians—a shocking thought, no doubt, for people reared in the conviction that Sex is the meeting of time and eternity, the one natural sacrament it is blasphemous to reject. Both can ruin our lives and the lives of those to whom we owe most loyalty. Both are unavoidably present in the lives of all who have not made an express commitment to some other guardian deity: pacifism and virginity are parallel vows, unsafe for anyone who has no hope of Heaven. Cosmologists investigating even the world revealed to science seem constantly to invoke the pair, the powers of attraction and repulsion, love and strife. One Neo-platonic exegesis of the story I hinted at in the first paragraph of this chapter is that Ares and Aphrodite are caught in the delightful, glittering net that is the phenomenal universe, cast by the divine craftsman. That aspect of Olympianism, seen through Neo-platonic eyes, I must reserve for another volume. Here I reiterate that the proper ordering of human life requires us to take seriously all its different forms and expressions. The very gods or demons that most threaten us may perhaps be woven together to uphold the whole. The Peace of Dives, you will remember, rests not on supernatural virtue but the god of trade and trickery. Ares too is not just a devil, any more than Aphrodite: our fear of him is not unlike the terror that in other ages made Aphrodite into the great Temptress; our professions of pacific virtue are as hypocritical as the double standards of past sexual morality; our good liberal contempt for fighting men is as understandable, and as damaging to all, as older contempt for women.

> For it's Tommy this, an' Tommy that,
> and 'Chuck him out, the brute!'
> but it's 'Saviour of 'is Country'
> when the guns begin to shoot.
>
> (Kipling 1927: 392.)

Why does Plato so often take the soldier as his model for the would-be virtuous life? Why does Hopkins think that Christ himself would approve the soldier?

> Mark Christ our King. He knows war, served this soldiering through;
> He of all can reeve a rope best. There he bides in bliss
> Now, and seeing somewhere some man do all that man can do,
> for love he leans forth, needs his neck must fall on, kiss,
> and cry 'O Christ-done deed! So God-made-flesh does too:
> Were I come o'er again' cries Christ 'it should be this'.
>
> (Hopkins 1970: 99.)

Perhaps we should ask ourselves why we are so ready to assume the worst of those who would die for us?

The Rules of War

So how shall we set out the rules of war? The more usual route towards a discussion of international order begins from the absolute rights of states, especially nation-states. If states have only such rights as are or might be given them by the free consent of individuals (a thought that I have already criticized), any international authority, it is supposed, has only such rights as sovereign states may, temporarily, allow. My own argument, to recap, has been that if state governments have any rights at all, or any rights much like the rights they claim, it is by derivation from the wider international order—of which there are at present many possible models. That order in its turn—whatever its exact shape—gains its authority over any human heart only in so far as it embodies *Themis*. What we need to consider is the nature of the world order in its war mode.

War is the absence or the collapse of friendly relations between two or more communities, but it has never involved a total collapse of ethical judgement, never been an uninhibited display of 'animal aggression'. There have been times, indeed, when it seems reasonable to think that wars are complicated games, with their own rules of correct action—the more so, most probably, when the combatants do not entirely believe that they are only mortal creatures. In practice war cannot be understood either as a pure chaos, or as a well-regulated game: wars are fought with an eye to the rules of war, but breach of those rules (even if it is judged a war crime) is still war (while moving a pawn sideways is not chess). The rules can sometimes be made to sound ridiculous: a matter of not fighting on holy days, or allowing the enemy to take up their positions before attacking them. Would-be realists exclaim that it is absurd, even inhumane, to obey such rules when disobedience might bring victory and an end at any rate of the present war. Few of those 'realists', in my experience, have troubled to imagine just what it is that they thereby endorse; most of them somehow retain the category of 'war crime' while denying that war has any laws. A longer view would reason that it is better to retain such limits on the use of military force. Without them wars would be bloodier. Customs and negotiated agreements reduce the damage done by war. Even if we lost by obedience on this occasion we shall benefit in the end. A general who ignores the rules is taking a grave responsibility for an increase in military violence in the long run.

But the rules of war do not all rest on such long-term calculation of the greater good (whatever that is). If they did it would be all too easy to dismiss them: how can we know what will happen in the long term? Is it not so important that we win this war that the escalation of future wars can be ignored? Is this not the war to end wars? If this is to be the last war, whose outcome will determine all our future, must not all means be used to win it, including the killing of prisoners, the slaughter or torture of non-combatants, betrayal of allies, and deception of one's fellow-citizens (who might judge otherwise)? Customary or negotiated agreements not to use all possible violence only have force if we expect to fight again another day, or judge that defeat in this war will not be the end of all things worthy.

Genuine realists may reasonably doubt that any war will 'end war' save by the expedient of ending human life. The destruction of Hiroshima did not inaugurate a new era of peace and tranquillity! They may also point out that if peace is achieved we shall have the task of living peaceably with our neighbours.

No State at war with another shall permit such acts of hostility as would make mutual confidence impossible during a future time of peace. Such acts would include the employment of assassins or poisoners, breach of agreements, the instigation of treason within the enemy state etc. . . . A war of extermination in which both parties and right itself might be simultaneously annihilated, would allow perpetual peace only on the vast graveyard of the human race. A war of this kind and the employment of all means which might bring it about must thus be absolutely prohibited. (Kant 1970: 96.)

The Laws of Manu also prohibited the burning of enemy camps, night attacks and assassinations, poison and fire weapons, and the killing of non-combatants (Aho 1981: 166). But all crimes are forgotten in the end, new generations—supposing that the final graveyard has been avoided—come who do not fully recall the horrors committed on their ancestors (or if they do we can brand them dangerous romantics). Utilitarian calculation is difficult at the best of times: in the heat of war it is impossible. Better to rely on other rulings—not least, of course, because 'utility' itself disguises a host of prior value judgements.

The traditional theory of the 'just war' has two parts: *ius in bellum* and *ius in bello*. The first deals with the decision to go to war, and the second with how war is to be waged. Both are concerned with justice as well as with utility, though there is some reason to think that the first part has a more clearly religious provenance, and the latter arises in the tacit bargaining of mercenary soldiers. Every human person is to be respected: all have rights which cannot justly be infringed, even for the sake (as the agent supposes) of some greater good in the future. One human may not murder, enslave, rob, or torment another. All are to be allowed a say in what is done to them, and on some issues close to their vital concerns they are to be allowed a decisive say. They are, by derivation, sacred. No social engineer, no leader, no general has any right to treat other humans merely as means to her own ends. To enforce those rules against those who let their immediate self-interest lead them astray we support the existence of law-courts, police, and military—and would do so even in a strictly anarchical society. In those days when 'there was no king in Israel, [and] every man did that which was right in his own eyes' (*Judges* 21: 25), yet the people of Israel could gather together, 'knit together as one man', against those who committed outrageous wickedness (*Judges* 20: 11). But even those congregations, even standing armies and appointed officers of the law may not with impunity disregard the rights of those they pursue, may not undertake pre-emptive strikes against suspected would-be bank-robbers, may not use such weaponry against them as will kill or injure innocent bystanders, may not shoot the robbers when they have surrendered, torture them to extract confessions, or hold their children hostage for their good behaviour. If this makes them less effective guardians of the law (if it does) then that is a price that others must be prepared to accept. We allow the police a right to halt and to arrest us all (though this right can be challenged later): we do not allow them a right to kill, torment, enslave, or rob us—for that is what we deny to everyone, and pay them to prevent. Even the courts and prisons must respect the rights of convicted criminals: even if we think they have forfeited the right to liberty, or life, we do not think them fair game for any device of our imagination. Sometimes, when it is clear that the police cannot capture some very dangerous wrongdoer except by methods that involve the death of innocents—a technical term that means no more than non-combatants—we allow this practice, so long as the police did not intend those innocent deaths, and did their utmost to avoid them. We are prepared to say that we would not complain at our death on such occasions, so long as this is the only and an effective way of preventing further wrongdoing of a serious kind. But our agreement is very limited, and some innocent deaths (as those of children) we would not readily think acceptable at all. The state is not above the law, nor is *'suprema regis voluntas lex'*.

These rules of proper police practice rest upon our conviction that all human persons have definite 'rights', which may not be overridden save under very special circumstances (and even then the victim must be compensated). Or rather, to put the same point in the way that a traditionalist like myself should prefer, they rest on the conviction that 'God has commanded [us] to act, or refrain from acting, in these ways' (Watt 1968: 96; see p. 121). The same sort of rules obtain in war: non-combatants may not be directly and deliberately harmed (although we are sometimes willing to countenance such harm if it is a by-product of the only effective way of halting a dreadful enemy); prisoners of war may not be killed, tortured, or starved. Only such force is to be used as is necessary to halt and disarm the enemy and certain weapons whose effects are long-lasting, widespread, and dangerous to non-combatants may not be used at all. Those rules are not always kept, and some of them have been allowed to recede from our collective moral consciousness. We are now in the odd position that the crew of a plane who have been bombing a civilian target in clear breach of the rules of war may be shot down, captured, and claim humane treatment under those same rules of war. It is understandable that some insurrectionists have held that the proposed rules are upheld by the great powers only when it is convenient, and that it would be folly for them to keep prisoners of war alive and well (at cost to their own war-effort) who have themselves ignored the long-standing conventions about not offering direct harm to non-combatants. It is understandable: I do not say that it is correct.

Some rules of war rest upon agreements between the warring nations—or, of course, their mercenary soldiers: not to use gas or bacteriological weapons. The dangers involved in weaponry of this kind are such that all parties are prepared to forswear them, knowing that if they break their word they will have begun a new cycle of military violence. Other rules do not rest for their force on any agreement at all, but on the laws of God, the outline of the sacred cosmos in which such nations find themselves. If our enemy used gas against our soldiers we would, perhaps, have less reason not to use it against enemy soldiers. If our enemy took to slaughtering children, we should have no less reason not to slaughter children in our turn. The former rule, perhaps, rests on mutual contract; not the latter.

If the rules are not wholly kept, nor all war crimes punished, what is the point of reaffirming them? First, that they are correct—failure does not invalidate them, but incriminate us. 'To say that the rules of war are out of date because people nowadays do not keep them is as absurd as to say that the law of contract is now superannuated because so many people shoplift' (Kenny 1985: 11). Second, that by reaffirming them we may at least reduce the number of occasions when they are violated. But how exactly are such rules to be enforced in the absence of a world governor, and of one coherent world order? If there were a world state, of course, 'the rules of war' would simply be the rules of proper police procedure to which I have likened them—or, alternatively, simple banditry. Criminals within a civil community are not usually promoting any radically different order of things, but merely preying on their fellow citizens: burglars have as much interest as the rest of us in the security of property, and in civil peace. It is that peace that allows them to be burglars. Crime may sometimes become something like a war, when there are two or more communities within the boundaries of a single nation-state, when the nation has lost what sense it had of solidarity. But war is characteristically a conflict between communities who owe no joint allegiance to any higher authority of a kingly kind, and who may even disagree precisely about the nature of a just solution to their disagreement. 'What would constitute moderation in a conflict between [Ayn Rand] and a communist, when [her] views are that she has an inalienable right to her life, liberty and happiness, and his views are that the "public good" of the state permits him to rob, enslave or murder [her]?' (Rand 1967: 206.) The present world community is divided among many nations whose internal affairs are held—within limits—to be their own concern. The police forces of one state have no authority in any other, save by specific agreements. How then does one state acquire a right to take arms against its neighbour, even if that neighbour is behaving in what would be a criminal way if it were a faction within a state? What can ever justify us in going to war?

One reply has been that nothing can, that war is so dreadful a thing that no one should embark on it. Paradoxically the result has sometimes been to convince people that if we do embark on war we must fight without any inhibitions at all. If war is hell, then all things diabolical are permitted there. Just war theorists since Augustine have preferred a more complex response.

If the lawful government of a state depended solely on the contract of obedience that its citizens are supposed to have made—the sub-Lockean model that I have already criticized—there would, it seems to me, be only two options. Either such a state has no rights whatsoever over any foreigner, or it has all such liberties as Hobbes supposed that any of us would have 'in nature'. We might have a weak 'right to command' such foreigners (in that we did no wrong in doing so), but no strong right, because they have no duty to obey. Neither option allows for rules of war beyond the merely contractual, and these only as *façons de parler*. They would be not laws so much as common practices, broken at our peril, but without any blame. If state governments, as I have argued, derive what rights they have from a wider community and a superior authority, we can spell out something of what they are licensed to do. A lawful government may institute police proceedings against wrongdoers within its boundaries. There are good reasons why it is taboo for it to act against wrongdoers elsewhere in the world. No nation has so much power as to be an effective guardian of all human rights wherever they may be; nor so much wisdom as to use such power to the best effect. Remember please just who it was that launched America on its Vietnamese adventure. It is better in general to leave distant communities to manage their own affairs. But some acts are so outrageous as to license any bystander who can effectively restrain them to take arms against them (see Locke 2. 8: 1963: 313). The point is not, as is sometimes supposed, that all wars must be self-defensive if they are to be just. The distinction between *Jihad* and *Defa'*, war at the Imam's command to spread the Islamic laws through-out the world and war to defend one's independence, needing no Imam to command (Khomeyni, *Kashf Asrar*, 229: Rajaee 1983: 89), is doubtless a real one. But on the one hand, not every territorial invasion threatens one's integrity as a slave of God. And on the other, other crimes than violation of our territorial integrity may justify us in taking military action. An act of violence against a neighbouring people, or against some class of the wrongdoer's own people, or—as I shall say at greater length later—against the integrity of the whole earth, may be so gross as to justify, even to require, our military intervention. How my neighbour rears her children, to take an analogous case, is in large measure her business, but we do not allow her to do just anything to them with impunity. Within a civil community the next step must be an appeal to authority; in the absence of such a single effective arbiter, we may have to come to blows.

Outrageous injustice may give us cause to go to war. But though it is a piece of flabby rhetoric to say that war never did anyone any good, war does remain something very dreadful, not least because it will be fought across the bodies of people who have been forced into combat (for even the enemy soldiers will rarely be dedicated fighters for evil). Rulers and princes—any who have power and authority to speak and act for all—should seek all other just means of settling the matter; should never embark on so hazardous an effort unless there is a reasonable probability of success (though just occasionally it may even be right to fight a lost cause to the bitter end, or at least to be prepared to do so); should weigh the deaths and suffering that will be caused, and the moral evils that will be occasioned, against the death and suf-fering and moral evil that will be caused by failing to fight it. No war should be fought unless some gross injustice touching the whole community of nations has been committed, all non-military solutions have failed, there is a reasonable chance of righting the wrong by fighting, and the costs of the war are not disproportionate to the goal. Even if all these conditions apply, it may still be wicked to go to war, if we do so with a wicked motive (arrogant pride or hatred or blood-lust), or without any readiness to resubmit the matter to non-military arbitration. Sensible rulers should consider that they are entering a world where their own moral principles may be corrupted; they may in the end commit as many deliberate injustices as their enemy (a fact which is one of the pacifist's strongest arguments).

Should we entertain another, and less comfortable, thought? If there are occasions when a lost cause should be fought out to the end, we cannot quite rule out the possibility that we might go to war without any hope at all of righting wrongs. Just war theorists, like modern liberals, have denied the claim, seeing it only as an expression of self-righteous bellicosity. I would certainly prefer to share that view. But maybe there will be, and have been, occasions when it is right to do our acts 'as worship', regardless of the immediate consequences. Maybe we thereby leave an image of hope for those who come after, a proof that there are those who cannot be intimidated, whom no threat at all will stir from the right way (if right it was).

The virtue of the barbarian who dies fighting for his tribe against hopeless odds—undismayed by the calculation that, on an 'enlightenedly self-interested' reckoning, he is sacrificing his life in vain—was exhibited on [2 Sep 1898] by the aged standard-bearer who charged a battalion armed with magazine rifles. (Toynbee 1954: 519.)

But we should not be too ready to think that we are in that extreme position, nor is it obvious that such faith-holders should involve other and more ordinarily decent people in their battle. Most of the time the rules of war apply.

Atrocities have always been committed, whether by undisciplined soldiers or the deliberate choice of rulers. The Emperor Titus starved Jerusalem into submission, and crucified all Jews who sought to escape from the dying city. But siege warfare apart, it has been possible in the past for armies to fight in obedience to the laws of justice. Soldiers have been the agents and principal victims of international disputes, and even if they have not freely volunteered themselves for danger, it is possible to hold that they may justly be opposed as long as they bear arms against our community (always assuming that we are in the right).

If they are in the wrong, they are still not wholly to be blamed, unless the case is obvious to all, and even then it would not be just to arraign them before our courts once they have surrendered. They are our route to their unjust leaders, and may justly be fought so long as we remember that they too are human—though I am not sure that I share Kant's disdain for assassination as a superior programme, unless his objection was merely to undeclared war, the known possibility of which would seriously undermine the civil peace. Tyrannicide is sometimes, to put it mildly, a better policy than war. Sevener Shiites, or Ismailites, adopted that procedure under al-Hasan in 1090 (Watt 1968: 113), and thereby alarmed the rulers more than ordinary Muslims. Assassination would at least be better than obliteration bombing of civilian targets, or germ warfare. The difference made by the invention of nuclear weapons is that such bombing is no longer, by comparison with the military and economic costs of raising the Dresden firestorm, outrageously expensive. The huge arsenals of the great powers serve no military purpose: even a poor nation, if it chooses, can acquire the capacity to obliterate its enemies. Even the IRA may do so one day soon. We must therefore reconsider the steps that have brought us so far from the just war justly fought.

The use of such weapons, nuclear, chemical, and biological, as we now have, within the earth's atmosphere, could never be justified. Of their nature, they kill indiscriminately. If employed as 'counter-value' weapons they are expressly intended to kill non-combatants—an act at least as outrageous as the practice of killing children in reprisal for guerrilla activity. If they are used as 'counter-force' weapons it is impossible to guarantee that millions of non-combatants will not perish miserably as well, far in excess of any lives gained by the exercise. Polaris or Trident would be the only fairly legitimate target for a nuclear attack (though polluting the ocean would have dreadful effects!). Nuclear weapons will devastate the biosphere, and no one has any clear idea of how long such damage will take to repair. Their use would leave little or nothing worth fighting for, and certainly not the civil institutions on which we currently pride ourselves.

The inhabitants of Warsaw already suffer what we would have to suffer if we surrendered to Russian blackmail. Yet in the worst days of martial law, can anyone really believe that what the Polish people wanted was for the West to put them out of their agony by dropping a nuclear device upon the centre of Warsaw? (Kenny 1985: 36.)

We should probably, if the event we fear occurred, be left with a choice between tribalism and military dictatorship—if any of us survived at all. This is not to say that it would be incredibly wicked to use such weapons first (as if this were a military convention like that barring the use of gas against military targets), but that it would always be incredibly wicked to use them. A reprisal even for a nuclear attack that took the form of nuclear retaliation lies so far beyond the limits of the just war as not to be worth discussing at all: it involves the deliberate killing of non-combatants; it makes a return to civil peace less and not more likely; it is motivated only by hatred and outraged pride. Those who have lent their tacit support to such a policy of genocidal retaliation should ask themselves what they would think of a terrorist group who took children hostage and tortured them to death in revenge for their enemy's failure to meet their demands.

Any state using nuclear weapons, so the General Assembly of the United Nations determined in 1961, 'would be acting contrary to the laws of humanity and committing a crime against mankind and civilization'. It is, notoriously, not quite so clear that a state which merely *threatened* to use them, or let it be thought that it might use them, under certain circumstances, is acting wickedly. 'Secular moralists', so far as there are such creatures, may well conclude that such a strategy is forced on them, precisely to reduce the chances of a conflagration. Those animals who make it clear that, if cornered, they will fight to the death are likelier to be left alone. Unfortunately, the strategy is unstable. It rests upon the conviction of all parties that a nuclear first-strike would result in massive nuclear retaliation. So we must persuade ourselves that if our enemy did launch a nuclear attack we should at once respond in kind even though there would then be no point in doing so, and though this act would merely increase the devastation. A merely vengeful act that may elicit further enemy attacks and will probably cost the whole earth dear even if it does not is not sensible military behaviour. So how can we, and our enemy, be persuaded that we shall in fact retaliate? We may say, with one American strategist, that 'regardless of strategic reasoning the [American] President would order a volley be fired back for the sake of national honour [*sic*!] or even just to satisfy the primitive motive of revenge. Millions of dead Americans would constitute a debt of blood to be repaid, inappropriate and even fatal though such repayment might prove to be' (cited by Kenny 1985: 20). If the Soviets believe that the Americans are as wicked and as stupid as that, it is hardly surprising that their strategists in turn remark that 'capitalism, in leaving the historical scene is ready to take with it all life on earth' (cited by Shenfield in Windass 1985: 67). A strategy predicated on the pretence of extreme wickedness runs the risk of persuading one's enemy that one is indeed so wicked that pre-emptive strikes are in order. The alternative is to persuade ourselves and our enemies that we think we could actually win a nuclear war by continuing the exchanges. But the belief that we could win is incompatible with the belief on which MAD (the strategy of Mutual Assured Destruction) is founded, that to initiate a nuclear exchange would destroy us all. If we could win even if we did not begin the exchanges, we could certainly do so if we did. Accordingly MAD is founded on two incompatible theses: that no one could win a nuclear war, and that we could.

Anyone who retains the romantic delusion that war could be prevented if only it were made horrible enough (a thesis long since tested to destruction) should surely be worried by the contradiction implicit in such reasoning. To be fair, I think we all are, including President Reagan, whose belated and partial conversion to the theory of the just war, and thence to the search for just techniques of neutralizing nuclear assaults, deserves more sympathy than it has received from the liberal establishment. 'Star Wars' may 'destabilize the balance', but the balance never was stable anyway.

Even those who accept the secular necessity of appearing to be wicked or obtuse may conclude that the multiplication of such weapons serves no purpose, and merely increases the likelihood of accident, miscalculation, or terrified pre-emptive strike. It is difficult to believe that any sensible person would ever have initiated the present 'balance of terror' as a way of securing 'peace', or rather 'a cessation of arms for terror of the sword'. I have, at any rate, never met anyone who thinks that the Middle East would be at peace if all contending nations, factions, and sects had nuclear bombs! But the secularist must in the end, in fear and trembling, put her trust in princes to play the game adroitly. I do not understand how any merely secular moralist, distrusting as they do the media through which they get their scanty information, can possibly believe themselves to be better informed upon the likely costs and benefits of adopting this strategy, or propaganda release, or that, than the existing governments. Theists, though, have one more hope, and one more judgement.

Those who put their trust in 'the horses of Egypt' (Isaiah 31), the military engine of their day, against the commandments of the Holy One of Israel, risk more than life.

> This man's purpose is lawless,
> lawless are the plans of his mind;
> for his thought is only to destroy
> and to wipe out nation after nation . . .
> Therefore the Lord, the LORD of Hosts,
> will send disease on his sturdy frame,
> from head to toe . . .
> The light of Israel shall become a fire
> and his Holy One a flame . . .

On that day the remnant of Israel shall cease to lean on him that proved their destroyer, but shall loyally lean on the Lord, the Holy One of Israel (Isaiah 10: 7–20).

The LORD, the Holy One of Israel, is 'a man of battle' (Exodus 15: 3), but His warfare is to establish justice. If we must sometimes fight for the welfare of strangers, of the widows and orphans, we do so as God's agents in the world and under His rulings. If we cannot now fight without breaking the rules, then we must not fight, and must instead rely upon His promises. The Lord is not Ares, even if 'joy of battle' is not wholly excluded from the sacred realm.

> O rebel sons, says the Lord,
> you make plans, but not of my devising,
> you weave schemes but not inspired by me,
> piling sin upon sin;
> you hurry down to Egypt without consulting me,
> to seek protection under Pharaoh's shelter
> and take refuge under Egypt's wing.
> Pharaoh's protection will bring you disappointment
> and refuge under Egypt's wing humiliation
>
> (Isaiah 30: 1–3)

The God who is more than all the gods is made known in the war on wickedness, such wickedness as arrogant inhospitality, pride, blood-lust, destruction of the natural ties that are our first experience of duty and the self. If we fight, and it must be conceded that we will, it must be in obedience to that God, not any national demon or Titanic power: obedience, and trust. To believe in God is to suppose that what we partly see and hear of the demands of justice is what will in the end triumph. In Anscombe's words (1961: 62):

Those who think they must be prepared to wage a war with Russia involving the deliberate massacre of cities, must be prepared to say to God: 'We had to break your law, lest your Church fail. We could not obey your commandments, for we did not believe your promises'.

That the house of Israel is with us still, and all the great empires have gone down to Sheol, is some sign, to the believing eye, that its God is indeed the Lord. 'It is the Torah and only the Torah that has pre-served the Jewish people through millenia of dispersion, persecution, and repeated decimation' (Eidelberg 1983: 316). Eidelberg's judge-ment that 'Israel is the one nation in the world' (1983: 320), because the only nation that has chosen *HaShem* rather than its own beliefs and inclinations, should not be dismissed too readily and smugly. Certainly other God-fearing peoples have distinguished between themselves and 'the tribes', the great mass of undisciplined heathen, *Dar al-Harb*, 'the land of Shinar' (Ellul 1970: 13 f.), of piracy and destruction. It would certainly be easy enough to argue that Israel itself, as an historical and national entity (sinking, like Notting Hill, to the status of a mere empire), has often enough deserved its own rebuke. But the image remains, and the undoubted fact that the whole modern world, for good or ill, rests upon Israel and its offspring (which is to say: Chris-tendom, Islam, and Communism).

Gangsters, Insurgents, and 'The Evil Empire'

Just war theory was originally directed at established rulers, princes with the presumed Mandate of Heaven to defend their people's lives and ways of living, or—occasionally—to 'spread the Islamic laws throughout the world' (see Rajaee 1983: 89), or mount a crusade against the infidel. But if we have no clear reason to suppose that pre-sent rulers rule by Heaven's command (though Heaven allows them space), how can we distinguish between the use of military force by state rulers, and its use by any bunch of more or less high-minded brigands?

Reason and experience alike tell us that the governments now existing in the world were established by bayonet-point, by force. None of the monarchies or governments that we see in the world are based on justice or on a correct foundation that is acceptable to reason. Their foundations are all rotten, being nothing but coercion and force. (Khomeyni, *Kashf Asrar*, 221: Rajaee 1983: 76.)

And if that is so, how shall we who serve existing states complain if another bunch of brigands seeks to establish its control? Must we accept that all such struggling states and would-be states exist in a Hobbesian state of nature, bound to defend themselves and what they see as theirs against invasion, but without any general moral right to condemn as wicked in the IRA or PLO or Khmer Rouge or Mafia what they allow as pardonable when ordered by a state? Governments that grew from bayonet-wielding bands, or that have in living memory purported to authorize the bombing of civilian targets, cannot consistently condemn all younger bands (which might, after all, grow up to be new states), or the use of explosives, poison, or assassination. They may often choose to fight them, but how can they claim the higher moral ground? Even the usual liberal plea, that lawful governments rule with the (implicit) consent of most of their people, is useless here, as long as lesser brigands can claim support of a kind (however terrorized) from the surrounding population. If the authority of the Queen in Parliament rests only on the tacit approval of the British people, why does not a similar divinity hedge the ruling council of any number of 'freedom-fighting', 'terrorist', or 'gangster' organizations? Is it as simple and amoral a distinction as this: state governments not only control, but are judged to control, the area they claim? Once any brigand-gang has earned the accolade of 'recognition' from a sufficient number of already successful brigands, it may claim the right to do what all existing states already do: it may coerce and kill, or make its citizens give up their lives and living, without eliciting much more than ritual disapproval from offended neighbours. Until it has that recognition, its members must be criminals, and the international order mobilized to contain or capture them. Whether it wins recognition or not will depend, amorally, upon the perceived interests and powers of present states, and not on any ideal law. Pol Pot, as I have pointed out before, is not denied his status merely for crimes against humanity.

One other reply is available: Berkeley's plea—of considerable political moment at the time—to disaffected Tories in the early eighteenth century reminded them that, as they would agree, the civil peace requires a stable ruler.[1] Even if a present prince once had no right to the crown, 'once [he is] in possession of it and you have sworn allegiance to him, you are no longer at liberty to enquire by what unrighteous means he might have obtained it' (Berkeley 1948: vi. 57).

---

[1] Articles on Berkeley's moral, political, and economic theories are collected in Clark 1988d.

A present civil peace is not to be disturbed, even if it weighs more heavily on some than others, even if it were once achieved by force. But Berkeley concedes at once that madmen and usurpers do not enjoy such sovereign immunity (Berkeley 1948: vi. 44 f.). To suppose that there is any 'right of rebellion' is inconsistent with the need for sovereign decision: a law that I ought only to obey if I agree to do so is no law at all. But a law that is not backed by God's clear purpose in providing peace has no authority. What may at first seem ambivalent in Berkeley's attitude to the Glorious Revolution of 1688 (and apparently did cost him court approval at one stage) was actually Anglican:

It was not that the king had been too absolute, but that the wrong king had been too absolute; it was not that the monarchy was to be thoroughly limited, but that a Catholic monarchy was to be excluded. The Revolution, as the expression of the *via media*, was a rejection of revolutionary innovation in favor of a church and state polity approved by the long usage of history, the ancient precedent of the law, and the spirit of reformed Christianity. (Straka 1962: 37; see Burke 1975: 280 ff.)

Berkeley, and other Tories of the time, were thinking of God-fearing princes, ones who might occasionally or often be 'inconvenient', but who did maintain as reasonably just a peace as we could reasonably expect. Even if they had, on particular occasion, no right to exercise authority within this field or that, it would be wrong, forbidden, to resist (Berkeley 1948: vi. 37)—though the ruler, acting beyond his rightful authority, committed a grave sin. Madmen and usurpers on the other hand, acknowledging no limit to their power, could not be makers or preservers of the peace. Confronted by such enemies of God and humankind we are driven back to war (even if caution teaches us to pause, and to prepare).

Early Muslim jurists divided the world into the *Dar al-Islam* (the sphere of Islam, submission to God's law) and the *Dar al-Harb*, the sphere of war. A third sphere, the sphere of truce, had very limited range, merely for those non-Muslims who accepted Muslim suzerainty without acknowledging the *Shari'a* (Watt 1968: 91). Within the *Dar al-Harb*, the kingdom of darkness (see Hobbes 1968: 627 ff.), it may be that such careful and amoral power-play is all that can be expected. Only within the *Dar al-Islam*, the kingdom of God, are clear rules laid down as to how disputes are to be settled. Wars within that kingdom are always temporary police-actions, aimed at the restoration of just order and the civil peace. Outside that kingdom there is no just order, and insurgents struggle to establish their own power-base.

The unity of Mankind can be achieved only as an incidental result of acting on a belief in the unity of God, and by seeing this unitary terrestrial society *sub specie aeternitatis* as a province of a Commonwealth of God which must be singular, not plural, *ex hypothesi*. (Toynbee 1954: 510.)

For perhaps there is a less cynical response, though it is one that must cause some heart-searching in established rulers. Some highly organized gangs are recognizably criminal despite the consent of many of those they work among. Their secrecy is not the point, nor yet their readiness to rely—when it suits them—on existing legalities. The hypocrisy of those who righteously complain when gunmen they have supported are gunned down is evident, as is the hypocrisy of petty criminals who can think that they are wronged by theft or extradition. Those who will not respect the decencies have no *contractual* claim on decency. But it is easy enough to remember that Resistance workers might exploit such regulations as an occupying force allowed without thereby endorsing them. As Spooner pointed out (in passages I cited in chapter four), it is absurd to infer a real consent in those who take such steps as they have been allowed to defend themselves against unjust expropriation. The distinction that we are implicitly relying on is something like the following: justified insurgents obey the rules of war and those of peace. Any organization that fails to do so is suspect (at the least). Those rules are the ones that I have already sketched, and foremost among them is the need for 'God's Mandate'—which is to say, some evidence that there is indeed a real wrong to be righted, and that the insurgents are the likeliest to mend the world. They must be 'slaves of God', not simply people with a grievance or a romantic wish to be 'doing something' about something wrong. Only those with a clear capacity and call to remedy injustice, and a proven willingness themselves to be accountable for what they do, can earn the accolade of moral recognition.

Even this much, of course, will be most difficult to judge: my point here is not to identify those groups that I might think deserving—how much, after all, do I or my acquaintances know of what goes on? It is to insist that the nations do already make distinctions between non-governmental groups (as we do between governments). Not all the former are unjustified, any more than all the latter are authentic rulers. In both cases, both their ends and means are relevant: we mind that their goal is justice, and that they use just means. Those who fail on either count are brigands. But there will still be questions: something of what 'justice' means is clear to all of us, but all such images are, inevitably, historically conditioned and all-too-likely to ignore deep troubles among those peoples who have in the past not been allowed a voice. It is all too easy to deny insurgents access to the only means of war they have, while at the same time letting pass all manner of habitual inject- ice in the stronger power. Those in present power have no absolute moral edge, but in another sense of that strange term they almost always have the 'moral' edge, like birds in their own territory. 'Mora- lizing' is itself a weapon of war, a way of putting down opponents, mak- ing them feel small. And any methodological conservative will have to agree that present power is vindicated just this much: that it is pre- sently in power, and likely to give some heed to winning over any oppo- sition, whereas that opposition is so far untried (and likely to be unbending lest it lose its way). 'The ills of rebellion are certain, but the event doubtful' (Berkeley 1948: vi. 55). It is at least alarmingly naive to take for granted that a just insurgent group, compelled to battle by whatever means within an established order (however formally unjust) will, once it is successful, lay aside its grudge. The record of our his- tory does not suggest that 'good insurgents' (even if they are) often make 'good rulers'. 'Bad insurgents', even with good causes, must be feared. It is not obvious that people prepared to execute their enemies by placing rubber tyres, filled with petrol, around their necks and set- ting them alight (an act, it seems, carried out with all the panoply of moralizing mockery that tyrants love), could ever be trusted with the sovereign power, no matter what the provocation was that gave them their 'excuse'.

On the one hand, therefore, people who—from a safe distance and without any risk of ever themselves enduring the kindly rule of the vic- torious rebels—lend moral and financial support to insurgents (of whatever party) are taking a grave risk. Those who do so in a friendly country, knit close to them by kinship and common purposes, should be despised. On the other hand, those who support existing tyrannies are likely enough to be judged, after the event, as vile appeasers. The God-fearing anarchist desires neither tyrant states nor would-be tyrants: in place of all those moralizing, murderous powers, she places 'God's Arky', *Dar al-Islam*, the Commonwealth of God. No group has moral authority that does not follow the commands of God: there are many disagreements, to be sure, about God's Law, but few of them are relevant to a debate about insurgency. We can agree, in this historical moment, about quite a lot, even if we also identify the Evil Empire, or the Great Satan, with different presently existing powers. At least we all know that there is such an empire, or the possibility of it, and that those who can rightly claim authority do so only as empowered to oppose its coming into being, in themselves or others.

7
Gaia and the Great City

Dear City of Zeus

The final context of our worldly activity is not our immediate nation-state, nor yet the socio-political nexus of suffering humanity, but the whole earth. It is of that 'Great City, whose author and founder is God', so Berkeley said (1948: iii. 129), that we should think ourselves citizens. That principle of mutual attraction which draws us 'together in communities, clubs, families, friendships and all the various species of society' (vii. 226), leads on to a loving appreciation of the whole earth and the spirit that guides its doings. One of the many not-so-peculiar oddities of the present age is that the theologically inclined have shied away from any doctrine of God's activity in nature at the very same time as the Earth herself has come to be seen as a proper object of pious adoration and concern. Traditional theism is attacked on the one hand for supposing that our God is active in the world, and on the other for neglecting to see the lineaments of the divine cosmos in the terrestrial biosphere. On the one hand, the divine is not active; on the other hand, what is active is the divine. Modernists hardly seem to know whether it is best to think of the world as a howling desert, where 'even the spring that spake is dry', or as the earth mother, Gaia, the goddess violated by two or three or more millenia of masculinist religion. That there is anything which rides within and guides the world, as a charioteer his chariot, is superstitious. We are not to believe that there are powers working invisibly for good, like the horses and chariots of fire revealed to Elisha's servant (2 Kings 6: 17). But a good many people also find it obvious that we should love and admire and care for the whole earth, that Nature herself gives us a standard to steer by. Ecomystics and secularists alike are opposed to what they think they know of theism: it is my object in this chapter to suggest that 'the earth is the Lord's' (Psalm 24: 1) and therefore estimable. 'The poet says, dear city of Cecrops, and will you not say, dear city of Zeus?' (Aurelius, *Meditations* 4. 23).

I should in passing dispel one misapprehension. It is very common for commentators to contrast the 'pantheistic' or 'immanentist' conception of the divine found in Greek, or at any rate Stoic sources, and the Hebrew 'transcendentalist' or 'monotheistic' view. Did not the Stoics say that the cosmos itself was called Zeus, because it is the cause of our living (Arnim 1904 ii. fr. 528, see Diogenes Laertius, *Lives of the Philosophers* 7. 147)? Did not the Hebrews, or at least the Psalmist, carefully distinguish between the Lord who 'is our refuge and strength' and the earth that might be removed and the mountains thereof carried into the midst of the sea (Psalm 46: 1f.)? There is perhaps a distinction to be made, but those who say so usually add that the Hebrews did not have our conception of 'Nature' as a power distinct from God. It is He 'that causeth the grass to grow for the cattle, and herb for the service of man' (Psalm 104: 14), not an hypostatized nature. But in that case, how does the Hebraic vision differ from the Hellenic? *Natura naturans* is simply God, for the Stoic as much as for the Psalmist.

And this is why the end may be defined as life in accordance with nature, that is according to one's own as well as that of the whole, a life in which we refrain from everything that the common law forbids, which is to say the right reason that pervades all things, which is this Zeus, who is the lord and ruler of all that is. And this very thing is the virtue of the *eudaimon* and the smooth current of life, when everything is done so that the *daimon* in each man agrees with the will of the ruler of the whole. (Diogenes Laertius 7. 88.)[1]

Natura naturans, the spiritual cause and principle that governs the entire phenomenal world, is also what is experienced in us as right reason, conscience, the command of God. So to find out what we should do we must, among other things, ask what the plan for the whole might be.

A wise man . . . does not look upon himself as a whole, separated and detached from every other part of nature, to be taken care of by itself and for itself. He regards himself in the light in which he imagines the great genius [= *daimon*] of human nature, and of the world regards him. He enters, if I may say so, into the sentiments of that divine Being, and considers himself as an atom, a particle, of an immense and infinite system, which must and ought to be disposed of, according to the conveniency of the whole. Assured of the wisdom which directs all the events of human life, whatever lot befalls him, he accepts it with joy, satisfied that if he had known all the connections and dependencies of the different parts of the universe, it is the very lot which he himself would have wished for. If it is life, he is contented to live, and if it is death, as nature

---

[1] I shall have more to say about that controlling *daimon* in the second volume.

must have no further occasion for his presence here, he willingly goes where he is appointed. (Smith 1976 (vii. 2. 1. 20) 276.)

Adam Smith's account of Stoicism on this point differs from Berkeley's simply in that Berkeley was rather more alive to the difficulty of so satisfying oneself. 'It becomes us with thankfulness to use the good things we receive from the hand of God, and patiently to abide the evil, which when thoroughly considered and understood may perhaps appear to be good, it being no sure sign that a thing is good, because we desire, or evil because we are displeased with it' (1948: vii. 134). But to say simply and without qualification that whatever happens to anyone must be conceived to be the will of God, the purpose of the universal genius and of one's own 'real Self', leaves us without any positive guidance as to what to do to others. Whatever one succeeds in doing, by the co-operative power of Zeus, will be what God and Nature intended for one's victim—so that one might reasonably attempt all sorts of things and leave it to God to select what He approves (and is that so absurd?).

The possibility—which seems to be a necessary postulate of practical reason—that one might offer a reasoned criticism of what goes on in the world has generally persuaded modern moral commentators that the universal genius cannot be the only standard or the only agent in the world. Could we not find out that the God of this world is the very devil, the order he is bent upon developing a merely satanic one? It seems fair to agree with Inge's comment (1920: 16) that the choice proposed by Russell between the worship of a Devil that does exist (the way of the world) and a God who does not (the way of conscience) is wholly unreal, since we could not worship either; but a refusal to bow down before iniquity, or copy the quaint practices of the 'natural world' has its own nobility. Nevertheless, as I pointed out a few years ago (Clark 1977b), and as Philo did several centuries before, there are some logical difficulties about defiance.

Refusal to reverence God implies refusal to honour parents and country and benefactors. And if so what depths of depravity remain for him to reach who besides refusing reverence dares also to revile [and curse] Him? . . . Answer me, thou man, does anyone curse God? Then what other god does he call on to make good the curse, or is it clear that he invokes the help of God against Himself? (Philo, *Moses* 2. 198 f.: 1930, vi. 546.)

To defy is to do more than merely to resent: it is to denounce as iniquitous, as something one will not countenance. But how can we thus set

ourselves apart from God and *natura naturans*? I can only be denouncing God in the light of that perception of the moral law as I find in my
heart: but who, by hypothesis, put that light there? I might as well
declare that my brain is the ground of all my thinking and is irreparably
and finally diseased. Either the God I denounce is not the one principle on which all things are based (in which case my denunciation is
out of order), or He is (in which case my very denunciation and the
'reasons' I offer for it are as unreliable as He). The first principle on
which we found our lives has got to be 'Honour the Origin'. How can
we respect our 'own' judgement if we don't respect that which provides
for it?

'Honor thy father and thy mother,' since life in truth is not your own but a gift
you receive at their hands. Not theirs only—every moment of life is the gift of
the world around us and of the God of that world. To honor, the ability to
honor—is both a distinctive human trait and the crucial component of humanity at peace. We are the beings able to cherish and give thanks. Hence,
'remember the Sabbath day, to keep it holy': it is not a day of rest only. Far
more it is a day of thanksgiving. Not the absence of activity but the act of
honoring, of giving thanks, is what restores the human soul and puts it at
peace. (Kohak 1984: 80.)

Thanksgiving and obedience are the necessary steps, as I have urged
elsewhere, to the discovering of God's presence. The reason we have
ceased—so far as we have in fact ceased—to be aware of 'God's presence with us' is simply that we have stopped worshipping. Thinking
itself, in its original form, is thanking (Heidegger 1968: 139 ff.).

Humans, as a species, throughout the millenia and all over the globe, have
been worshippers of the Holy. The awareness of God's presence is and ever
has been the most persistent specific trait of our species being . . . The question that humans have posed through the ages is not whether there is a god but
rather, 'What does the Lord require of me?' (Kohak 1984: 186.)

The ontological issues raised here will concern me again in my third
volume. What I am emphasizing here is that the principle on which the
whole world is understood to be founded must be one that we can
respect, by which we can let ourselves be moved without involving
ourselves in desperate contortions and self-contradictions. 'What
beauty can be found', Berkeley's Euphranor inquires in criticism of
the high-minded atheist, 'in a moral system, formed, connected and
governed by chance, fate or any other blind unthinking principle?'
(Berkeley 1948: iii. 128.) If, for example, our moral—which includes

our epistemic—codes were generated in us solely as those which once gave chances of evolutionary 'advantage' to our ancestors, how could we rationally regard them as anything but disposable and accidental inhibitions? This is not to say that we could then determine ourselves to act more directly for our evolutionary advantage, as if that preference were not itself an accidental product of past history. Mark Studdock, in Lewis's *That Hideous Strength*, inquires of the 'moral objectivist'—a man who believes 'that all which appears in the mind as motive or intention is merely a by-product of what the body is doing' (Lewis 1945: 444)—whether the aims of the macrobes—which is to say the demons who control the NICE—are 'compatible with our own'.

'What do you mean by our own aims?'
'Well—I suppose—the scientific reconstruction of the human race in the direction of increased efficiency—the elimination of war and poverty and other forms of waste—a fuller exploitation of nature—the preservation and extension of our species, in fact.'
'I do not think this pseudo-scientific language really modifies the essentially subjective and instinctive basis of the ethics you are describing . . . Your view of war and your reference to the preservation of the species suggest a profound misconception. They are mere generalizations from affectional feelings.' (Lewis 1945: 317; see also Lewis 1943.)

Those who think or choose to think that the Origin is blind, lazy or inane can hardly give much honour to what stems from it. But what basis of action and belief can they then find? How can we possibly go on taking ourselves or our species seriously as determinants of right action? How can we think that what strikes 'us' (whom?) as elegant or comprehensive explanation has any particular prospect of being 'true-in-fact'? How can we pretend to ourselves that we have no alternative but to carry on valuing just what we accidentally do, when it is obvious that our values and associations are illusory? As long as we believed that Aphrodite was a real, though deadly, god we could honour her as such. 'When the partner assumes an incandescent beauty, this moment has a peaceful perfection, for one has been granted a vision of eternity by Golden Aphrodite' (Paris 1986: 17). The Homeric Hymn that brings her striding over the mountain in search of Anchises depicts a real epiphany: once the world is radically disenchanted, and we can no longer honour or worship the Origin of gods and men, she must be no more than a kind of itch, a glamour on a fundamentally unmeaning world. Maybe we can pretend to ourselves that she is more than that, but this is to admit that everything that matters to us is a fantasy, that nothing counts. Shaw's intelligent Christian, Lavinia, in *Androcles and the Lion*, is a profoundly unhistorical figure, but her profession of faith is true enough in spirit, even if no Christian of that time would actually have said this:

Religion is such a great thing that when I meet really religious people we are friends at once, no matter what name we give to the divine will that made us and moves us. Do you think that I, a woman, would quarrel with you for sacrificing to a woman god like Diana, if Diana meant to you what Christ means to me? No, we should kneel side by side before her altar. But when men who believe neither in my god nor in their own—men who do not know the meaning of the word religion—when these men . . . ask me to pledge my soul before the people that this hideous [symbol of the terror and darkness through which they walk] is God and that all this wickedness and falsehood is divine truth, I cannot do it. . . . And all the time I should believe more in Diana than my persecutors have ever believed in anything. (Shaw 1934: 689.)

To take anything seriously and sacredly, even one's own whims and pleasures, it is necessary to engage in worshipful obedience. If the Origin and Principle of things is not to be obeyed and worshipped how can anything it originates be worshipful? If it *is* to be obeyed and worshipped then we have to consider not simply what our individual *daimon* demands, as if it and we ourselves could exist in isolation, but what the universal *daimon*, Blake's Poetic Genius, requires in all its elements. We must draw ourselves ever closer to the command that can be conceived to be given to all the world.

Deep Environmentalism and the Liberal Tradition

Those humanistic moralists, in Greece, Israel, or China, who first proclaimed the sacredness of every human person, did not appeal directly to absolute rights of self-ownership (restricted by the equal rights of others), nor to an intuitively perceived intrinsic value possessed by all and only members of our species. Individual right, Kipling's 'leave to live by no man's leave underneath the Law', and private property were defended as the likeliest way of enabling a society of freemen to subsist in mutual harmony, and cultivate their virtues: if we each had some portion of the land to tend we would be less likely to fall prey to tyrants, and the land itself would prosper. What we owned, however, was not the land itself, but the lawfully acquired fruits, and we owned these only for their lawful use. 'Nothing was made by God for Man to spoil or destroy' (Locke 2. 31: 1963: 332). Individual liberty rested on the value God placed in every soul, as a unique expression of His glory, such that any despotism, however benevolent in purpose, must issue in a decline of valuable diversity. Each of us has a profound and vital interest in the virtue of our fellow-citizens, and in the continued viability of the ecosystems within which we live.[2]

Leopold's vision, which has been the inspiration of much recent environmentalism:

We abuse land because we regard it as a commodity belonging to us. When we see land as a community to which we belong, we may begin to use it with love and respect. . . . That land is a community is the basic concept of ecology, but that land is to be loved and respected is an extension of ethics. (Leopold 1968: p. viii.)

This can be used to ground both libertarian and zoophile intuitions in a necessary moral synthesis. Our moralizing predecessors defended their moral views in the context of the moral universe they inherited or posited. Where modern moralists think that the universe which would be maintained by the rules they advocate is to be justified solely by its value to 'us' (whoever 'we' may be), the ancients thought it obvious that it was the whole world which was to be admired:

It is a visible living creature, it contains all creatures that are visible and is itself an image of the intelligible; and it has thus become a visible god, supreme in greatness and excellence, beauty and perfection, a single, uniquely created heaven. (Plato, *Timaeus* 92 D.)

Our individual selves, so far from being thought absolute self-owners, were considered elements and partners in the whole universe, even by those of a liberal persuasion. Universal 'self-ownership', which is to say the duty and prerogative of each element of the universe to maintain its own integrity as a part of that diverse and lovely whole, is not an abstract, logical requirement, but an aspect of the way the 'visible god' works. When Berkeley, for example, set himself to show the value of righteousness, he appealed to our understanding of ourselves as

---

[2] Some of the following material was originally printed in Clark 1987b, as a discussion of Regan's attempt to ground 'rights' simply on the characteristic of 'being the subject of a life'. I do not myself believe that this extension of contemporary liberal ideology is useful, but this does not alter my general agreement with Regan's goals in this matter, namely to secure decent treatment for creatures very ill-served by anthropocentric philosophy.

'member[s] of a great City, whose author and founder is God' (*Alci-phron* 3. 10: 1948: iii. 129). He was Cartesian enough to forget, some-times, that there were other spirits than the merely human whose welfare might be considered, but his intention here was clear. We should not be misled by the word 'city': what Berkeley meant was the whole created universe (see Clark 1985a, 1988d). It would be absurd, said Aristotle, to suppose that human beings were the most important things in the world (*Nicomachean Ethics* 6, 1141^a 20 f.). The value which Aristotle urged us to 'contemplate and serve' (Aristotle, *Eudem-ian Ethics* 8, 1249^b 20) was the same god which the universe reflected in its continuing activity: the honour due to us as rational beings rested on the value of the universe we understand. It is because the cosmos is worth knowing and preserving that those who can know and preserve it deserve their status: we are the servants, the 'shepherds of being' (see Sprigge 1984: 456, after Heidegger). The cosmic whole was main-tained in being, at the behest of God, through the integrity and mutual co-operation of its elements. That world, in Philo of Alexandria's graphic phrase (*Quod Deus Immutabilis* 176: 1930: iii. 97, 489), was a sort of cosmic democracy—not a mob rule, but a genuinely 'liberal' society, where none are allowed to lord it over others, but must all take their place, and their turn.

Accordingly, the view which Regan dubs 'environmental fascism' (Regan 1983: 362), that 'the integrity, stability and beauty of the biotic community' is the proper criterion of right action (Leopold 1968: 217), is nothing like as novel as Leopold and others supposed (nor is it fas-cist). That certain Amerindians 'conceive of themselves as belonging to the land' (Lee 1959: 169), is no surprise. What sane intelligence supposes that she owns the Land, or that all moral agents should bow down before her own inherent and absolute value? What sane com-munity of merely human individuals? We certainly do not need to look back to imaginary matriarchies to discover reason here.

The enjoyment of the good things available to us is conditional— 'for the earth is the Lord's', say the Christians, and it is not as owners that we make use of it. The fear of demons (inhabiting inanimate matter or haunting the dark corners of the world) which has been found so widely among 'primitive' peoples and dismissed by anthropologists as animism or the personification of natural forces, is a vestigial trace of the once universal knowledge that all things have a claim upon us, a claim which, if it is ignored, must bring certain consequences in its train. It is not demons but consequences that haunt the dark forest, as they do the madman's dreams. (Eaton 1977: 128.)

We may 'own' the fruits of the land, but we cannot justly dispose of the Land itself (as Jefferson well knew: see Clark 1985b). The disenchantment of the world, the 'objective gaze', has clearly ideological and political motives. We 'disenchant' it in order to make it absolutely available to us, as we also 'objectify' the animals we seek to use at our pleasure. In neither case, of course, do we really 'disenchant' what we see: on the contrary, we elect to treat animals, plants, and habitats as tools, structured by our present purposes. The tribes we evict from lands they think sacred could justly retort that it is they who allow the objects real power, that it is they who make themselves available to truth. Our supposed 'objectivity', all too often, is merely a failure to acknowledge our own purposes.

The main theoretical objections usually made to 'deep environmentalism' (as distinct from the 'shallow' kind that rests environmental concern on our need to maintain the 'environment' as an economic resource) are as follows. Firstly, it denies to individuals any absolute or inherent value. Secondly, it allows inherent value to things other than the merely sentient, whereas it has been a moral commonplace for most of this century that states of mind and experience are all that can be 'really' good or bad. Thirdly,

the practical implications . . . are reminiscent of the morally objectionable views and attitudes of primitive moralities. To treat a person, a dog, a fly, a flea, an ant, a malaria organism, a tree, a thistle, a stone, a grain of sand, a pool of water, an ocean, as equals, as ends in themselves, would be to act in a grossly immoral and morally insensitive way. (McCloskey 1983: 56.)

Intuitionism, as a meta-moral theory, unfortunately leads to the substitution of abuse for argument (see MacIntyre 1981: 16 ff.)—though I am certainly myself in no position to deny the importance of fundamental intuitions, and the right of those who have them to denounce wickedness! But in so far as the doctrine under discussion precisely denies that any of these individuals can justly or reasonably be considered end-in-themselves, the attack in this case is sophistical.

The objections to 'very deep environmentalism', that is, come from individualists, 'mentalists' and non-egalitarians. What all these lack is the patience to consider what the real political implications of a reasonable holism are. The simple answer to individualism is that there are no individuals. There are, to be sure, people, frogs, and beech-trees, breaths of wind and drops of acid rain, but none of these countable entities are self-sufficient, with essences and welfares

atomically distinct from that of others. The doctrine which Regan
(1984: 152) finds unaccountable, that I am something conceived four
thousand million years ago or more, that 'we are the rocks dancing' is
the merest scientific realism. Only if there is a distinct spiritual being
descended upon this portion of the immortal substance of the universe
(Clark 1984: 175 ff.) is there any sense in taking Me seriously as a separate thing, and if there is such a spiritual eye—as, of course, I think
there is—that too cannot be conceived solipsistically. It is, exactly, the
universal *daimon*.[3] My being and my welfare cannot be disentangled
from the being and welfare of the created universe. The living world
(which is itself an element or function of the cosmic whole) is like 'the
federation or community of interdependent organs and tissues that go
to make up [a physician's] patient' (Gregg 1955; see Lovelock 1979).
Claiming a spurious advantage for individuals at the price of damage to
the whole is simply silly. 'If men spit upon the ground they spit upon
themselves. Man did not weave the web of life, he is merely a strand of
it. Whatever he does to the web he does to himself' (Seattle 1854).
That this is not an empty or a frivolous dictum is evidenced, for
example, by what can only be described as the criminal folly of current
agro-industrial practices in Brazil. 'Criminal' because the ecosystemic
catastrophe developing there has been supported in the face of precise
and (as it turns out) accurate predictions of exactly what would happen
if the forest were chopped down to make way for smallholdings and for
ranches: the land's fertility (which was locked up in the great trees), the
peoples who had lived there, and the livelihoods of the too optimistic
colonists are all destroyed.

What are we for?

The question faced by all of us, especially in the developed West, is the
one constantly raised by Doris Lessing's characters: 'What are we for?'
(See Lessing 1980.)

Are we a higher species? A disinterested observer, coolly examining the evidence and assessing humanity's impact upon the globe, would not be likely to
come to that conclusion. At best we are one species among others. But then,

---

[3] There is no point in appealing to current English usage, or the etiolated version of
such usage that 'descriptive metaphysicians' usually rely upon, to settle the metaphysical
disputes to which I here refer. I shall deal more carefully with them in my second and
third volumes.

what justifies the totally disproportionate cost of our presence? Ask it for once without presupposing the answer of the egotism of our species, as God might ask it about his creatures: why should a dog or a guinea pig die an agonizing death in a laboratory experiment so that some human need not suffer just such a fate? (Kohak 1984: 92.)

—even supposing that the experiment was genuinely vital to our own concerns. One of the many oddities of modernists is that the very people who most insist on the merely 'subjective' and 'unscientific' character of moral judgement become morally incensed when such questions are raised, accusing the questioner of species treachery and the like. Oyarsa's words to Weston, the spokesman for a debased species imperialism, in Lewis's Malacandra:

'You do not love any one of your race—you would have let me kill Ransom. You do not love the mind of your race, nor the body. Any kind of creature will please you if only it is begotten by your kind as they now are. It seems too, Thick One, that what you really love is no completed creature but the very seed itself: for that is all that is left.'

'Tell him', said Weston when he had been made to understand this, 'that I don't pretend to be a metaphysician. I have not come to chop logic. If he cannot understand—as apparently you can't either—anything so fundamental as a man's loyalty to humanity, I can't make him understand it.'

Oyarsa continued: 'I see now how the lord of the silent world has bent you. There are laws that all *hnau* know, of pity and straight dealing and shame and the like and one of these is the love of kindred. He has taught you to break all of them except this one, which is not one of the greatest laws; this one he has bent till it becomes folly and has set it up, thus bent, to be a little, blind Oyarsa in your brain. And now you can do nothing but obey it, though if we ask you why it is a law you can give no other reason for it than for all the other and greater laws which it drives you to disobey.' (Lewis 1952: 162 f.)

Even Lewis did not quite anticipate that some such Westerners would admit to serving only the seed, the 'selfish gene' (on which see my second volume), though he caught the exact note of moral outrage mingled with contempt for the laws of logic as well as of morality that modernists so frequently display! Ancient humanists saw value in humanity because they saw value in the world of which we are a part, and which we can come to know.

So how do those who really strike us as spiritually alive and saintly beings treat the natural world? What do the saints say and do? Can we imagine a real saint, one who practises 'the presence of God', who acknowledges with every breath her own dependence on the spirit and her own unworthiness of it, behaving toward the natural order as a good modernist would? Saints, of course, come in many guises, and many who have the title for political or ecclesiastical reasons are not convincingly saintly. The most convincing saints characteristically welcome the non-human, greet them as fellow-strugglers and worshippers of the most high, not because they have any naive or sentimental belief about what, say, a sky-lark believes, but because they see the lark's fulfilment of its God-given nature as at once a pledge and an example. John the Divine heard 'every created thing in heaven and on earth and under the earth and in the sea, all that is in them crying: Praise and honour, glory and might, to him that sits on the throne and to the Lamb for ever and ever!' (Revelation 5: 13). Whereas the modernist, in effect, sees the natural world as merely a vast heap of more or less usable material, having no significance until the handyman has arrived to make something of it, the saint understands herself to live within a meaningful and orderly universe, even if its meaning is sometimes simply that our action is needed. We are at once the audience and a part of God's speech with himself and with creation. To interfere too radically in the natural order, to forget our own nature as terrestrial mammals and demand the right to remake all things only in our own image, for our own purposes, is to corrupt the text, to surrender to the worst of fairies.[4]

Saintliness requires that we respect the natures of our fellow creatures, and the order of which we are all a part. Some saints have concluded, in practice, that they should live in complete and open dependence, fitting themselves entirely into the natural order, and so offending the squeamishness of gentlemanly humanists. It is a minor irony that Christ's own sardonic instruction to rely upon the Lord who is with the falling sparrow, who clothes the anemones and finds the ravens their food, is usually quoted to 'prove' that he thought people— or at least his followers—more valuable than sparrows, and so licensed to take unfair advantage of sparrows, anemones, and ravens. Such saints live within the promised covenant, 'with the beasts of the field and the fowls of heaven and with the creeping things of the land' when God shall have broken the bow and the sword and the battle out of the land and made them to lie down safely (Hosea 2: 18). The beasts will be at peace with us, said an early commentator on the gospel of Mark,

---

[4] Part of the material in this section was first published in Clark 1986c as a meditation on the biblical conception of our place 'in nature'.

'when in the shrine of our souls we tame the clean and unclean animals and lie down with the lions, like Daniel' (see Clark 1977a: 131).

Most religious traditions, unsurprisingly, have found a place not only for these saints but for the mass of pious and more or less well-intentioned persons. How shall we, who do not yet feel called to go out into the wilderness (on which see my next chapter), singly or in groups, think and act toward the natural order? It is, as Aldo Leopold remarked, the temptation of town-dwellers to think that food comes from the grocery store, and heat from the boiler. It is easy to believe that we do not live 'in nature' but in human culture, although everything we have and are is a transformation of natural product. We need above all to remember that we do not live in a human technosphere, surrounded by an 'environment' that we may take a casual interest in if we choose. We live in the same natural world as alligators, elks, and human saints, though our dependency is of a more complex and easily disrupted kind.

In the Book of Job 'Yahweh describes himself as the wisdom that makes for the survival of the wild ass, the hamster, the eagle, the ostrich, of all living nature, and the wisdom that uproots mountains and annihilates angels' (Kallen 1969). The vision of things before which Job at last bowed his head, and repented in dust and ashes, was a cosmic democracy, in which each creature gets its turn, and is allowed its own integrity. So far from dictating that we human beings should think all nature at our own disposal, the Bible constantly insists that humankind is not alone, not privileged above all others, not like God.

Do you not know, have you not heard, were you not told long ago, have you not perceived ever since the world began, that God sits throned on the vaulted roof of earth, whose inhabitants are like grasshoppers? He stretches out the skies like a curtain, he spreads them out like a tent to live in; he reduces the great to nothing and makes all the earth's princes less than nothing. To whom then will you liken me, whom set up as my equal? asks the Holy One. (Isaiah 40: 21 ff.)

The Bible, like the post-Platonic Greek philosophers, expects us to accept our place within the creation, to live by the rules God imposes, to take what we need, no more, and to give up our demands so that life may go on. Every seventh and every fiftieth year the land must be unploughed, and all live together off its natural produce, citizen and stranger and the wild animals of the country (Leviticus 26: 6 f.). If the law is not kept the people shall be driven from the land, and 'the land shall enjoy its sabbaths to the full' (Leviticus 26: 34). None shall eat the life, which is the blood, of any creature, even if in the post-Noahic days meat-eating is allowed. This is not to say that the Bible contains many specific injunctions of a kind to appeal to zoophiles. It was a sterner world than ours, and the animals who shared the Israelites' land or houses could not have had an easier life than the Israelites themselves. But there was affection there, and acknowledgement of duty. A donkey fallen into a ditch must be hauled out even on the sabbath, even if it is the property of one's enemy (Deuteronomy 22: 4). The poor man's pet sheep, whom Nathan the prophet used to shame King David (1 Kings 12), was loved as a daughter (and no one had the brass nerve to say that he shouldn't have wasted good affection on a mere beast).

Northrop Frye, in his attempt to see the Bible whole, concludes that one of its messages is that we shall not regain the world we have lost, the world where we might easily live in nature, with all creatures as our friend, 'until [we] know thoroughly what hell is, and realize that the pleasure gained by dominating and exploiting, whether of [our] fellow man or of nature itself, is a part of that hell-world' (Frye 1982: 76). Things are not wholly at our disposal, and never will be, either in the sense that we can or that we ought to use them with an eye solely to our benefit, and avoid all inconveniences of this mortal life. We cannot by any technical means transform this world into a pleasure garden, nor ought we to try. Nor can we retreat within a denatured city, and imagine that we thereby fulfil the biblical prophecy of a world wholly suffused with humanly significant meaning, 'when there shall be no more sea', no more image of the unaccountable. The city that the Bible praises was imagined as a part of the land within which it stood, the holy mountain where wolf shall dwell with lamb, leopard lie down with kid (Isaiah 11: 6), and the leaves of the trees serve for the healing of the nations (Revelation 22: 2). The city that it dispraises, Babylon, 'is a tower to seize for herself what belonged to God, a wall to protect herself against God's interventions' (Ellul 1970: 16): but the attempt is hopeless from the start.

No one who reads the Bible can doubt that its human authors were deeply conscious of the natural world, the creation, the land flowing with milk and honey. Where we see 'nature', the non-human environment ruled by powers alien to humankind, they saw God's creation, a world continually offering embodied images of the spiritual values they pursued. 'The God of Israel spoke, the Rock of Israel spoke of [David]: He who rules men in justice, who rules in the fear of God, is

like the light of morning at sunrise, a morning that is cloudless after
rain and makes the grass sparkle from the earth' (2 Samuel 23: 3 f.). In
the mouths of poets and prophets this is more than simile, more than a
rather strained declaration that a just ruler is like the sun after rain.
The prophet sees God's liberating justice in the light when God sets
His rainbow in the sky 'sign of the covenant between [Himself] and
earth' (Genesis 9: 14), as another people 'saw' God's rebuke to the
powerful in the lightning flash. 'As the hills enfold Jerusalem, so the
Lord enfolds His people' (Psalm 125: 2). 'Once the Lord called you an
olive-tree, leafy and fair; but now with a great roaring noise you will
feel sharp anguish; fire sets its leaves alight and consumes its branches.
The Lord of Hosts who planted you has threatened you with disaster'
(Jeremiah 11: 16). When Babylon the great has fallen at last, 'there no
Arab shall pitch his tent, no shepherds fold their flocks. There mar-
mots shall have their lairs, and porcupines shall overrun her houses;
there desert owls shall dwell, and there he-goats shall gambol; jackals
shall occupy her mansions, and wolves her gorgeous palaces' (Isaiah
13: 20 f.). 'The whole world has rest and is at peace; it breaks into
cries of joy. The pines themselves and the cedars of Lebanon exult
over you: since you have been laid low, they say, no man comes up to
fell us' (Isaiah 14: 7 f.). The whole world, not merely human history,
embodies God's purposes to the prophetic eye, and no general distinction is drawn between human and non-human. God's purposes,
indeed, may be more fully and obviously embodied in the non-human,
and moral examples drawn from them: 'Mothers, cherish your sons.
Rear them joyfully as a dove rears her nestlings' (2 Esdras 2: 15).

Why, if all this is so, are there so few general injunctions to behave
decently to the non-human? The word of the Lord to Ezra: 'champion
the widow, defend the cause of the fatherless, give to the poor, protect
the orphan, clothe the naked. Care for the weak and the helpless, and
do not mock at the cripple; watch over the disabled, and bring the
blind to the vision of my brightness. Keep safe within your walls both
old and young' (2 Esdras 2: 20 ff.). These commands could certainly
be read as applying to non-human creatures, but just as certainly were
not. The non-human rested directly on the Lord, and did not turn
aside from Him. There were few occasions when the Israelites could
do much hurt to the wild things, unless by overhunting them or keeping them away from all the crops. The creatures they used for sacrifice—which was the only licensed way of getting meat—were being
returned to God. And the prophets disapproved: 'your countless

sacrifices, what are they to me? says the Lord. I am sated with the whole-offering of rams and the fat of buffaloes; I have no desire for the blood of bulls, of sheep and of he-goats. Though you offer countless prayers, I will not listen. There is blood on your hands. Put away the evil of your deeds, away out of my sight. Cease to do evil and learn to do right, pursue justice and champion the oppressed; give the orphan his rights, plead the widow's cause' (Isaiah 1: 11, 15 f.). The God of Israel, in short, is made known in the demand for justice, the insistence that no human being is entitled to oppress God's creatures or claim equality with God.

So what should God-fearers feel obliged to do in this new age, when God has, with His usual sardonic humour, given us the power to remake things if we choose, and in the remaking find disaster? 'For the Lord of Hosts has a day of doom awaiting for all that is proud and lofty, for all that is high and lifted up, for all the cedars of Lebanon, lofty and high, and for all the oaks of Bashan, for all lofty mountains and for all high hills, for every high tower and for every sheer wall, for all ships of Tarshish and all the dhows of Arabia. Then man's pride shall be brought low, and the loftiness of man shall be humbled' (Isaiah 2: 12 f.). So far from lending support to the sort of modernism which puts its trust in human resourcefulness, the biblical tradition recognizes that our powers are no different in kind from those of any other creature, and the Lord stands over all. Philo's cosmic democracy is fiercely defended.

The first step then is simply not to aim too high, not to expect a pleasure garden, not to demand our human comforts at whatever cost, not to 'turn the world into a desert and lay its cities in ruins' (Isaiah 14: 17). If we cannot live in the land on the terms allotted to us, of allowing others their place, not disregarding the needs of the apparently defenceless, not claiming the right to decide how all things should go, then we shall find that we have lost the land. The natural historian of a future age may be able to point to the particular follies that brought ruin—chopping down the tropical rain-forests, meditating nuclear war, introducing hybrid monocultures, spreading poisons, financing grain-mountains, and rearing cattle in conditions that clearly breach the spirit of the commandment not to muzzle the ox that treads out the corn (Deuteronomy 25: 4). The historian whose eyes are opened to the acts of God will have no doubt that we brought that ruin on ourselves, that it is God's answer to the arrogant. In those days our survivors will have to be saints, unless we have taken a step back from the furnace and consented to be ordinarily decent and God-fearing folk. 'How long must the land lie parched and its green grass wither? No birds and beasts are left, because its people are so wicked, because they say, God will not see what we are doing' (Jeremiah 12: 4).

If we set ourselves to live as citizens, denizens, of the cosmos, in accordance with those laws that can be conceived to govern the lives and livelihood of all, we cannot at the same time think only of our own nation's good, or our own species, or even of the Kantian kingdom of rational ends. The destruction of ecosystems is a 'cause of war' as much as genocide. The place of tribal peoples and of the non-human is as great a matter of political concern as the price of oil or the privileges of the rich. It should be clear that I am not advocating a bureaucratic plan for the management of the whole earth. On the contrary, the plan for the whole earth is something that cannot be captured in the programme of a single species, or a single finite mind. It is by our several actions, our perseverance in the path to which we are called, that the whole is best maintained. 'Think globally; act locally' (Eller 1987: 18: after Jacques Ellul). We can't put it all together, in the words of the *Last Whole Earth Catalogue*: it is together. So long as we see the world as a mere jumble of competing interests, we can give no special weight even to our 'own' for we have no uncontroversial grasp even of who 'we' are, nor any right to respect the products of that jumble.

That we inhabit a cosmos, not a chaos, and that we are the servants of being, is one of those doctrines whose truth is only evident to those who seek to live as if it were.

You never enjoy the world aright, till the Sea itself floweth in your veins, till you are clothed with the heavens, and crowned with the stars; and perceive yourself to be the sole heir of the whole world, and more than so, because men are in it who are every one sole heirs as well as you. Till you can sing and rejoice and delight in God, as misers do in gold, and kings in sceptres, you never enjoy the world . . . The world is a Temple of Majesty, yet no man regards it. It is a region of Light and Peace, did not men disquiet it. It is the Paradise of God. It is the place of Angels and the Gate of Heaven. When Jacob waked out of his dream, he said, 'God is here, and I wist it not. How dreadful is this place! This is none other than the House of God, and the Gate of Heaven'. (Traherne 1. 31: 1960: 15.)

The crucial difficulty for piety, of course, is that while it is necessary, on the one hand, to accept that God is King ('everything obeys God, therefore everything is perfect beauty' (Weil 1957: 194)), we can hardly forget, on the other, that things are not as they should be. God shall arise and His enemies be scattered, but the Transfiguration is a promise, not yet a perfect reality. Put otherwise: in the light of eternity God's victory is, perhaps, already won; in history, the darkness is still strong.

The Kingdom of God is what appears, what is made apparent, when our earthly passions, of anger and concupiscence and sloth, are 'blown out'. In the Mahayana tradition, similarly, Nirvana will turn out to have been 'here' all along. The Kingdom, and Nirvana, are precisely not abstract ideals which we must turn aside from the present in order to realize, somehow or other, in some distant future. They are present realities of which we are constantly forgetful. It is because they are real, that we can have some assurance of victory: if they were only 'ideals' (still more so, if they were ideals of the curious kind that are tarnished by being actualized), what possible reason could we have to believe that they ever would be actualized? If God is not 'now' victorious then prophecies of His eventual success can only be more or less unreasonable hopes. A god that lives only in its worshippers' hearts, only by their acquiescence, is not God at all, but the Satan whom modernists have unknowingly been praising, 'that archetypal dropout, the Lie that knows no End, the primeval Parent-sponsored Rebel, the Eternal Enemy, the Great Nothing itself' (Blish 1972: 113).

The Lie in question is that I (this ego here) am an independent creator of value, religious or otherwise, that I have no need to be freed from the petty devils of rage, greed, and ennui, that truth is to be found in 'a vision and understanding of that great and ultimate Nothingness which lurks behind those signs [we] call matter and energy'. This absolute nihilism, which modernists like Cupitt hope to acknowledge and forget, is inflicted, in Blish's fable, on a pious scientist 'until such time as he despise his soul for its endeavours, and destroy the life of his body' (Blish 1968: 87). What he should have remembered, and Cupitt should have acknowledged, is that the Nothing is itself only a by-product of the divine imagining, that our very capacity to look down into the abyss is evidence of the Poetic Genius, that the Buddha's discovery that all is Void, all is illusion, is immediately followed by the great awakening.

All of us, humans together with all creation, need not be. There is, in nature and the human mind, no ultimate reason why the massive boulder, the oak sapling rising beside it, the chipmunk searching for seed, and I, the human who watches them in wonder, should be rather than not be. And yet, we are— and our being testifies to its Creator. It is not an argument, and would fail if so presented. Rather, it is a testimony, the presence of God made manifest. (Kohak 1984: 189.)

To experience the presence of God is to know ourselves, and all others, to have been chosen out of an infinite number of possible worlds. This is the world, and these the companions, that we are to love. The question of course is: how?

The City of the Wise

The ancients taught that all the wise were friends. 'Not one tower hath my country, nor one roof, but wide as the whole earth its citadel and home prepared for us to dwell therein' (Crates: Diogenes Laertius (D. L. hereafter) 6. 98). The wise acknowledged the whole earth as their 'city', the place where they were at home, and claimed that whole earth as theirs by virtue of their friendship with the gods. Whiggish commentators regularly, and wrongly, conclude that this was a plea for the 'unity of humankind', whereas the philosophers clearly intended only that the *wise* were one (Clark 1987c). Wise and foolish are not friends, though the wise—no doubt—wish the fools well (i.e. that they stop being fools). Some of the wise denied that local laws and customs could have any weight at all: why should the wise consent to obey the fools? Aristippus placed the virtue of philosophy just in this: that the philosopher was at ease everywhere, and would not alter his (*sic*) behaviour even if the local laws were all repealed (D.L. 2. 68). Some of those self-styled wise might be lucky enough to live in a community whose expectations were not too far astray from wisdom, but in all cases the wise would do only what they saw was right. How exactly the rest of us would manage if the wise once took control is never entirely clear.

The wise are identified, in this tradition, by their devotion to the laws of God and Nature, by their recognition of wisdom wherever it may be found, in whatever race or creed or country. Some of them— perhaps the wiser of them—do admit their debt of loyalty and gratitude to their immediate peoples, and take pleasure in the welfare of their fatherland (D.L. 2. 89). Pythagoras is said to have written to Anaximenes to say that 'always to be watching the heavens is not good, and it is nobler to care for one's fatherland' (D.L. 8. 50). Asked how someone could best educate his son, he replied, 'by making him a citizen of some well-governed State' (D.L. 8. 16). But there is not one Law in Rome and another in Athens (Cicero, *De Republica* 3. 33), and it is that Great City, 'walled and governed by reason' (D.L. 7. 40), to which their first loyalty is given. At the same time, in the tradition, non-rational beings are often classed as 'merely material'—which is to say, without moral standing. ' "It's only electricity" implies that electricity as belonging to the natural order is no more than a thing to be manipulated by man' (Galloway 1951: 33)—but perhaps the proper appreciation of such natural forces and the beauty of those organic forms they mould must lead to a more respectful attitude.

A community of the wise across the world, united by their wish to understand and appreciate the laws of nature, and with a tendency to think that creatures which cannot share that appreciation have no moral standing: this is not to be identified with all humankind, but with what we would now call the international scientific (or more generally academic) community. Because the world is marvellous beyond imagining, those people who co-operate to understand and love the world through the exercise of scientific reason are themselves the acolytes of something marvellous. 'Scientists' do not much care to be subjected to merely political control, requiring as of right a freedom to investigate and to collaborate. I have remarked before that servants of Apollo are as shocked as servants of Aphrodite at any suggestion that their goals are not the only good! There are, perhaps, fewer people now than once there were to think that our hope of peace and order lies with 'the scientists', that we ought all to hear and obey what 'science', through its servitors, declares. Fewer fantasies are written which nominate 'the Council of Scientists' or the like as world-rulers, never to be challenged by us lesser mortals. Scientists themselves are now prepared to criticize the easy and self-serving assumption that no one but a scientist is entitled to raise moral doubts about experimental practices or military–industrial involvement. It is unfortunate that their self-criticism is sometimes rather poorly researched, probably because—without much thinking about the point—they think that 'rational thought' is only possible to scientists. The British Association Study Group whose report was published as Morley (1978), at any rate, seem not to have realized the extent to which they were repeating, misrepresenting, and ignoring ancient argument.

Scientists have no more right than anyone else to ravage or destroy: 'I was curious to see what would happen' is no better reason for invasive experimentation than 'I get a sexual kick from torturing things'.

Those who think it is are egotists, and far removed from any proper worship of the world they study. I have never been able to see any reason to suppose that people with a university degree in physics or biology (or, of course, philosophy) are especially suited to be rulers, or have more right to choose their own experimental objectives or designs than soldiers have to choose their own targets—especially so when they are paid by state expropriation (i.e. taxation). But the ancient dream that the wise, self-dedicated to the ideals of objectivity, honesty, tolerance, doubt of certitude, selflessness, and humane generosity (Morley 1978: 122), constitute the central thrust of human or cosmic evolution, should not be quite forgotten. Individual scientists need not now be moral paragons: Merton's summary of the scientific ethos in the four institutional imperatives of universalism, communism, disinterestedness and organized scepticism (Merton 1967: 551) makes it clear that these rest not on individual virtue but on the complex of critical and self-opinionated scientists forming invisible colleges across the world. In that developing and ambiguous body of knowledge, served and increased by ordinarily sinful people, is mirrored—so we may believe—the world from which we grow. Sperry's declaration that 'the grand design of nature perceived broadly in four dimensions to include the forces that move the universe and created man, with special focus on evolution in our own biosphere, is something intrinsically good that it is right to preserve and enhance, and wrong to destroy and degrade' (Sperry 1982: 22) catches the spirit of a pious science, even if it is not entirely clear that Sperry has himself thought clearly enough about the implications of that principle. 'Human society [on this principle] would no longer be justified in destroying or downgrading the rest of creation for its own homocentric ends' (Sperry 1982: 23). Right on: but what does that suggest about a great deal of scientific experimentation on 'the rest of creation'?

The love of knowledge, in itself, may only be a prurient curiosity (on which see my second volume): the love that is proper is a wish to know something that is worth knowing, and a wish to worship it. That pious science is still, no doubt, the moving spirit of our noblest scientists— even if 'Science' has profited, and suffered, from its social success quite as much as the Christian Church did from Constantine. For many, no doubt, science of whatever kind is 'just a job', and their allegiance to the norms of science is quite as 'slavish' as the 'morality' of those who obey the law only so long as they are frightened of the police, or see some personal advantage in obedience. Free people do not act from greed or fear: they follow their vocation. This vision, of an international brotherhood dedicated to the discovery and love of truth, disdainful of local prejudice and of worldly gain, should not be mocked too much. The ancients—despite the disregard of merely animal interests to which I have so often before referred—did not suppose that wisdom was shown in torturing or wasting things in order to discover how they worked. Nor did they suppose that even human welfare was well served by multiplying the opportunities for luxurious living, or learning to evade the natural costs of these. Both these motives, of mere curiosity or greed (masquerading as benevolence), would be beneath the wise. True science, and philosophy, acknowledges no boundaries, and seeks only to be united with the truth of things in rational contemplation.

That vision and vocation, and the social class that seeks to embody it, might well seem to represent the Brahminical function of which I spoke before: a class without direct political power, and rather inclined to despise it, which none the less embodies a necessary check on power, a reminder of the world outside the mere conveniences of the state. It is understandable, as Lewis remarked (in somewhat Stapledonian mood), that some people should resent that calm intelligence:

If we were all on board ship and there was trouble among the stewards I can just conceive their chief spokesmen looking with disfavour on anyone who stole away from their fierce debates in the saloon or pantry to take a breather on deck. For up there, he would taste the salt, he would see the vastness of the water, he would remember that the ship had a whither and a whence. He would remember things like fogs, storms and icebergs, and what seemed in the hot lighted rooms down below to be merely the scene for a political crisis would appear once more as a thin egg-shell moving rapidly through an immense darkness over an element in which men cannot live. (Lewis 1966: 59 f.)

This is the truth in the slogan—more often heard in scorn, from its opponents, than from those supposed to believe it—that 'academic life has nothing to do with politics'. Those who seek the truth of things, unperturbed by questions of race, creed, or party politics, can regard the twists and turns of national or international life with equanimity. What will it matter in a hundred years, or fifty million? To take sides on this immediate quarrel or that as if it mattered *sub specie aeternitatis*, or to disregard the discoveries and arguments of our fellow philosophers because they have—as mortal individuals—a different political master, would be to betray a vocation. At the same time, this does itself constitute a political—or para-political—stance. Just because devoted scientists, philosophers, and 'academics' in general seek truth wherever it is found, and recognize no barriers of race, creed, culture, or political allegiance, they must wish it to be true that no barriers to communication be erected, that everyone with something to contribute to the pursuit of wisdom have the chance to seek it out, and to be heard. Anyone at all may chance to hold a necessary key to some further room in the palace of wisdom: refusing to listen to them, or denying to some class of our potential fellows any chance of help, is a sin against the light. The academy must therefore be open to all classes and conditions of humankind, with the solitary proviso that they be sincere and capable seekers after truth. Academics, to be true to their calling, and to merit the respect that some at any rate have thought their due, must favour open societies, with multiple routes into that relatively sheltered world of the truth-seeker.

At this point moralists divide: Apollo, it must be agreed, is a god, like others, that must be made to serve 'the infinite and eternal of the human form'. Outside that order he is become Apollyon, slayer of cities. Some conclude that academics must 'take a stand' against political evils such as apartheid or the Bomb, and preach the moral duty of academic boycott. No 'decent person' should visit South Africa; international conferences should exclude South Africans (even if the academics in question are themselves acknowledged enemies of apartheid); anyone who seeks to question this 'rough justice' is abused by all right-thinking moralists as an 'ivory tower academic' indifferent to and ignorant of the plight of millions. Similar noises are made about association with Israel, or sometimes America (by left-wingers), or (with somewhat clearer reason in that this latter is a centralized society whose academic conferences are intrinsically and openly propagandist) the USSR (by right-wingers). Other moralists believe that academic boycotts are themselves a sin, for just the same reason as apartheid or collectivism: namely that they amount to the creation of just those barriers to free expression and debate that the open society should abhor. Just as sane people do not do everything possible to win even a just war, let alone those things that they are fighting the war to halt, so good academics do not betray academic principle even to 'punish' those who do academic wrong, let alone those whose masters do such wrong. Keeping channels of communication open, and accepting evidence and argument from any source, is what the academic life is all about. Those who claim the respect due to that craft and at the same time act as short-term (and almost always very ignorant) politicians have forgotten themselves.

The impulse to 'do something' about observable injustice is a very powerful one, but there seems little reason to believe that 'direct action'—whether this be ritual excoriation of South Africans or the purchasing of sub-machine guns for use on 'enemies of the people'—has any very beneficial result. If the international academy does have any claim to be, despite its manifold absurdities and the undoubted sins of its members, an image of 'the city of the wise', a partly realized 'Brahminical' check on power, it is because it uses the para-political or pre-political network. The best thing to do with tyranny is not necessarily to oppose it by means that will themselves establish tyranny.

If God is willing to put up with a stinker like the Roman Empire, you ought to be willing to put up with it, too. There is no indication God has called *you* to clear it out of the way or get it converted for him. You can't fight the Roman Empire without becoming *like* the Roman Empire; so you had better leave such matters in God's hands where they belong. (Eller 1987: 11, paraphrasing St Paul, Romans ch. 13.)

The best thing to do with tyranny—unless we truly have the Mandate of Heaven—is to ignore it, and continue in good heart and conscience to make such connections, academic, economic, personal as will outlast the Caesars.

8

Pagans, Drop-outs, and Renouncers

The Pagan Way

I have been laboriously pointing out that we all live within networks of familial and friendly relationships, that states gain such authority as they have only by embodying moral and sacred values that transcend the merely economic and contractual, that businesses, sects, and nations all have a part to play in a civilized world order whose lineaments are visible in times of war as well as in times of peace. I have also insisted that we human beings live within and upon a world whose ecosystemic health is essential to any purposes we might have for the future, that the beauty of the whole earth is a sacred value, something that any world order must recognize and serve if it is to deserve our loyalty. That order is itself a pluralistic, uncentralized 'cosmic democracy'. What I have sought to describe is the tangled web of our fundamental loyalties and worship, with a view to uncovering just what gods we still acknowledge. The world of our human experience—which is not simply the Globe rolling through emptiness, the delusion of Ulro—is still structured by familial affection, sexual desire, and trade, by the demands of hospitality and word once given, by the spirits of our different nations, by war and innocence and the world's beauty. The gods, in other words, keep just their ancient places, although we pretend to ourselves that we know nothing of that many-splendoured thing. Pure polytheism, the radical plurality and incommensurability of value preferred by some modern secularists,[1] is a partial, scattered vision of the Olympian order, that magnificent celebration of sacred value where each separate deity is held in obedience to *Themis*. The figure of *Themis*, what is proper, assigns to each its own, and decrees that no one value step outside the 'infinite and eternal of the human form'. Human beings take shape in their splendid service of the powers; the powers themselves, the angels of the nations, have their meaning only as elements within the whole divinely sanctioned order.

---

[1] 'Why *must* there be a conceivable amalgam, the Good Life for Man?' (Austin 1964: 28.) In a godless world, no reason, any more than there *must* be a single, humanly accessible theory of what causes things to happen.

Maybe no single individual can embody the Ideal: it does not follow that there is no such ideal, within which each of us is as it were a fragment, an experiment. Our modern image of Dame Nature, holding the balance between competing kinds and values, comes close to *Themis*. In more operational or pragmatic terms: we ought so to organize our political and economic lives as to provide for the health and diversity of the whole earth, and allow each kind and family its own integrity. We ought to encourage in others and in ourselves those virtues as will maintain the whole.

I have, in short, attempted to write like an educated, philosophical pagan, an enterprise which I believe is a necessary prelude to any exposition of the Christian—or more radically Abrahamic—faith. Cicero, speaking through Cotta in *De Natura Deorum*:

> I ought to uphold the beliefs about the immortal gods which have come down to us from our ancestors, and the rites and ceremonies and duties of religion. . . . You, Balbus, are a philosopher, and I ought to receive from you a proof of your religion, whereas I must believe the word of our ancestors even without proof. (*De Natura Deorum* 3. 2. 5–6.)

Philosophers too must believe many things without proof, but those who demand proofs from the ordinarily religious can hardly complain if they are asked to 'prove' their own ideological convictions on the same terms.

You may also have registered that I side with Celsus against Origen, John Hick, and other liberal theologians (joke), in holding that the world does not exist purely for human benefit (see Rokeah 1982: 12). 'The world does not exist for the sake of man, but man exists for its sake' (Plato, *Laws* 903 CD). Hick (1968: 295 f.) does acknowledge 'man's solidarity as an embodied being with the whole natural order in which he is embedded', and 'the permanent significance and value of the natural order', but still endorses a vision in which all the manifold evils of material existence are justified by their end-product, us.

Although I have occasionally cited Hebrew and other scriptures, I doubt if anything I have said would be unacceptable to a Stoic or Neoplatonic philosopher disposed to recognize the Hebrews' God, the God of Gods, as the philosopher's Zeus. Ancient philosophy, I should remind you, was not merely analytical enquiry.[2] When ancient com-

---

[2] Some of what follows was read to the triennial meeting of the Classical Association in Glasgow in 1986. Another part of that presentation, a defence of the ancient view that this world, the world of our present experience, is indeed a dream and a delirium, will reappear in the third volume of this present series (see also Clark 1983c).

mentators sometimes called the Hebrews a nation of philosophers (see Hengel 1974: 255 f.; Momigliano 1975: 82 ff.), it was not because Jews were always asking questions—as the Sceptics and some moderns do.[3] Josephus does remark that the Sadducees make a practice of contradicting their teachers (*Antiquities* 18. 16 ff.), but he probably only means that they were very rude! Whereas modern philosophers, at least since Descartes, are constantly claiming that all previous philosophers have got things wrong, that they 'raise a dust, and then complain they cannot see'—a stylistic trick that often deceives the innocent as to the real provenance of the sophist's own ideas—the ancients were happy enough to draw on ancient testimony, even if they hoped to clarify or expand it, and even if this did quite often involve them in contradicting their teachers. Nor did the commentators have Rabbinic exegesis and casuistry in mind, though this too may strike the modern as familiar enough. The Hebrews were philosophers because (it was supposed) they worshipped an unimaged deity, and dedicated all their lives to virtue. Theophrastus' comment that the Jews were philosophical because they looked up to the stars (Fragmente der Griechischen Historiker 737 fr. 6: Hengel 1974: 256) betrays some misunderstanding of the Hebrews' calling—but the distinction between even Vitruvius' claim that the highest good lies in contemplating *mundi et astrorum magnificentia* (34. 26) and the requirement to worship God only, and not his creatures, is not easily spelled out (as I observed in the last chapter). Greek commentators did tend to downgrade or ignore those aspects of Mosaic Law that struck them as vulgar or irrational, just as they tended to ignore Brahminical doctrine that did not fit well with their picture of the Hindu *sannyasin* as a 'gymnosophist', a naked philosopher. Moses, so Strabo says (16. 3. 35), was a *philosophical* monotheist, even if later generations declined into superstition, circumcision, dietary regulation. Such practices, of course, could be interpreted as outward and visible signs of an inner discipline (as the cloak and long hair of the pagan philosopher should be). Epictetus confesses that he and his disciples are, as it were, Jews in word but not in deed: parabaptistai, not dyed-in-the-wool (*Discourses* 2. 9. 21), very far from applying the principles they preach: 'so although we are unable even to fulfil the profession of man, we take on the additional profession of the philosopher'.

---

[3] 'Why does a Jew always answer a question with a question?' 'And why shouldn't a Jew always answer a question with a question?'

Moses, so Josephus said (*contra Apionem* 2. 16 f.: see Schurer 1979:
ii. 416) combined the best of practical, or Spartan, and theoretical, or
Athenian, wisdom. It was necessary both to know and do the Torah.
What was known was easily identified with that natural law, the divine
Logos active in the universe, whose reality was acknowledged at least by
Epictetus' sort of philosopher. 'Israel is loved', said the Rabbi Akiba,
'for to her was given an instrument with which the world was created'
(Hengel 1974: 170; see Eidelberg 1983: 274). To know the Torah was
not just to know what was required of us in any particular circumstance
(and why): it was to appreciate God's action in the world at large, to see
His glory in the heavens. 'The universe is a most sacred temple most
worthy of God. Man is initiated into this temple by being born into it
and by becoming an awed spectator of this resplendent reality' (Plu-
tarch, *De Tranquillitate Animi*, 20). Or as a later philosopher wrote, of
his childhood world:

Beside (the schoolboy's) world there existed another realm, like a temple in
which anyone who entered was transformed and suddenly overpowered by a
vision of the whole cosmos, so that he could only marvel and admire, forgetful
of himself. Here lived the Other, who knew God as a hidden, personal and at
the same time suprapersonal secret. (Jung 1967: 61 ff.)

The Greek philosopher, perhaps, saw the pattern of God's action in
the cosmos first, and sought to model his life on that; the Hebrew, perhaps, was first acquainted with the Mosaic Law, and understood the
cosmos as dependent upon Israel's obedience: 'the world stands on
three things', said Simon the Just: 'on the Torah, on the cult and on
acts of love' (Hengel 1974: 161). There is a distinction still between
those who think that the *Logos*, the reason that things exist, preceded
Jesus (and the man Jesus only brought the word to us) and those who
think that Jesus identically is the Word (that the Man Jesus *is* the
Reason Why, that Jesus *is* The Man: see Clark 1986b)—a point to
which I shall return in a later volume. Distinctions and misunder-
standings certainly abound: my object here is not to deny that there are
differences, nor yet to discuss them, but to remind you of the shared
doctrine, experience, and practice within which Christian understanding took shape. In identifying those shared doctrines I do not (as must
be obvious from earlier comments) mean to suggest that we can somehow dispense with them and still retain the 'essential core' of Christian
faith. Some modern theologians seem to find it sufficient to accuse the
Church Fathers of Hellenizing or 'philosophizing' the faith without

ever saying what it is that 'Hellenism' was, or what was wrong with it. On the one hand, there was a classical Greek pattern, springing 'particularly from the Plato of the *Phaedo* [that] stresse[d] the radical separation of the divine from the phenomenal realm of our experience' (Wiles 1986: 3). On the other, this tradition had been 'tainted [by the Christian era] by eclectic, Hellenistic philosophy' (Smalley 1978: 42), equally damnable but different. Philosophers trained in the classical tradition do not easily recognize either the supposedly 'pure' Platonic doctrine, or the 'tainted' Hellenistic one, as a correct account of what the philosophically inclined believed. Nor is it always easy to see what theologians have against the doctrinal language they dismiss:

The Johannine *Logos* is *not* the supreme divine realm which encompasses the worlds, nor a primal divine unity prior to the emanations, *but* the bearer of the fulness of the divine salvation. (Schnackenburg 1968: i. 275.)

Pelikan (1984: 12) remarks that the Christian tradition has often 'manifested considerable skill at [the] practice of affirming in the concrete what it denied in the abstract'—namely the Platonic (or Neo-platonic) tradition which later Christians 'in the doctrinal tradition of Jerusalem' need to relearn in order to understand the doctrinal formulae they profess.

Philosophical paganism, as I understand it, is the celebration of the human world within which we grow to virtue. The denial of a human meaning in the world as we seriously conceive it to be is what atheism amounts to—and that is an atheism of which 'the Plato of the *Phaedo*' is certainly not guilty. Pagan theists respect the landscape and architecture of their ancestors, the overwhelming presences of love, war, trade, objectifying knowledge, the immediate impact of a child abused, or the natural universe profaned. The little gods of household and sect take shape within a deeply imagined universe. That imagined (which is not to say imaginary) world is the one that the Creator produces out of chaos, out of the merely unmeaning material universe whose ghastly shape we glimpse behind or within the cosmos. As I have pointed out before, the lightning that is attributed to Zeus is the lightning endowed with human meaning, not that limit of imagination, the large electric spark that would exist even in a humanly unmeaning world—or that is thus made available for unlimited human use. It is true of the Hellenic as of the Hebraic vision, and indeed of all ordinary pagan visions, that the God and Creator is not an arbitrarily postulated explanation of a world seen without religious or moral affect: the God, the guardian of *Themis* for that tribe, is the spirit experienced within the ritual and ceremonial observance of the tribe. 'It is not just any imaginable Creator or Spiritual Cause that religious cosmology hypothesizes: instead it welcomes the discovery that the whole world can be explained by the same presence that is known in prayer and ritual and sacred text' (Clark 1986a: 123). In this matter I can endorse Wiles's judgement on Bultmann: where Bultmann (1952: 228 f.) declares that 'God's creatorship is not, for Paul, a cosmological theory. . . . [but] a proposition that concerns man's existence . . . man, that is, in his creatureliness and in his situation of being one to whom God has laid claim', Wiles comments that 'personal and scientific ways of knowing cannot be [so] sharply separated off' (Wiles 1986: 32). If the Hebrew knew the *Logos* first as Torah and only later as natural law, while the Hellenic philosopher saw the *Logos* first in the natural universe, it is still the case that the 'natural universe' of the Hellene was one imbued with human meaning, a suitable home for the virtuous intelligence. Genuinely and firmly religious people attempt to find in their whole life something like the unforced gaity, exaltation of spirit, creative contrition that can be evoked and channelled by great ritual occasions. They find the God of ritual even in non-ritualized event. The world He makes is the life-world within which they find their ultimate significance, outside of which they are lost. I do not mean that it makes no sense to ask whether such a God 'really' exists, or 'really' acts in the world. I do mean that the question amounts to an enquiry about the 'real nature' of the whole world which cannot be answered without a deal of preliminary discussion about what is to count as 'real', what is to count as 'evidence' of reality.

Paganism, in its many forms, is a celebration of human life, as we find ourselves within a life-world that already contains the natural universe. That life-world takes shape within the hidden framework of the great dead giant, the world as it is for itself: consider just how many mythologies ascribe our origin to a prehistoric, pre-temporal sacrifice. What is sacrificed is what the world would be without us; and myths about that primordial event are not about the merely temporal occasions traced by scientific cosmologists. The erosion of our sacred order, in so far as it is a real event at all, presages the wolf-age, the axe-age before the world's ruin. Out of that ruin will arise another order, as Yeats prophesied, blended and knit together from the strands of sacred duty.

Philosophical paganism, of course, does not rest content with cere-monial duty, or unselfconscious absorption in the socio-political nexus. The Hebrews were 'philosophers', remember, because their God was strictly incorporeal, not to be identified with any mortal image.

'Anarchy' ('unarkyness') is simply the state of being unimpressed with, disin-terested in [sic], skeptical of, nonchalant toward and uninfluenced by the high-falutin claims of any and all arkys (i.e. all principles of governance claiming to be of primal value for society). . . . Precisely because *God* is the Lord of His-tory we dare never grant that it is in the outcome of the human arky contest that the determination of history lies. (Eller 1987: 1 f.)

Eller's book is entitled *Christian Anarchy*, but he would recognize that this is not a feature only of the Christian strand of Abrahamic thought. According to Philo's analysis, Abraham followed his divine vocation precisely by abandoning the Chaldaean identification of visible world (and visible state) and God:

Then opening the soul's eye as though after a profound sleep and beginning to see the pure beam instead of the deep darkness he followed the ray and dis-cerned what he had not beheld before, a charioteer and pilot presiding over the world and directing in safety his own work, assuming the charge and super-intendence of that work and of all such parts of it as are worthy of the divine care. (*On Abraham* 70: Philo 1930: vi. 41.)

Abraham was driven away from 'all city life into pathless tracts where the traveller could hardly find his way' (*On Abraham* 86: vi. 47). The divine was to be known in its own nature only to those prepared to put aside the images and homely comforts of a cosmos organized on the lines of an earthly, human city. We must trust in the Lord, and not 'the horses of Egypt'. 'It is precisely by the creation of idols [the gods in whom each people sees its own unity and strength], that the city closes herself up to God . . . And so Yahweh's intervention is to be charac-terized by the destruction of her idols' (Ellul 1970: 54). Here we have no continuing city; we are to think of ourselves as tourists, or resident aliens—as Aristotle implied before Paul, and before Philo.[4] 'To philo-sophize means to withdraw—not from the things of everyday life—but from the currently accepted meaning attached to them, or to question

---

[4] For Aristotle the life of the good citizen in a well-conducted *polis* was strictly infer-ior to the unattached, untroubled life of the contemplative philosopher. He was himself a resident alien, but perhaps not entirely untroubled by 'political connections'.

the value placed upon them' (Pieper 1965b: 103). And if we do so withdraw, shall we still be worried about our pension rights?

It is written of Cain that he founded a commonwealth; but Abel—true to the type of pilgrim and sojourner that he was—did not do the like. For the Commonwealth of the Saints is not of This World, though it does give birth to citizens here in whose persons it performs its pilgrimage until the time of its kingdom shall come—the time when it will gather them all together. (Augustine, *De Civitate Dei* 15. 1; see Toynbee 1954: 561.)

The pagan philosopher, unless he was a Sceptic or Cynic, might well think that there were traditional customs and distinctions that the wise man ought to abide by, as demonstrating his indifference to personal profit or pleasure, his willingness to abide by cosmic law. He might aim to keep himself pure, through sacrifice and abstinence (D.L. 7. 119). He might think that he should play a part in the defence of his ordinary *patris*. But there remained a sense in which he must expect to go away into solitude to uncover the gods' will for himself and for humankind, and might find it impossible to participate in what seemed an irredeemably corrupt *politeia*. Philo was in a long tradition when he spoke with approval of those 'who flee society and seek solitude in order to be able to lead a life of contemplation' (Wolfson 1946: ii. 264). Thus Heracleitos, found playing knuckle bones with the boys, retorted that it was better to do that than join in the Ephesians' civil life, and ended his days as a misanthrope in the mountains, eating grass and herbs (D.L. 9. 3). Vernant's comment applies to more than the earliest sages:

[Their] teachings, like the revelations of the mysteries, claimed to transform the individual from within, to lift him to a higher state, to make of him a unique being, almost a god. When the city fell victim to disorder and pollution and turned to such a sage to ask the way out of its difficulties it did so precisely because he seemed a being apart and exceptional, a holy man isolated and removed to the fringes of the community by his whole manner of life. (Vernant 1982: 58 f.)

Such sages, fellow citizens with the gods of the cosmos, were not engaged in the later Enlightenment project of reinventing human knowledge on the basis of their immediate sense-experience and of such aphorisms as struck them as self-evident. They were seeking to burrow down to the god-given principles on which even corrupt and shallow societies had once been founded, and to that state of the soul that united them with the soul of the world. In identifying themselves as citizens of the cosmos, not simply or at all of any mortal city, they sought to 'return to Nature', to live like animals. The image of that return still haunts us:

Prior to hunting the relations of our ancestors must have been very much like those of the other non-carnivores. . . . With the origin of hunting the peaceful relationship was destroyed, and for at least half a million years man has been the enemy of even the largest mammals. In this way the whole human view of what is natural and normal in the relation of man to animals is a product of hunting, and the world of flight and fear is a result of the efficiency of the hunter. (Washburn & Lancaster 1972: 299.)

It is always helpful to have an ancestor to blame. Once upon a time, in the Dreamtime days, the days of the very beginning, there was a garden. It seems to be necessary for us to suppose that the Unfallen World was real then, whether we think of that happy life as the world 'before hunting' or 'before patriarchy' or 'before possessiveness'. But whether there has even been an earthly paradise does not touch the present significance of the image: it functions, like fairyland, as an escape from present pain into a larger universe.

Even when a man does not directly participate in the social order conceived as something sacred, even when he evades it, this is not to assert his own value as an individual but to re-enter an ordered whole by another route by identifying himself to the fullest extent with the divine. (Vernant 1983: 335.)

Or as Eller puts it: 'the dying off of arky (or our dying to arky) is of value only as a making room for the Arky of God' (Eller 1987: 12). It is, once again, an oddity of modernist thought that the Flight of the Alone to the Alone is not well thought of, although the divine is held not to be really active within the circles of this world. If God simply is Nature, and the phenomenal universe His only body, then it would seem reasonable to accept a properly pagan culture: what God requires of us would simply be to live in accordance with the nature openly displayed in Nature. Local affections, loyalties, and natural responses, within a universe controlled by *Themis*, should be enough for us. If that is an inadequate response, on the other hand, then it must be that there is a God who transcends—and demands that we transcend—the orderly pattern of a Chaldaean universe. Though modern liberal theologians would often be in complete agreement, say, with Celsus' attack on Christian superstition and self-righteous dogmatism, they would obviously be just as disconcerted by Celsus' own allegiance to the gods of the nations and the divinely ordained cosmos.

It is, of course, unsurprising that these two movements of the spirit—Chaldaeanism and Abrahamism—can both seem very compelling. Aristotle's implicit claim that the life of the foreigner, the resident alien, is superior to that of the politically involved citizen was always paradoxical. Abraham's migration served in the end to establish yet another nation, yet another vision of the cosmos centred on an earthly Jerusalem. A merely Gnostic insistence that the divine truth is to be found only by turning away from all earthly ties, ignoring all natural images, deserves Plotinus' magisterial rebuke: 'If God is not in the world, He is not in you' (*Enneads* 2. 9. 16). On the other hand, a merely, and unphilosophically, pagan view that God is to be known only in the patterns in which we have grown, amounts to that worship of the little *baalim* that Hebraic prophecy renounced.[5]

The pattern of events in the humanly conceived cosmos is what makes us 'at home' in the world: but we are not to think of ourselves as at home for ever. One sort of believer runs the risk that she may see the Emperor and the world He rules as a living law, an embodied virtue, and forget that an infinite deity transcends all images, and does not exist for our sakes. The other kind runs the risk of seeking God only in the desert, and forgetting that we can only have a chance of success here if He has not left us entirely without witnesses. A merely natural and uncontentious God offers no standard from which to reject the way things sometimes are. A merely ideal or trans-natural God is unattainable. The radicals' 'rejection of culture is easily combined with a suspicion of nature and nature's God; their reliance on Christ is often converted into a reliance on the Spirit immanent in him and the believer . . . [leading to] loss of contact with the historical Jesus Christ . . . for whom a spiritual principle is substituted' (Niebuhr 1951: 81). Or as an eminent Cambridge theologian remarked some years ago: 'Christ-centred Christianity [divorced from Hebraic monotheism] must eventually evolve into humanism, and so lose touch with everything that Jesus himself stood for (Cupitt 1979: p. viii).

Tramps and Holy Men

The socio-political nexus within which we grow (and which grows with us) is not something we, as individuals, create or license. I have urged us to respect the gods and the gathering order amongst which we live,

---

[5] I am of course well aware that Israel as a whole did not renounce the *baalim*, and that early Yahwism was knit together with other Palestinian divinities.

as our chance of sanity. The first lesson of sane piety is 'Know Thy-
self'—which is to say, remember that you are mortal, and live by the
grace of gods within a world carved out of emptiness. Piety is the service and contemplation of a cosmic order, achieved through that slow
coming-to-oneself that rests upon our gradual recognition of our
duties within that order. Those who deny the cosmos, and objective
obligation, end up by losing track even of the self in whose name they
first rebelled. There is a certain wry amusement to be had from the
contemplation of modern philosophical, and other, debunking of those
rationalist and individualistic pretensions that were used in the past to
counter the claims of traditional religion. But the time has perhaps
now come to turn my argument around. It is exactly a feature of traditional religion, after all, that there are some—perhaps the very best
of us—who turn aside from the celebration of cosmic religion, paganism. 'It is a mark of an authentic and living tradition that it points us
beyond itself' (Pelikan 1984: 54). If the cosmos is, mythologically,
founded on a giant's sacrifice, or laid out within the abiding forest that
must always encroach upon our careful clearings, might we not go into
the forest, or give the giant a voice?

The *sannyasin* or the wandering sage constitutes a reminder, within
the traditionally conceived cosmos, that the cosmos we inhabit
depends upon an unseen world. They may go aside from the city into
the literal forest or wilderness, to dwell with the wild things, but their
goal is not simply to live as members of the earthly cosmos, the wider
community that I described in the last chapter. The wilderness, the
'natural world', is itself part of our human universe, filled with ancestral memory and moral lesson. The *sannyasin* aims even beyond that
wider world, to live towards the Unknown. 'Our conscious world is a
kind of illusion, like a dream which seems a reality as long as we are in
it. . . . The man driven by his *daimon* steps beyond the limits of the
intermediary stage, and enters the untrodden, untreadable regions'
(Jung 1967: 356, 377). Markandeya falls out of the mouth of Vishnu,
into 'the immense silence of the night of Brahma', out of our common
dream (Zimmer 1946: 38 ff.)

It is uncomfortably and obviously true that this is not how we now
feel about tramps. Although Western as well as Hindu tradition speaks
well of wandering sages, unconcerned with worldly fortune, we do not
expect to encounter unwashed saints. Even in classical times, of
course, many of the penniless wanderers who professed to follow the
example of Diogenes the Cynic were frauds. Even in Hindu society we

can be sure that many professed *sannyasin* are miserable failures. 'For but a week I lived the holy life with tranquil heart in quest of merit. The life I've lived for fifty years since then, I've lived against my will' (quoted by Zimmer 1952: 168, from the Tale of Yannadatta). But in those other settings even the attempt to live 'rooted in the Eternal' deserved some credit. We have so entirely lost the suspicion that saints—or even philosophers—should be detached from worldly cares, should sell up and follow Christ, without thought for tomorrow or need to hang on to their possessions, that even professed Christians automatically discount the possibility that a tramp might really be a holy man. If tramps deserve our charity, it is only (as Aristotle said) because they are human, not because they are themselves deserving. If we give them charity, it is with great care lest they abuse the gift. Nothing that such a drop-out does is taken with the respect due between equals: it is *obvious* that, if a charitable passer-by wishes to see them properly fed on a freezing night, they must be taken to a hot-dog stand, and not (however well-behaved they seem) to a warm eating-house. It is *obvious* that, if not drunk now, they will be soon, and that, even if they are not actually 'psychologically disturbed', they cannot possibly be 'nice to know'.

I am not saying that these ways of treating tramps are incomprehensible: there are excellent reasons for them. We should perhaps recognize that there is a class of human being composed of 'natural slaves', people who cannot take proper responsibility for their own lives, can contribute nothing to society, and must accept in slavishly grateful manner whatever freemen choose to give. A good many such tramps have learnt the necessary tricks of flattery and emotional blackmail that slaves have always had to practise, and those who must deal with them may do better to recognize that 'pity' is an insult, and a disease. But in seeing how easily we slip into thinking of others as slaves, frauds, and vagabonds, we might also remember the mere possibility that we are speaking to St Francis, or Gautama Buddha. Other cultures have included that possibility in the structure conveyed to their young, the possibility that the whole of orderly, respectable society might be rightly challenged by people who 'drop out'. 'The fourth function [in Dumezil's construction of Indo-European society] . . . personified by serfs and outcastes, is the lowliest in the hierarchy, but as the embodiment of sacrifice it is at one with the highest gods' (Rees & Rees 1961: 139). Perhaps if we too remembered that, the great subculture of tramps, layabouts, and drunkards that we encounter might be leavened once again by would-be-holy men, or we might notice that it already is. 'You never know who may be concealed under the appearance of a poor man' (Eaton 1977: 114 f.). Perhaps the truly Brahminical comment on society is not to be found amongst 'professionals'. 'The essence of philosophizing is that it transcends the world of work' (Pieper 1965b: 85): state-kept schoolmen like myself seek to serve two masters.

It is worth adding in this context that one way in which genuine religion and spiritual discernment can be slipped into the great mass of secular or worse than secular entertainment, is through the adventures of a mendicant Chinese warrior-priest, televised at peak viewing times under the title of 'Kung Fu' for many years. Because he has no more possessions than he can carry, no secular position to establish, and because he comes from a supposedly mysterious East, he can expound, through action, simple rules of emotional self-discipline and contemplative prayer that would be laughed at in the mouth of earnest and respectable Christians. Part of the advantage he has derives simply from the dreadful ignorance of our own heritage of spiritual learning that pervades Western culture, and from the normal human habit of supposing that what is foreign and exotic must be more learned than the familiar. 'I cannot help wondering', remarked Broad in a somewhat different context, and about Wittgenstein, 'whether, if the same things had been said quietly and by an Englishman, they would have seemed so impressive as when said excitedly and in broken English with a great deal of play-acting by a picturesque foreigner . . . '(Letter to G. E. Moore, cited in Sotheby's *Catalogue of the Papers of G. E. Moore* 1979). But the warrior-priest also gains from being, in effect, a tramp—and not one easily identified with drunken or neurotic imbecility. Some of the same credit, sometimes, goes to monks, friars, or priests who recognizably have given up their all to serve God and the congregation, who have no wealth or property or spouse. But those professions have career structures, and a chance to shine. Real drop-outs are unknown, except to those they meet 'down at the roots'.

Dies Irae, Dies Illa

The alien way may even lead its devotees to the conviction that there will, one day, be a final reckoning. Where merely pagan devotion expects to see the cosmos revolve forever down time's highway, the millenarian expects an end. Sometimes the cosmos of our ordinary living is perceived as the province of the evil one. God's true servants turn aside from it, and wait for the judgement. Consciousness of acute and humanly irremediable sin may create its own fantasies of punishment which it will be almost a relief actually to endure (see Ellul 1970: 65 on the story of Sodom). 'The Aztec empire, one may suspect, was toppled so easily because its ruling peoples could no longer endure the headless corpse that wandered their hallucinatory forest, the hideous wound in its chest opening and closing with the sound of a woodman's axe. The arrival of Quetzalcoatl, even in the unpromising guise of Cortes and his men, was a welcome relief' (Clark 1986a: 240). Other travellers on the alien way have conceived this cosmos in all its manifold realms as merely indifferent, rather than as evil. It is not something to be destroyed utterly when the Husbandman breaks in, but something to be abandoned when we walk out from it. True life lies outside, and breaks in upon us only in the sense that our desire is aroused to leave Ur and Haran till we come at last to the land of Seeing (which is the esoteric significance of 'Israel').

The idea of Judgement Day, of an irresistible and final breaking in, is not one that much appeals to liberal theologians. Prophecies of such a day are regularly interpreted to convey a present moral: Christ judges the nations only in the sense that their pretensions are thrown into a bad light when contrasted with his virtue. Whenever a ruler seeks to condemn a saint she runs the risk of finding that it is she who stands at the tribunal of history, that their roles are subtly reversed. The curse on the descendants of Ham, that they shall be servants, is an irony of this kind, as Ellul (1970: 10 f., 25 f.) observes: for it was Ham's children who ruled the Hebrew world as Egypt and Babylon. Judgement Day is simply the reversal experienced in any human heart when what had seemed permissible or obligatory is suddenly seen to be wicked. A sensible pagan, of course, and even a philosophical pagan, would not take these reversals too much to heart: absolute purity is unattainable, even an affront to those gods under whose sway we live. Those who say simultaneously that such purity is required of us, but that the Lord will never arise to scatter all His enemies, or even that the Lord exists solely as an impossible ideal in our own human minds, seem wilfully obscure. Those who insist that they do indeed believe in a real God, a power that frames and is not contained within the cosmos of our human meaning, should either agree that God does not much mind what happens in this world, or that the days of His patience may at last run out. What is perhaps even odder is that it is the more conservatively inclined theologian who simultaneously doubts that God much minds about 'social justice' or ecological catastrophe, and expects a genuine Day of Reckoning, and the liberal theologian who denies that any such Day is to be expected while simultaneously insisting that almost our only pious duty is to socialize the economy, with a view to providing for all inhabitants of the region just those goodies that our predecessors thought were least important in the face of Heaven. If what God minds about is that we do our duty in the here-and-now and not turn aside to follow any alien way, why should He forever leave the cosmos unreformed? If, on the other hand, what happens here is only prologue, and the Real World something we achieve once we've abandoned this unfortunate beginning, why should He need to correct it?

Or to put the same problem in another way, and so look ahead to the issues to be debated in my third volume: Wiles (1986: 51) sees the need to have confidence in God's 'ultimate triumph', but feels obliged to place that triumph 'outside the physical finite world of our present experience' (p. 52), thereby reintroducing a dualism that he would normally dismiss as 'Platonic'. 'Whatever Christians may properly mean by their hope for the resurrection of the body, it cannot reasonably be understood to involve continuity of our existing bodily substance' (Wiles 1986: 91). But in that case the relationship between the resurrected saint and her (putative) earthly being, as well as the relationship between Church Triumphant and Church Militant, God's realized Kingdom and the world labouring in child-birth, remain wholly obscure.

A genuine ending, of the kind that traditional piety has so often expected, would be so unlike any ordinary event in time that it is understandable that we should not be quite sure what it would involve. Ordinary 'world's ends' are catastrophes, sudden reversals of the wheel of fortune, new beginnings that are rapidly perceived as ancient errors. Hiroshima did not inaugurate the Kingdom, and neither did the Conquistadors, though worlds ended there. The Day of Judgement cannot be something that we will have a chance to reconstruct, to fit into our myth-histories and happy stories. It is meant to be a final breaking in upon the human cosmos as irrevocable as Nirvana, not another stage to be transcended, or another mood or mode of mental being that will have its own karmic consequences. Nirvana is not a state of mind,[6] and the Day of Judgement is no ordinary day. Since it has to be the end of time, to expect it is to expect something that, when

---

[6] And certainly not the hive-mind or collective consciousness that I have heard confused Westerners suppose. I shall consider minds, states of minds, and what lies 'beyond' in my second volume.

it happens, will have happened already: if time is at an end, this is not just to say that there will then be no hereafter, but to say that the very divisions of past, present, future that we live by will be overthrown. Once time is at an end, and eternity—to which all times are present—has resumed its reign, the here-and-now will be, will already have been, transformed. Once again, I postpone to my third volume any attempt to analyse this ontologically. What matters here is the constantly recreated image of an 'Outside Over There', in whose light all our preoccupations with family and friends, crafts and countries and historic memories, may seem paltry, distracting, soon to be dismissed, and yet be, somehow, the present being of that celestial Outside. The paradox is obvious, and I suspect inescapable: I am trying to offer an account, in the broadest sense, of the socio-political significance within the cosmic realms of the attempt to testify to something that lies entirely beyond the cosmos of our present imaginings. The *sannyasin*, in renouncing his former life, privilege, and duty, becomes a meaningful figure, having quite specific privileges and duties. The rejection of cosmic religion is a calling that has a part to play in cosmic religion.

HaShem Elohim

In Hebraic religion Yahweh Himself is at once the One that will not allow His people to settle down in faithful obedience to the cosmic powers, and the World-Ruler. Distinctions were drawn in Rabbinic exegesis between Yahweh as *Elohim*, and Yahweh as *HaShem*. *Elohim* is more like Zeus, the philosophical order of the cosmic powers; *HaShem* is the incomprehensible Unity that requires a special worship. 'Were it not for the laws or constraints which the Creator imposes on nature—these laws or confined forces are sometimes called angels—the world could not exist' (Eidelberg 1983: 11). *HaShem* is known to us only 'from the rear', as It is imaged in the cosmic order, but the image must always be of something that is not to be identified with any such angel. Or in Philo's terms: the One is to be distinguished from the *Logos*, and the children of the One are a higher tribe than the children of the *Logos* (Dey 1975: 31f.). The author of John's Gospel insisted that to know the *Logos* was to know the One, in the only way open to anyone but the Christ. Mainstream Christianity, in insisting that only Jesus was the child of the One, defined him as the *Logos* itself, the very centre and beginning of creation. By Rabbinic testimony, the Lord created the world beginning from Zion: by Christian He began from Bethlehem, or Calvary. But that is by the way: the point is that both Hebrew and pagan would in the end have agreed that there was One God, and there were also many. We were spiritual amphibia, bound to revere the gods of nature and the nations, but also bound to look aside, or through, to the One Incomprehensible.

The creator is the common father and king of all, but the various nations have been divided by him among nation-ruling gods, ethnarchs, and city-protecting gods, each one of whom controls his allotment in accordance with his own nature. And since in the father all things are perfect and unified whereas in each separate deity a different capacity predominates, Ares accordingly rules over the warlike nations, Athena over those that are both warlike and wise, Hermes over those whose understanding exceeds their daring: thus, each essential quality of their specific gods is adopted by the nations subject to their rule . . . If one is unable to perceive any reason for these variations among nations, but rather asserts that they occurred spontaneously, how can he continue to believe that the universe is administered by providence? (Julian, *contra Galilaeos* 115 DE: Rokeah 1982: 157.)

The fundamental pagan complaint against Christians was that they had abandoned the religion and piety of their ancestors in favour of an unknown God that encouraged them to despise the human cosmos and its elements. 'For all the gods of the nations are idols [or *daimones*], but the Lord made the heavens' (Psalm 96: 5). Their complaint may often have been justified, as it might also have been when directed against some philosophers. Pieper's summary of Plato's message, in the *Phaedrus*:

One can recover [the original state of beginning, and the true end of life] when one 'stands aside from the busy doings of mankind', and steps forth out of the workaday world. But he who does so 'is rebuked by the multitude as being out of his wits', for they know not that he is full of a god. (249 D 2: Pieper 1965a: 81.)

But Plato did hang on to the notion that our earthly world, the cosmos, was at least a true reflection of the Undying, and not to be despised.

The radical message, on the other hand, hovers on the brink of rejecting every earthly, cosmic value in the name of the One beyond, the Great First Light. If this is only an individual vocation, to celibacy, absolute non-violence, poverty, and the like it can be accommodated well enough within the cosmic order. Even whole communities can practise such 'withdrawal', though they are rarely much approved by liberal theologians—who combine, as I have remarked before, a strong disinclination to see God as active in the world with an equally strong disinclination to locate the divine anywhere else than in the world.

Where pagans could sensibly rebuke the radicals for despising the gifts and earning the enmity of the cosmic gods, liberals simultaneously deny that those forces are divine and that any of us has any right to withdraw our customary allegiance from them.

My sympathies, you must long since have concluded, are with the pagans, and not with the radical Christians, least of all those strange creatures who despise their only origin in the name of an ideal in their own heads. But the worldly Church, so to speak, cannot be left unchallenged. The radical Christians genuinely frightened people, and did not merely irritate them: if they owed no final allegiance to the natural powers and constitutions of our earthly lives together, how could they be trusted? If the gods are dead, everything is permitted! If they refused to rest content with tradition and consensus, but preferred the judgement of their inspired saints, who could tell what it would occur to them to do? The God of any new age coming must, as Yeats saw, be destructive of the old. They could, in their turn, deploy a fine range of philosophical rebukes against the foolish majorities, the traditions engineered by rebel angels. If we have an inspired prophet or infallible Imam it would be absurd not to obey him, and it takes little effort to acquire inductive evidence that majorities and complacent *kosmikoi* are almost always wrong. 'Athanasius contra Mundum' is a slogan that has strengthened many foolish people in their self-righteous ways, but it would be just as foolish to deny that the world is often, almost always, wrong. The pagans, being inheritors of a cosmos that was in many respects humane and lovely, could pose as shocked observers of the Christians' ill-tempered and self-righteous argument. Julian, having been brought up Christian, is almost the only pagan to forget his manners! But I at least can hardly complain that the Christians took their stand against animal sacrifice and lethal sports, and disapproved of capital punishment and military action as casual tools of policy. We must be able to criticize the cosmos in all its realms and levels: we can only intelligibly do so if we have a place 'outside the world' on which to stand. And if we—or some of us—have just that, who can predict what the judgement against the world will be? Maybe the very things that we are most proud of will indeed be revealed as splendid vices. Cosmic success cannot be our only criterion, even if we believe that the God of our devotion will—in the end—remake the world.

Gordon Dickson, a science-fiction writer, in the latest novel of his Childe sequence, imagines amongst the various 'Splinter Cultures' of an interstellar humanity, each embodying a particular archetype, a society of 'faith-holders', turned aside from every ordinary goal to serve the Lord of their devotion, and standing firm against the tyranny of merely material men. Dickson's achievement, despite the limitations of his genre and his own skill, is to play fair both by the faith-holders and their critics, who see them—unsurprisingly but inaccurately—as cold and self-righteous ignoramuses. One of their Elect, self-defined as the Chosen of the Lord, addresses a crowd after some small military success against the oppressors:

When did you come to fear death? There is no death to fear. Our forefathers knew this, when they came from Earth. Why do you fail to know it now? They knew as we should know that it does not matter if our bodies die as long as the People of God continue. For then all are saved, and will live forever. There is . . . a teacher of lies in this city—Antichrist incarnate. He envies us our immortality for he is only mortal and he knows that he will die. He can be killed. For God alone is independently immortal. He would exist even if Mankind did not; and because we are part of God, you and I, we are immortal also. But Antichrist has no hope of long life except in Mankind. Only if we accept him, and his like can they hope to live. But because Mankind is of God, though the Enemy may slay our bodies he cannot touch our souls unless we give them freely to him. If we do, we are lost indeed. But if we do not, then though we may seem to suffer death we will live eternally—not only in the Lord but in those who come after us, who will because of us continue to know our God. . . . Even if it was possible for our enemies to kill all who are steadfast in the Faith that killing would be useless to them. For even in their slaves the seeds of Faith would still lie dormant, awaiting the proper hour and the voice of God to flower once more. Come, join me in putting off our fear of death, which is only like a child's fear of the dark . . . For there is no reward like the reward of those who fight for Him, knowing that they cannot lose because He cannot be defeated. (Dickson 1985: 351 f.; see Eaton 1977: 101.)

I could, of course, have selected passages from the pagan philosophers that would have made a similar point—Epictetus' refrain is that the oppressor can only harm one's body, which is the least significant element of the enlightened being. But the Abrahamic or Mosaic message carries some different implications. For the enlightened pagan death can only be a separation of the soul and body, a waking-up to the real life of which this world is but a phantom. This life, Aurelius declared, is a dream and a delirium (*Meditations* 2. 17. 1): we are in the strictest sense the sort of brains-in-a-vat that have become the staple of modern epistemological enquiry. Death is a triviality, and only the philosophers' virtue relieves us of the fear—which I mentioned in an earlier chapter—that those who fear no death are strictly uncontrollable. As I said there, those who make it their business to root out from men a proper fear of death, along with any remaining convictions that there is a real difference between right and wrong, are in effect endeavouring to fill their country with terrorists, crazed killers, and criminally reckless drivers! But Dickson's preacher does not deny that death is an evil, nor seek to root it out from anyone at all: it is those who are, in her phrase, 'part' of God that will live forever in Him and in His people. The natural fear of death, as well as other natural and expectable emotions and inhibitions, may serve as traffic signals, *preparatio evangelica*, reminders of our mortal station.

The true voice of the Alien God is known in the victim of earthly catastrophe, and not in the lords of our present age. Plotinus, who was certainly as great a philosopher and spiritual leader as Hellenic civilization ever produced, remarked that Pheidias' statue of Olympian Zeus was what Zeus would look like if He did indeed 'take flesh and dwell among us' (*Enneads* 5. 8. 1). There is a sense in which he was surely right. But maybe that is only how the *Logos* would be manifest (is manifest) in the Unfallen World. In this world, after all, maybe Plato and the Christians were correct, and the Undying Light made flesh only in Christ crucified.

One other major difference from the merely pagan creed—though it is one foreshadowed in Aristotle—is that the attempt to live in the knowledge and the love of God is not a solitary occupation. What it involves is not, after all, a Flight of the Alone to the Alone. 'There is no true being without communion. Nothing exists as an individual, conceivable in itself' (Zizioulas 1985: 18)—not even God, let alone ourselves. Some pagans, admiring the cosmos, identified Zeus as 'nature's inflexible law and mind dwelling in mortal men, leading according to justice all that happens below' (Euripides, *Troades* 884 ff.: Zizioulas 1985: 30). For that school of thought we are inextricably part of the cosmos, tied forever to the turning wheel.[7] The other, more Platonic school of thought allowed us an escape from the wheel, but only as isolated intelligences, so far separated from our individuality in this world as to render it doubtful whether there were many such spirits or just one. The vision approved by Dickson's preacher is of a People, freely consenting to praise God alone, and immortal in its praising.

The vision is terrifying enough to those of us who can with difficulty

---

[7] I cannot resist mentioning that the name of one factory I passed on the way from Liverpool to Cambridge to give the lectures which are the basis of this volume, is the Universal Grinding Wheel Company.

maintain our homely, civic, cosmic virtue. We would all much rather be told that we should so live as to secure a comfortable life in the here-and-now. Preaching Radical Christianity is an honest option only for those who live it! Most of us are on the side of those baffled magistrates who begged the Christians to pay their due respect to the emperor's genius with a little pinch of incense. We rather suspect that a good many Christians did just that, and did not really feel much guilt about it. Why should anyone elect to defy the powers? Heroic self-sacrifice, even if we cannot imagine ourselves performing it, we can just understand, when something is to be gained by it, like the life of another. What we have neglected, perhaps, is that the spiritual meaning of a people might be just such a worthy end. To die rather than offer incense, or rather than eat pig, or shave one's beard (Epictetus, *Discourses* 1. 2. 29), or rather than see the sacred places ploughed under all seem faintly absurd or self-indulgent to us, precisely because we have forgotten that the body is more than raiment. To die for the Spirit that makes us a people, that makes each one of us a person rather than a mortal animal, is not so silly. If there are no such faith-holders and testifiers among us to experience and make known the presence of their God, then we, being a godless people, will soon perish just because we are no longer a people, but 'a collection of citizens of nowhere who have banded together for their mutual protection' (MacIntyre 1981: 147).

The cosmic religion that I have been sketching in this volume is, so it seems to me, a necessary element in piety and in a decent polity. But the presence amongst us of those who see themselves as members also of a heavenly kingdom should not be forgotten. 'The impulse to pray', William James commented, 'is a necessary consequence of the fact that whilst the innermost of the empirical Selves of a man is a self of a social sort it yet can find its only adequate *Socius* in an ideal world' (James 1890: i. 316). *Kosmikoi* and *hyperkosmikoi*, so to call them, fulfil a divine vocation. The former—which is most of us bourgeois intelligences—should be on the lookout for the elect, for those who will serve the One in ways that go beyond our ordinary sense of duty. The latter should remember what powers of blindness and self-deception stalk the earth: it is after all no proof that one is a prophet that the people persecute one! In practice we can do no better than to put our prayerful trust in the traditions of a godly people. A theocentric polity, one that enshrines such values as can be understood to ground and beautify the cosmos, lasts only as long as its people are enabled to maintain the delicate balance between cosmical and hypercosmical religion, their service of *HaShem Elohim*, the One and the *Logos*.

References

AHO, J. P. (1981), *Religious Mythology and the Art of War* (Aldwych Press: London).

ALLCHIN, A. M. (1978), *The World is a Wedding* (Darton, Longman & Todd: London).

ANSCHOMBE, G. E. M. (1958), 'Modern Moral Philosophy', *Philosophy*, 33: 1–19.

—— (1961), 'War and Morality', in W. Stein (ed.), *Nuclear Weapons: A Catholic Response* (Sheed & Ward: New York), 45–62.

ARNIM, H. VON (1904), *Stoicorum Veterorum Fragmenta* (Teubner: Leipzig).

AUSTIN, J. L. (1964), 'A Plea for Excuses', in D. F. Gustafson (ed.), *Essays in Philosophical Psychology* (Macmillan: London), 1–29 (1st pub. in *Proceedings of the Aristotelian Society*, 57 (1956–7)).

BANC (1987), *The Ecological Conscience* (BANC: GlosCAT, Gloucester).

BARKER, E. (1915), *Political Thought in England* (Williams & Norgate: London).

BELLOC, H. (1927), *The Servile State* (Constable: London; 3rd edn.).

BERKELEY, G. (1948), *Collected Works*, ed. A. A. Luce & T. E. Jessop (Thomas Nelson: Edinburgh).

BINNEY, M. (1977), 'England: Loss', in M. Binney & P. Burman (eds.), *Change and Decay* (Studio Vista: London), 27–41.

BLAKE, W. (1966), *Collected Works*, ed. G. Keynes (Clarendon Press: Oxford).

BLISH, J. (1968), *Black Easter* (Faber: London).

—— (1972), *The Day after Judgement* (Faber: London).

BLUSTEIN, J. (1982), *Parents and Children* (Oxford University Press: New York).

BOSWELL, J. (1953), *Life of Johnson* (Oxford University Press: London).

BRIGGS, K. (1967), *The Fairies in Tradition and Literature* (Routledge & Kegan Paul: London).

BULTMANN, R. (1952), *Theology of the New Testament*, vol. i (SCM Press: London).

BURKE, E. (1975), *On Government, Politics and Society*, ed. J. W. Hill (Fontana: Glasgow).

BURRELL, D. (1972), *Analogy and Philosophical Language* (Yale University Press: New Haven).

BURTON, J. W. (1968), *Systems, States, Diplomacy and Rules* (Cambridge University Press: Cambridge).

CAPOUYA, E. & TOMPKINS, K. (1976), *The Essential Kropotkin* (Macmillan: London).

CARROLL, J. (1974), *Break-Out from the Crystal Palace* (Routledge & Kegan Paul: London).

CHESTERTON, G. K. (1946), *The Napoleon of Notting Hill* (Penguin: Harmondsworth; 1st edn. 1904).

—— (1961), *Orthodoxy* (Fontana: London; 1st edn. 1908).

CLARK, S. R. L. (1975), *Aristotle's Man* (Clarendon Press: Oxford).

—— (1977a), *The Moral Status of Animals* (Oxford University Press: Oxford; reprinted 1983).

—— (1977b), 'God, Good and Evil', *Proceedings of the Aristotelian Society*, 77: 247–64.

—— (1982a), 'God's Law and Morality', *Philosophical Quarterly*, 32: 339–47.

—— (1982b), 'Aristotle's Woman', *History of Political Thought*, 3: 177–91.

—— (1983a), 'Waking-Up: A Neglected Model for the Afterlife', *Inquiry*, 26: 209–30.

—— (1983b), 'Gaia and the Forms of Life', in R. Elliot & A. Gare (eds.), *Environmental Philosophy* (Open University Press: Milton Keynes), 182–97.

—— (1983c), 'Sexual Ontology and the Group Marriage', *Philosophy*, 58: 215–27.

—— (1984), *From Athens to Jerusalem* (Clarendon Press: Oxford).

—— (1985a), 'God-appointed Berkeley and the General Good', in H. Robinson & J. Foster (eds.), *Essays on Berkeley* (Clarendon Press: Oxford), 233–53.

—— (1985b), 'Slaves and Citizens', *Philosophy*, 60: 27–46.

—— (1986a), *The Mysteries of Religion* (Blackwell: Oxford).

—— (1986b), 'Abstraction, Possession, Incarnation', in A. Kee & E. T. Long (eds.), *Being and Truth* (SCM: London), 293–317.

—— (1986c), 'Christian Responsibility for the Environment', *Modern Churchman*, 28: 24–31.

—— (1986d), 'Icons, Sacred Relics, Obsolescent Plant', *Journal of Applied Philosophy*', 3: 201–10.

—— (1987a), 'God's Law and Chandler', *Philosophical Quarterly*, 37: 200–6.

—— (1987b), 'Animals, Ecosystems and the Liberal Ethic', *Monist*, 70: 114–33.

—— (1987c), 'The City of the Wise', *Apeiron*, 20: 63–80.

—— (1988a), 'How to Believe in Fairies', *Inquiry*, 30: 337–55.

—— (1988b), 'Mackie and the Moral Order', *Philosophical Quarterly*, 39: 98–144.

—— (1988c), 'Cupitt and Divine Imagining', *Modern Theology*, 5: 45–59.

—— (1988d) (ed.), *Berkeley: Money, Obedience and Affection* (Garland Press: New York).

—— (1988e), 'Introducing Berkeley's Moral Philosophy', in Clark 1988d: 1–30.

—— (1988f), 'Abstract Morality, Concrete Cases', in J. D. G. Evans (ed.), *Moral Philosophy and Contemporary Problems* (Cambridge University Press: Cambridge), 35–53.

—— (1988g), 'Children and the Mammalian Order', in G. Scarre (ed.), *Children, Parents and Politics* (Cambridge University Press: New York).

—— (1988h), 'Good Ethology and the Decent *Polis*', in A. Loizou & H. Lesser (eds.), *The Good of Community* (Gower Press: Aldershot).

—— & Clark, E. G. (1988), 'Friendship in Christian Tradition', in S. Tomaselli & R. Porter (eds.), *The Dialectics of Friendship* (Tavistock Press: London).

CLASTRES, P. (1977), *Society against the State*, tr. R. Hurley (Urizen Books: New York).

CLIFTON-TAYLOR, A. (1974), *English Parish Churches as Works of Art* (Batsford: London).

COOMBS, H. C. (1978), *Australia's Policy towards Aborigines 1967–77* (Minority Rights Group 35; MRG: London).

COREA, G. (1988), *The Mother Machine* (Women's Press: London).

COSTONIS, J. J. (1974), *Space Adrift* (University of Illinois Press: Urbana).

CUPITT, D. (1979), *Christ and the Hiddenness of God* (Lutterworth Press: London).

—— (1980), *Taking Leave of God* (SCM: London).

—— (1982), *The World to Come* (SCM: London).

DANTE (1954), *Monarchy and Three Political Letters*, ed. D. Nicholl & C. Hardie (Weidenfeld & Nicholson: London).

DAWKINS, R. (1986), *The Blind Watchmaker* (Longman Scientific & Technical: Harlow).

D'ENTREVES, A. P. (1951), *Natural Law: An Introduction to Legal Philosophy* (Hutchinson University Library: London).

DERRETT, J. D. M. (1973), *Jesus's Audience* (Darton, Longman & Todd: London).

DETIENNE, M. & VERNANT, J. P. (1978), *Cunning Intelligence in Greek Culture and Society*, tr. J. Lloyd (Harvester Press: Hassocks).

DEY, L. K. K. (1975), *The Intermediary World and Patterns of Perfection in Philo and Hebrews* (Scholars Press: Nissoula, Montana).

DICKSON, G. R. (1985), *The Final Encyclopedia* (Sphere: London & Sydney).

DOMBROWSKI, D. A. (1984), *The Philosophy of Vegetarianism* (University of Massachusetts Press: Amherst).

DONAGAN, A. (1977), *The Theory of Morality* (University of Chicago Press: Chicago).

DOUGLAS, M. (1973), *Natural Symbols* (Pelican: Harmondsworth; 2nd edn.).

DUERR, H. P. (1985), *Dreamtime: Concerning the Boundary between Wilderness and Civilization*, tr. F. Goodman (Blackwell: Oxford).

DUNN, J. (1986), *Rethinking Modern Political Theory* (Cambridge University Press: Cambridge).

EATON, G. (1977), *King of the Castle: Choice and Responsibility in the Modern World* (Bodley Head: London).

EIDELBERG, P. (1983), *Jerusalem versus Athens* (University Press of America: Lanham).

ELLER, V. (1987), *Christian Anarchy* (Eerdmans: Grand Rapids, Mich.).

ELLUL, J. (1970), *The Meaning of the City*, tr. D. Pardee (Eerdmans: Grand Rapids, Mich.).

ENAYAT, H. (1982), *Modern Islamic Political Thought* (Macmillan: London).

ENGELS, F. (1985), *The Origin of the Family, Private Property and the State*, intr. M. Barrett (Penguin: Harmondsworth; 1st edn. 1884).

EVANS-WENTZ, W. Y. (1911), *The Fairy Faith in Celtic Countries* (Oxford University Press: Oxford).

FAWCETT, J. (1979), *The International Protection of Minorities* (Minority Rights Group 41; MRG: London).

FEYERABEND, P. (1987), *Farewell to Reason* (Verso: London & New York).

FOX, R. (1975), 'Primate Kind and Human Kinship', in R. Fox (ed.), *Biosocial Anthropology* (Maleby Press: London), 10 ff.

FRYE, N. (1982), *The Great Code* (Routledge & Kegan Paul: London).

GADAMER, H. G. (1980), *Dialogue and Dialectic*, tr. P. C. Smith (Yale University Press: New Haven).

—— (1981), *Reason in the Age of Science*, tr. F. G. Lawrence (MIT Press: Cambridge, Mass.).

—— (1986), 'The Historicity of Understanding', in K. Mueller-Vollmer (ed.), *The Hermeneutics Reader* (Blackwell: Oxford), 256–92.

GALLOWAY, A. D. (1951), *The Cosmic Christ* (Nisbet & Co: London).

GOODENOUGH, E. R. (1967), *The Politics of Philo Judaeus* (George Olms: Hildesheim; 1st edn. 1938).

GOODIN, R. E. (1985), *Protecting the Vulnerable* (University of Chicago Press: Chicago).

GOODMAN, N. (1978), *Ways of World-making* (Harvester: Brighton).

GRAY, J. (1986), *Hayek on Liberty* (Blackwell: Oxford).

GRAY, J. GLENN (1970), *The Warriors: Reflections on Men in Battle* (Harper & Row: New York; 1st edn. 1959).

GREEN, C. E. (1969), *The Human Evasion* (Hamish Hamilton: London).

GREGG, A. (1955), 'A Medical Aspect of the Population Problem', *Science*, 121: 681–2.

HARPER, G. M. (1974), *Yeats's Golden Dawn* (Macmillan: London).

HAYEK, F. A. (1982), *Law, Legislation and Liberty* (Routledge & Kegan Paul: London).

HEIDEGGER, M. (1968), *What is Called Thinking?*, tr. F. D. Wieck & J. Glenn Gray (Harper & Row: New York).

HENGEL, M. (1974), *Judaism and Hellenism*, tr. J. Bowden (SCM Press: London).

HICK, J. (1968), *Evil and the God of Love* (Fontana: London).

HOBBES, T. (1968), *Leviathan*, ed. C. B. Macpherson (Pelican: Harmondsworth).

HOLBROOK, C. A. (1973), *The Ethics of Jonathan Edwards* (University of Michigan Press: Ann Arbor).

HOPKINS, G. M. (1970), *Poems*, ed. W. H. Gardner & N. H. Mackenzie (Oxford University Press: London; 4th edn.).

HUME, D. (1902), *Enquiries*, ed. L. A. Selby-Bigge (Clarendon Press: Oxford; 2nd edn.).

INGE, W. R. (1920), *The Idea of Progress* (Clarendon Press: Oxford).

—— (1926), *The Platonic Tradition in English Religious Thought* (Longmans Green & Co: London).

JAMES, W. (1890), *The Principles of Psychology* (Macmillan: London).

—— (1970), 'The Moral Equivalent of War', in R. Wasserstrom (ed.), *War and Morality* (Wadsworth: Belmont), 4–14.

JOHNSON, S. (1924), *Journey to the Western Isles* (Clarendon Press: Oxford).

JONES, G. (1977) (ed.), *Oxford Book of Welsh Verse in English* (Clarendon Press: Oxford).

JUNG, C. (1967), *Memories, Dreams, Reflections*, ed. A. Jaffe (Fontana: London).

KALLEN, H. M. (1969), 'The Book of Job' in N. N. Glatzer (ed.), *The Dimension of Job* (Schocken Books: New York), 17 ff.

KANT, I. (1930), *Lectures on Ethics*, tr. L. Infield (Methuen: London).

—— (1970), *Kant's Political Writings*, tr. H. B. Nisbet, ed. H. Reiss (Cambridge University Press: Cambridge).

KENNY, A. (1985), *The Logic of Deterrence* (Firethorn Press: London).

KIPLING, R. (1927), *Collected Verse* (Hodder & Stoughton: London).

KOHAK, E. (1984), *The Embers and the Stars* (University of Chicago Press: Chicago).

KUPER, L. (1982), *International Action against Genocide* (Minority Rights Group 53; MRG: London).

LEARY, D. E. (1977), 'Berkeley's Social Theory', *Journal of the History of Ideas*, 38: 635–49 (reprinted in Clark 1988d).

LEE, D. (1959), *Freedom and Culture* (Prentice-Hall: New York).

LEE, R. B. & DE VORE, I. (1972) (eds.), *Man the Hunter* (Aldine Atherton: Chicago).

LEOPOLD, A. (1968), *Sand County Almanac* (Oxford University Press: New York).

LESSING, D. (1980), *The Marriages between Zones Three, Four and Five* (Cape: London).

—— (1987), *Prisons We Choose to Live Inside* (Cape: London).

LEWIS, C. S. (1943), *The Abolition of Man* (Bles: London).

—— (1945), *That Hideous Strength* (Bles: London).

—— (1952), *Out of the Silent Planet* (Pan: London; 1st edn. 1937).

—— (1960), *The Four Loves* (Bles: London).

—— (1966), *Of Other Worlds*, ed. W. Hooper (Bles: London).

LIFTON, R. J. (1970), *Boundaries: Psychological Man in Revolution* (Random House: New York).

LOCKE, J. (1963), *Two Treatises on Government*, ed. P. Laslett (Cambridge University Press: Cambridge).

LOSSKY, N. O. (1928), *The World as an Organic Whole* (Oxford University Press: London).

LOVELOCK, J. (1979), *Gaia: A New Look at the Earth* (Oxford University Press: New York).

LOVIBOND, S. (1983), *Reason and the Use of Imagination in Ethics* (Blackwell: Oxford).

LUTOSLAWSKI, W. (1930), *The Knowledge of Reality* (Cambridge University Press: Cambridge).

LYNCH, K. (1972), *What Time is this Place?* (MIT Press: Cambridge, Mass.).

McCLOSKEY, H. J. (1983), *Ecological Ethics and Politics* (Rowman & Littlefield: New Jersey).

MACHAN, T. R. (1975), *Human Rights and Human Liberties* (Nelson Hall: Chicago).

McILWAIN, C. H. (1939), *Constitutionalism and the Changing World* (Cambridge University Press: Cambridge).

MacINTYRE. A. (1981), *After Virtue* (Duckworth: London).

MACKIE, J. L. (1976), *Ethics: Inventing Right and Wrong* (Pelican: Harmondsworth).

MACPHERSON, C. B. (1962), *The Political Theory of Possessive Individualism* (Clarendon Press: Oxford).

MACQUARRIE, J. (1981), *Twentieth-Century Religious Thought* (SCM: London).

—— (1984), *In Search of Deity* (SCM: London).

MAO ZEDONG, (1967), *Quotations from Chairman Mao* (Foreign Languages Press: Peking).

MARTIN, J. J. (1970), *Men against the State* (Ralph Myles: Colorado Springs).

MEILAENDER, G. (1981), *Friendship* (University of Notre Dame Press: Notre Dame & London).

MERLAN, P. (1963), *Monopsychism, Mysticism, Metaconsciousness* (Nijhoff: The Hague).

MERTON, R. (1967), *Social Theory and Social Structure* (Free Press: Glencoe, Illinois).

MILL, J. S. (1848), *Principles of Political Economy* (Parker: London).

MOMIGLIANO, A. (1975), *Alien Wisdom* (Cambridge University Press: Cambridge).

MONOD, J. (1972), *Chance and Necessity*, tr. A. Wainhouse (Collins: London).

MOORE, V. (1954), *The Unicorn: Yeats' Search for Reality* (Macmillan: London).

MORGAN, R. C. (1980), 'Non Angli sed Angeli: Some Anglican Reactions to German Gospel Criticism', in S. Sykes & D. Holmes (eds.), *New Studies in Theology* (Duckworth: London), 1–30.

MORLEY, D. (1978), *The Sensitive Scientist* (SCM: London).

MORRALL, J. B. (1958), *Political Thought in Mediaeval Times* (Hutchinson: London).

MUIR, E. (1960), *Collected Poems* (Faber: London).

NEWMAN, J. H. (1979), *An Essay in Aid of a Grammar of Assent* (University of Notre Dame Press: Indiana).

NIEBUHR, H. R. (1951), *Christ and Culture* (Harper & Row: New York).

—— (1963), *The Responsible Self* (Harper: New York).

NIETZSCHE, F. (1956), *The Birth of Tragedy & The Genealogy of Morals*, tr. F. Golffing (Doubleday & Co: New York).

O'DONOVAN, O. (1986), *Resurrection and Moral Order* (Intervarsity Press: Leicester).

OGILVY, J. A. (1978), *Many-dimensional Man* (Oxford University Press: New York).

O'NEILL, O. (1986), *Faces of Hunger* (Allen & Unwin: London).

OTTO, W. F. (1954), *The Homeric Gods*, tr. M. Hadas (Thames & Hudson: London).

PAINE, R. (1987), *The Rights of Man* (Penguin: Harmondsworth).

PARFIT, D. (1986), *Reasons and Persons* (Clarendon Press: Oxford).

PARIS, G. (1986), *Pagan Meditations: The Worlds of Aphrodite, Artemis and Hestia*, tr. G. Moore (Spring Publications Inc.: Dallas).

PATERNOSTER, M. (1976), *Man: The World's High Priest* (Fairacres Publication 58; SLG Press: Oxford).

PATON, H. J. (1948), *The Moral Law: Kant's Groundwork* (Hutchinson: London).

PEIRCE, C. S. (1931), *Collected Works*, ed. C. H. Hartshorne, P. Weiss, and A. W. Burks (Harvard University Press: Cambridge, Mass.).

PELIKAN, J. (1984), *The Vindication of Tradition* (Yale University Press: New Haven & London).

PESCHKE, C. H. (1978), *Christian Ethics* (C. Goodlife Neale: Alcester & Dublin).

PHILO (1930), *Complete Works*, tr. F. H. Colson & G. H. Whitaker (Loeb Classical Library: Heinemann: London; Putnams: New York).

PIEPER, J. (1965a), *Love and Inspiration* (Faber: London).

—— (1965b), *Leisure the Basis of Culture*, tr. A. Dru (Fontana: London; 1st pub. 1952).

PLANTINGA, A. & WOLTERSTORFF N. (1983) (eds.), *Faith and Rationality* (University of Notre Dame Press: Indiana).

POMPA, L. (1975), *Vico: A Study of the 'New Science'* (Cambridge University Press: Cambridge).

POWYS, J. C. (1974), *In Defence of Sensuality* (Village Press: London).

PRICE, R. (1974), *Review of the Principal Questions in Morals*, ed. D. D. Raphael (Clarendon Press: Oxford).

PUTNAM, H. (1983), *Realism and Reason* (Cambridge University Press: Cambridge).

RAINE, K. (1981), *Collected Poems* (Allen & Unwin: London).

RAJAEE, F. (1983), *Islamic Values and World View* (University Press of America: Lanham).

RAND, A. (1967), *Capitalism: The Unknown Ideal* (New American Library: New York).

RAWLS, J. (1971), *A Theory of Justice* (Clarendon Press: Oxford).

REES, A. & REES, B. (1961), *Celtic Heritage* (Thames & Hudson: London).

REGAN, T. (1983), *The Case for Animal Rights* (Routledge & Kegan Paul: London).

—— (1984), 'Honey dribbles down your fur': *Bowling Green Studies in Applied Philosophy*, 6: 138 ff.

ROKEAH, D. (1982), *Jews, Pagans and Christians in Conflict* (Brill: Leiden).

RORTY, R. (1979), *Philosophy and the Mirror of Nature* (Princeton University Press: Princeton).

ROYCE, J. (1908), *The Philosophy of Loyalty* (Macmillan: New York).

RUSSELL, J. B. (1977), *The Devil* (Cornell University Press: Ithaca).

RYKWERT, J. (1976), *The Idea of a Town* (Faber: London).

SATPREM (1968), *Sri Aurobindo: The Adventure of Consciousness*, tr. Tehmi (Aurobindo Ashram: Pondicherry).

SCHNACKENBURG, R. (1968), *Commentary on St. John's Gospel*, vol. i, tr. K. Smyth (Burns & Oates: London).

SCHURER, E. (1979), *The History of the Jewish People in the age of Jesus*, ed. G. Vermes, F. Millar, & M. Black, vol. ii (T. & T. Clark: Edinburgh).

SCHUSTER, E. M. (1970), *Native American Anarchism* (Da Capo Press: New York).

SCHUTZ, A. (1971), *Collected Papers*, vol. i, ed. M. Natanson (Nijhoff: The Hague).

SEATTLE (1854), *Chief Seattle's Testimony*, tr. D. Smith (Pax Christi & Friends of the Earth: London 1976).

SHAW, G. B. (1934), *Collected Plays* (Odhams Press: London).

SMALLEY, S. S. (1978), *John: Evangelist and Interpreter* (Paternoster Press: Exeter).

SMITH, A. (1976), *The Theory of Moral Sentiments*, eds. A. L. Macfie & D. D. Raphael (Clarendon Press: Oxford).

SPERRY, R. (1982), *Science and Moral Priority* (Blackwell: Oxford).

SPOONER, L. (1972), *Let's Abolish Government* (Arno Press: New York). Reprints two works, dated 1870 and 1886, in facsimile.

SPRIGGE, T. L. S. (1984), 'Non-human Rights: An Idealist Perspective', *Inquiry*, 27: 439–61 ff.

SQUIRE, A. (1969), *Aelred of Rievaulx* (SPCK: London).

STAPLEDON, O. (1972), *Last and First Men* and *Last Men in London* (Penguin: Harmondsworth; 1st edn. Methuen: 1930).

STEINER, F. (1967), *Taboo*, ed. L Bohannan, intr. E. E. Evans-Pritchard (Pelican: Harmondsworth; 1st edn. 1956).

STEPHENS, J. (1982), *The Demi-Gods* (Butler Sims Publishing Ltd: Dublin; 1st edn. Macmillan 1914).

STIRNER, M. (1971), *The Ego and His Own*, tr. John Carroll (Cape: London).

STONE, C. D. (1974), *Should Trees have Standing?* (William Kaufmann Inc.: Los Altos).

STRAKA, G. M. (1962), *Anglican Reaction to the Revolution of 1688* (State Historical Society of Wisconsin: Wisconsin).

THAYER, F. C. (1973), *An End to Hierarchy! An End to Competition* (Franklin Watts: New York).

THOMSON, J. J. (1971), 'In Defence of Abortion', *Philosophy and Public Affairs*, 1: 47–66.

TIGER, L. & FOX, R. (1974), *The Imperial Animal* (Paladin: St. Albans; first pub. 1971).

TINBERGEN, N. (1968), 'On War and Peace in Animals and Men', *Science*, 160: 1411–20.

TIVEY, L. J. (1981) (ed.), *The Nation-State: The Formation of Modern Politics* (Martin Robertson: Oxford).

TOLKIEN, J. R. R. (1966), *The Lord of the Rings* (Allen & Unwin: London).

TOYNBEE, A. (1954), *A Study of History*, vol. vii, *Universal States, Universal Churches* (Oxford University Press: London).

TRAHERNE, T. (1960), *Centuries* (Clarendon Press: Oxford).

TURNBULL, C. (1973), *The Mountain People* (Cape: London).

VERNANT, J. P. (1982), *The Origins of Greek Thought* (Methuen: London).

—— (1983), *Myth and Thought among the Greeks* (Routledge & Kegan Paul: London).

VOEGELIN, E. (1952), *The New Science of Politics* (Chicago University Press: Chicago).

VYCINAS, V. (1972), *Search for Gods* (Nijhoff: The Hague).

WASHBURN, S. L. & LANCASTER C. S. (1972), 'The Evolution of Hunting', in Lee & DeVore 1972: 293–303.

WATT, W. M. (1968), *Islamic Political Thought* (Edinburgh University Press: Edinburgh).

WAUGH, E. (1962), *Brideshead Revisited* (Penguin: London).

WEIL, S. (1957), *Intimations of Christianity*, tr. E. C. Geissbuhler (Routledge & Kegan Paul: London).

—— (1987), *The Need for Roots*, tr. A. F. Wills (Ark Paperbacks: London & New York).

WEST, M. I. (1971), *Early Greek Philosophy and the Orient* (Clarendon Press: Oxford).

WHEATLEY, P. (1971), *The Pivot of the Four Quarters* (University Press of Edinburgh: Edinburgh).

WHITE, H. B. (1970), *Copp'd Hills towards Heaven: Shakespeare and the Classical Polity* (Nijhoff: The Hague).

WILES, M. (1967), *The Making of Christian Doctrine* (Cambridge University Press: Cambridge).

—— (1976), *Working Papers on Doctrine* (SCM Press: London).

—— (1986), *God's Action in the World* (SCM Press: London).

WILLIAMS, L. (1967), *Man and Monkey* (Andre Deutsch: London).

—— (1977) *Challenge to Survival* (New York University Press: New York; 2nd edn.).

WILLS, G. (1978), *Inventing America* (Random House: New York).

WILSON, F. A. C. (1958), *W. B. Yeats and Tradition* (Gollancz: London).

WINDASS, S. (1985) (ed.), *Avoiding Nuclear War* (Brassey's Defence Publishers: London).

WOLFSON, H. A. (1946), *Philo: Foundations of Religious Philosophy* (Harvard University Press: Cambridge, Mass.).

YEATS, W. B. (1950), *Collected Poems* (Macmillan: London).

—— (1955), *Autobiographies* (Macmillan: London).

—— (1959), *Mythologies* (Macmillan: London).

—— (1962), *Explorations* (Macmillan: London).

ZIMMER, H. (1946), *Myths and Symbols in Indian Art and Civilization*, ed. J. Campbell (Pantheon: New York).

—— (1952), *Philosophies of India*, ed. J. Campbell (Routledge & Kegan Paul: London).

ZIZIOULAS, J. D. (1985), *Being and Communion* (Darton, Longman & Todd: London).

Index